Body–Self Dualism in Contemporary Ethics and Politics

Profoundly important ethical and political controversies turn on the question of whether biological life is an essential aspect of a human person or is only an extrinsic instrument. Patrick Lee and Robert P. George argue that human beings are physical, animal organisms – albeit essentially rational and free – and examine the implications of this understanding of human beings for some of the most controversial issues in contemporary ethics and politics. The authors argue that human beings are animal organisms and that their personal identity across time consists in the persistence of the animal organisms they are; they also argue that human beings are essentially rational and free and that there is a radical difference between human beings and other animals; furthermore, they criticize hedonism and hedonistic drug-taking, present detailed defenses of the pro-life positions on abortion and euthanasia, and defend the traditional moral position on marriage and sexual acts.

Patrick Lee is John N. and Jamie D. McAleer Professor of Bioethics and Director of the Bioethics Institute and Professor of Bioethics at Franciscan University of Steubenville. He is the author of *Abortion and Unborn Human Life* (1996), and his articles and review essays have appeared in *American Journal of Jurisprudence*, *Bioethics*, *Faith and Philosophy*, *Philosophy*, *The Thomist*, *International Philosophical Quarterly*, and other scholarly journals, as well as popular journals and online magazines.

Robert P. George is McCormick Professor of Jurisprudence and Director of the James Madison Program in American Ideals and Institutions at Princeton University. He is a member of the President's Council on Bioethics and the Council of Foreign Relations, as well as a former member of the U.S. Commission on Civil Rights. He is the author of numerous books, articles, and essays, including *In Defense of Natural Law* (1999) and *The Clash of Orthodoxies* (2001). He has also written for the *New York Times*, *Washington Post*, *Wall Street Journal*, *First Things*, *Boston Review*, *New Criterion*, and the *Times Literary Supplement*.

Body–Self Dualism in Contemporary Ethics and Politics

PATRICK LEE
Franciscan University of Steubenville

ROBERT P. GEORGE
Princeton University

CAMBRIDGE UNIVERSITY PRESS
Cambridge, New York, Melbourne, Madrid, Cape Town,
Singapore, São Paulo, Delhi, Mexico City

Cambridge University Press
32 Avenue of the Americas, New York, NY 10013-2473, USA

www.cambridge.org
Information on this title: www.cambridge.org/9780521124195

First published 2008
Reprinted 2009
First paperback edition 2009
Reprinted 2010, 2012

A catalog record for this publication is available from the British Library.

Library of Congress Cataloging in Publication Data

Lee, Patrick, 1952–
Body–self dualism in contemporary ethics and politics / Patrick Lee,
Robert P. George.
    p.   cm.
ISBN-13: 978-0-521-88248-4 (hardback)
ISBN-10: 0-521-88248-6 (hardback)
    1. Philosophical anthropology.   2. Ethics.   I. George, Robert P.   II. Title.
BD450.L3735   2007
171′.2–dc22   2007020753

ISBN 978-0-521-88248-4 Hardback
ISBN 978-0-521-12419-5 Paperback

For Germain Grisez

Contents

Acknowledgments

The authors have benefited from the assistance, advice, criticism, and support of many people. They wish particularly to thank the Earhart Foundation, the National Catholic Community Foundation, and Witherspoon Institute as well as Ryan Anderson; Luis Tellez; Carlos Cavalle; Herbert W. Vaughan, Esq.; Roger and Carol Naill; Howard and Roberta Ahmanson of Fieldstead and Co.; Joe and Debbie Duffy; William Saunders, Esq.; Edward Smith, Esq.; Ward Kischer, PhD; William Hurlbut, MD; Maureen Condic, PhD; Richard Doerflinger; Markus Grompe, MD; Thomas Berg, LC, PhD; Alfonso Gomez-Lobo, PhD; Gilbert Meilaender, PhD; Mary Ann Glendon, LLM; Leon Kass, MD, PhD; Edward Furton, PhD; Eric Cohen; Yuval Levin; John Finnis, PhD; Germain Grisez, PhD; Christian Brugger, PhD; Hadley Arkes; Joseph M. Boyle, PhD; John Crosby, PhD; Kevin Flannery, SJ, PhD; Nicanor Austriaco, OP, PhD; Beth Matanzo; Jane Hale; Bradford Wilson, PhD; Laurie Tollefsen, PhD; and Susan Carstensen.

Erratum:
On p. 124 of this work we discuss monozygotic twinning and the issues it raises for diachronic identity of the human organism. We wish to call attention to an important recent article on this subject by David Oderberg: "The Metaphysical Status of the Embryo: Some Arguments Revisited," Journal of Applied Philosophy 25 (2008), 263–76. In addition, we note that David Oderberg has independently developed an argument along the lines that we present on p. 124, using, as we do, examples of plant cuttings and dividing cells, in "Modal Properties, Moral Status and Identity," *Philosophy and Public Affairs* 26 (1997), 259–298, and *Applied Ethics* (Blackwell, 2000), pp. 17–18.

Introduction

Profoundly important ethical issues turn on the question whether biological life is an essential and intrinsic aspect of a human person or is only an extrinsic instrument. Consider, for example, the controversy concerning abortion. A key issue, of course, is the status of the developing human embryo or fetus that is deliberately destroyed by induced abortion. If the human person is not a particular type of *organism*, then one could hold that a human organism begins to exist at one time while the human person begins to exist at a later time. If, however, a human person *is* (whatever else he or she may be) a particular type of organism, then whenever the human organism begins to exist that is the time that the human person begins to exist. Now, consider the issue at the other "edge of life," namely, euthanasia. Here the issue is the status of the severely debilitated and, perhaps, permanently unconscious or minimally conscious individual. A supporter of euthanasia might look at such an individual and say, "that's the same living organism that used to be grandfather, but that is not grandfather anymore." The assumption the euthanasia supporter is making is that the "person" is something distinct from the living human organism, albeit associated with it, namely, the consciousness or perhaps a spiritual entity. If we reject that assumption and regard the human person as a particular type of bodily being, a particular type of organism, then the living human individual remains grandfather – the person – and is entitled, from an ethical vantage point, to be treated as such, despite his debilitated condition.

The relationship between the personal and the biological is also important for central issues in the domain of sexual ethics. Does sexual intercourse only *symbolize* a personal union? In that case the personal union itself would seem to be a purely spiritual reality (in essence only a union of wills or affections of the individuals), and demands on what structure the sexual act must take in order actually to symbolize union would have to be argued out extensively. If the biological is an intrinsic aspect of the human person, however, it might be that sexual intercourse does more, or can do more, than symbolize a union existing wholly in a different dimension of being; it may actualize or be an internal part of the union of bodily persons.

In this book we argue that human beings are physical, animal organisms, albeit essentially rational and free. We then examine the implications of this understanding of human beings for some of the most controversial issues in contemporary ethics and politics.

In Chapter 1 we provide positive evidence that human beings are animal organisms; that their personal identity across time consists in the persistence of the animal organisms they are; that they do endure through time (thus rejecting the perdurance theory of the human person, roughly, that a human person is a series of conscious experiences rather than a substance that endures through time); and that, as a consequence, the human person comes to be when the human animal organism comes to be, and the human person does not cease to be until the human animal organism dies.

In Chapter 2 we show that while human beings are animals, they are a specific kind of animal, and that there is a radical difference in kind between human beings and other animals. In this chapter we also show that the position that human beings are animals is fully compatible with holding that an aspect of the human being, that is, the rational-spiritual soul, transcends matter. We also show that our position on the nature of the human person is compatible with the one that the human soul is the sort of reality that could survive death and with the belief, held by faith by Christians and Jews, that there is a resurrection of the body at some point after death. (We do not enter the theological debate about whether, in fact, human persons will be resurrected. Our concern is merely to show the compatibility of our claim that human beings are rational-animal organisms with the Jewish and Christian belief that they will be.) In this chapter we also argue that this difference in kind (between us and other animals) grounds a moral obligation on our part to treat human beings in a way that is radically different from the way we may legitimately treat other beings that do not possess a rational nature, indeed, that we are morally obligated to give full moral respect to all human beings (irrespective of age, size, stage of development, or mental or physical condition) and treat them, as Kant rightly said, always as ends and never as mere means only.

Chapter 3 shows that body–self dualism is exemplified in the ethical theory of hedonism and, in particular, in (both the ethical defense and actual practice of) hedonistic drug-taking. To show this, we examine the different types of hedonism and different types of pleasure. We explore many of the arguments against hedonism, propose our own specific argument against it, and explain the ways in which pleasure is good and the ways in which it is not.

Chapter 4 shows that the main defenses of abortion are based on an implicit body–self dualism. This chapter sets out some of the embryological evidence which shows that human embryos and fetuses are human beings, provides philosophical evidence that from conception onward they are persons with full moral worth, and argues that since the parents have a special responsibility to care for their children, intentional abortion, even if in rare cases it is not intentional killing, is morally wrong (though there are rare cases in which it is not wrong intentionally to perform an act that one knows or believes will cause fetal death as a side effect).

Chapter 5 shows how the euthanasia debate, in many ways, mirrors the abortion debate, explains why euthanasia or assisted suicide is morally wrong, clarifies the distinction between intentional killing, on the one hand, and causing death as a side effect, on the other hand, defends the proposition that human life itself is a basic good of human persons, and clarifies the criterion of death.

In Chapter 6 we defend the position that within marriage, the marital sexual act (when performed with morally upright intentions) is not a mere symbol of love or affection, nor a mere means to procreation (positions that reflect at least an implicit body–self dualism), but embodies or makes present the intrinsic human good of marital union, a union that is itself bodily as well as emotional and spiritual. We also argue that nonmarital sexual acts, such as masturbation, fornication, and sodomy, cannot actualize any basic human good and therefore involve instrumentalizing one's (and perhaps others') body (or bodies) for the sake of a mere experience (without the reality) of unity or for the sake of self-affirmation. Thus, in this chapter we examine what marriage is, how sexual acts contribute to the good of marriage, and show the immorality of nonmarital sexual acts, such as those mentioned earlier.

I

Human Beings Are Animals

Is biological life an essential and intrinsic aspect of a human person or are our bodies merely extrinsic instruments? Stated abstractly, the question may seem rather distant from matters of ethics and public affairs. In truth, however, as we indicated in the introduction, it is logically connected to several morally charged political issues.

In this chapter we defend the position that human beings are living, bodily entities, that is, organisms, and indeed animals. The first argument we present is a development of Aquinas's argument against Plato's position on the relation of the soul to the body.[1] The overall, main argument is as follows:

1. Sensing is a living, bodily act, that is, an essentially bodily action performed by a living being.
2. Therefore the agent that performs the act of sensing is a bodily entity, an animal.
3. But in human beings, it is the same agent that performs the act of sensing and that performs the act of understanding, including conceptual self-awareness.
4. Therefore, in human beings, the agent that performs the act of understanding (including conceptual self-awareness, what everyone refers to as "I") is a bodily entity, not a spiritual entity making use of the body as an extrinsic instrument.

Each of these steps in the argument will be explained more fully. The main development, however, will occur in providing support for the first

[1] See St. Thomas Aquinas, *Summa Theologiae*, Pt. I, q. 75, a. 1 and q. 76, a. 1.

premise, since substance dualists as well as proponents of the no-subject view (the position that the person is not an enduring substance at all but is a set of experiences united by memory and other psychological connections)[2] deny that premise.

I. Main Challenges to Establishing the First Premise

We shall present two arguments to defend the first premise (that sensation is a bodily act). In our first argument we shall begin by concentrating on sensation in *non*human animals (and then compare sensation in human beings to sensation in nonhuman animals.) Before doing that, however, we shall consider the main challenges to that first premise. There are, we believe, four theories about what a human being is which in various ways block acceptance of the proposition that sensation (whether in nonhuman animals or in human beings) is a bodily or organic act. Two theories of material entities go against this proposition: mechanism[3] and the position that the ultimate entities are events rather than substances (as in process philosophy, which may be called "eventism," or as in perdurantism).[4] And two theories of mind go against it: the no-subject view (the denial that there are enduring substances) and substance dualism (the identification of mind with an independent spiritual substance).

Observing nonhuman animals, most of us do not hesitate to say that these animals, that is, these complex, moving bodily entities, sense and adapt to their sensations. When we see a dog chase a rabbit or sniff out the place of a hidden bone, and observe that dogs have bodily structures similar to our eyes, ears, and noses, we understand that dogs see, hear, and smell. But there are various ways of denying this position, that is, various

---

[2] Also called "the bundle theory of the self." See, for example, Derek Parfit, *Reasons and Person* (New York: Oxford University Press, 1989), Chapters 10–13.

[3] That is, the view that there are no *composite* substances. What appear to be composite substances are, according to those holding this view, mere aggregates of simple substances (similar to a machine, and hence the term "mechanism").

[4] "Perdurantism" refers to the position that there are no substances that *endure* throughout time. What appear to be enduring substances are, according to this view, entities that have extension in time as part of their being (analogous to songs or baseball games, which are said to *perdure* rather than endure). For a general treatment: Michael J. Loux, *Metaphysics: A Contemporary Introduction* (New York: Routledge, 1998), 201–232; a recent full-scale defense: Theodore Sider, *Four-Dimensionalism: An Ontology of Persistence and Time* (New York: Oxford University Press, 2001). This theory is often adopted in the context of considering the question of the identity of *persons*, and so we treat the specific arguments for and against it in the context of considering personal identity across time. See Section VII.

ways of denying that sensation is an action attributable to a bodily animal as its subject, the different ways corresponding to the theories mentioned earlier.

First, someone might say that sensation is not a unitary action at all, but an aggregate of electrical and chemical reactions: a mechanist would take this sort of position. Second, someone might say that sensation is really a mental episode *associated with* the body (rather than an act performed by a bodily being): a proponent of the no-subject view (or "bundle theory of the self") might take this position. Third, someone might say that sensation occurs, not in a bodily entity, but in a mind that is substantially distinct from the body. One might then hold either that there really is no sensation in nonhuman animals (it only appears that way; they really are automata, as Descartes held) or that in nonhuman animals also there are substantially distinct minds associated with them. So, to defend the first premise in the main argument stated earlier, we must defend the position that animals are enduring entities (against mechanism, eventism, and the no-subject view), and that sensation occurs in *them*, as opposed to occurring in substantially distinct minds associated with them. Our treatment of these positions will necessarily be brief, so we shall consider some, but not all, of the possible objections that our arguments might suggest.

II. Animals are Enduring Agents

A mechanist holds that the dog is just an aggregate of smaller entities, perhaps molecules, and perhaps these molecules are aggregates of atoms, and so on. On this view, dogs and other animals are only aggregates of smaller entities, and their actions are determined not by any intrinsic unitary direction but merely by the interaction of the smaller units. A proponent of this view might add that it is *convenient* to think of animals and other entities as unitary substances, but this convenience hardly translates into a truth descriptive of the world. This mechanistic view might then harmonize either with a functionalist view of the human mind or with the identification of the human self with a distinct substance as Platonists or Cartesians hold.

However, there is strong evidence that it is more than convenience that moves us to see dogs and other animals as real substantial units rather than as mere aggregates, *entia per accidens*.[5] Our viewing the dog as a unit is

---

[5] On the distinction between a composite substance and a mere aggregate, see Richard Connell, *Substance and Modern Science* (Houston, TX: Center for Thomistic Studies,

similar, as Aristotle pointed out, to our viewing houses or other composite artificial objects as units. Why do we think of the boards and bricks of a house as one? Because we grasp a certain type of unity, a functional unity, in those materials. We understand that the material components of the house are organized for the purpose of providing shelter and warmth. In this case the unity is extrinsic; it has been imposed from outside by human agency.[6]

Analogously, when we see a dog chase a rabbit or come up to us drooping his head and wagging his tail, we apprehend a unity in the materials that go into the makeup of the dog. In the dog's chase of the rabbit, we understand the canine feet and back and head as organized and directed to a single end, the catching of the rabbit. Even while the dog is sleeping, we understand the various parts of the dog, the cells, the tissues, the organs, as functional parts of a whole. Unlike the house, however, whose unity has been extrinsically imposed, the unity of the dog is intrinsic.

The things around us, and most obviously animals and other living things that exhibit behavior, are really various types of agents. And agents endure. An agent is a source of regular actions and reactions. We observe recurrent and predictable actions and reactions; the source or center of such patterns of action is a thing or agent. It is not reasonable to think of reality simply as events or as particles in random motion, because agents or natures are required to explain the recurrence of definite actions and reactions. We must think and act in relation to dogs as units, for example, because only in that way can we understand and predict the actions of the materials which together we refer to as a dog. The materials that together constitute a dog are in some ways similar to a multiplicity of chalk marks on a blackboard: why those bits of chalk dust are there can be explained mechanically, by reference to the properties of the chalk dust and the wood and other chemicals in the blackboard. But beyond that, there is an intelligibility in the chalk marks (though, unlike the dog, imposed from outside in the use made of them) which can be understood only by grasping their unity, which allows them to express a meaning.[7] Similarly, we cannot fully explain why the dog turned to the left and then to the right exactly

1988), 3–39; Joshua Hoffman and Gary Rosenkrantz, "On the Unity of Compound Things," in *Form and Matter: Themes in Contemporary Metaphysics*, ed. David Oderberg (Malden, MA: Blackwell Publishers, 1999), 76–102.

[6] Aristotle, *Parts of Animals*, Bk. I, 1 639b15–640a10; ibid., *Metaphysics*, Bk. VII, Chapter 17.

[7] See James Ross, "Christians Get the Best of Evolution," in *Evolution and Creation*, ed. Ernan McMullin (Notre Dame: University of Notre Dame Press, 1985), 223–251.

when he did without seeing the dog as a unitary agent, as an animal in pursuit of a prey. True, the motions of the parts of the dog can be explained on lower levels, that is, by reference to the smaller particles that go into the makeup of the dog. We can explain the dog's turning to the left by reference to muscle contractions, and these contractions can be explained as electrochemical reactions. But there is a unity in the turning this way and that way of a dog which can be understood only by understanding the materials in the makeup of the dog as parts of a single agent. But again unlike the house or chalk dust, here the unity is from within. It is a unity not imposed by us but recognized by us – that is, it is a unity that is antecedent to the meanings we impose on things by our use of them.[8] It is the same with trees, animals, and other composite substances.[9] Thus, the more reasonable position is that the unity of the materials consists in their intrinsic organization. Dogs, cats, trees, and perhaps, on the lower level, molecules and even detached atoms are composite units, understood as one in that they are distinct types of agents.

The position that animals and other entities are things or substances which endure through time is not an a priori necessary truth. It is not logically inconceivable that we could have a world with entities that do not endure at all, or endure for a very short time.[10] The evidence that there are persisting substances, and that animals are enduring substances, consists (in part) in all of the phenomena which show beyond reasonable doubt that animals and other entities are *agents* and they remain the same sort of agents, numerically the same ones, throughout stretches of time. The actions initiated and sustained by animals – such actions as chasing prey, eating meals, mating – are actions that take time. The life of a numerically single organism is maintained by continuous processes such as respiration, blood circulation, cell repair, and homeostatic operations. To suppose that there are only events or experiences strung together in various ways is, we believe, not easily made compatible with the fact that in countless cases an action and its structure is explained by the persistence of a numerically

---

[8] Cf. Aristotle, *Physics*, Bk. II.

[9] At the level of nonliving things, it is hard to say what are substances as opposed to aggregates. Is a water molecule a composite substance or an aggregate composed of two hydrogen elements and an oxygen element? We are inclined to think the former, but nothing in the argument we are advancing here depends on the answer to that question.

[10] This is not to suggest that a world without substances is logically possible. It is only to say that a world with substances whose duration was so brief as to be undetectable is perfectly conceivable.

singular agent that produced and sustained it.[11] A dog will chase a rabbit; a horse will not. This is partly because a dog is a carnivore while a horse is a herbivore. But this is most reasonably interpreted as meaning that a dog is a certain type of agent, that is, an enduring source of predictable actions and reactions – given certain circumstances, this type of agent will act or react in certain ways.[12]

This understanding of enduring agents is also challenged by process philosophy, more specifically, the view we referred to as eventism. A. N. Whitehead recognized that both difference and continuity must be included in our account of the realities we experience.[13] But rather than locating the continuity in an enduring substrate, such as a substantial agent, he located it in the commonality of universal features. For example, according to Whitehead, an animal is not an enduring substance, but a society of events, and the continuity is the commonality of features shared by the series of events (which he labeled "actual occasions").[14]

But the continuity which he recognized is continuity in a series, and so it *requires explanation*. If the commonality is not intrinsically determined, then the regularity with which such continuous sequences occur remains unexplained. Rather, that in reality which corresponds to sound explanations is a numerically singular subject or center of actions and reactions; this subject is the real counterpart of explanations and predictions of actions (and reactions) in various circumstances (within a suitable environmental range) and throughout stretches of time. Hence it seems that the real counterpart of such explanations must endure through time.

So, it is reasonable to hold that the dog is a persisting (enduring) organism. The dog chases the rabbit on Monday because the dog is a carnivore. The dog chases the rabbit on Tuesday because he is still a carnivore, and he remembers where he chased him on Monday. (This is evidenced by the fact that as he approaches the tree where he first saw the rabbit on Monday, he begins to salivate and turn his head quickly in various directions.)

---

[11] Cf. Michael Ayers, "Substance: Prolegomena to a Realist Theory of Identity," *Journal of Philosophy* 88 (1991), 69–90.

[12] Cf. Benedict Ashley, *Theologies of the Body: Humanist and Christian* (Braintree, MA: Pope John Center, 1985), 253–296; R. Harré and E. H. Madden, *Causal Powers: A Theory of Natural Necessity* (Totowa, NJ: Rowman and Littlefield, 1975), 44–118; T. D. J. Chappell, *Understanding Human Goods: A Theory of Ethics* (Edinburgh: Edinburgh University Press, 1998), 104–125.

[13] A. N. Whitehead, *Process and Reality* (New York: Macmillan, 1929), 34–35, 59–66, and 240–248.

[14] Ibid.

III. Sensation is a Bodily Act

St. Augustine, Descartes, and others held that in human beings sensation is not, strictly speaking, a bodily act (or state) at all, but an act performed by the soul on the occasion of the change produced in the body by stimuli acting on it.[15] According to this view, having a sensation is an act that occurs in one's consciousness, and so it is in one's soul, even though it is in some way informative of how things are modifying my body. In other words, the bodily processes in the sense organs and the brain would be merely preparatory to the sensation itself, which would be an act of *conscious experience* and would occur only in the mind.[16]

However, there are several problems with this view. The first difficulty concerns nonhuman animals. It is hard to believe that nonhuman animals have spiritual substances associated with their bodies in which sensations occur that guide their (nonbodily) desires and bodily movements. It was for this reason that Descartes, holding that sensation is a spiritual state, denied that nonhuman animals sense at all, claiming instead that nonhuman animals are mere automata.[17] But Descartes's denial is implausible. The movements of animals are clearly specified by information obtained through sensation. They turn their heads in order to obtain sensations; they cry out apparently with pain when struck and groan or cry when apparently suffering from constant pain. Also, much of their behavior can be explained only by admitting that they remember and have images. Dogs that seem to be sleeping often bark or moan, clearly reacting to what they are dreaming. So, there is sensation in, or at least associated with (if it occurs in their substantially distinct minds), nonhuman animals.

It may be objected, nevertheless, that sensation in nonhuman animals could guide the bodily parts of the dog from outside that body, and thus exist in the substantially distinct animal minds.[18] Indeed, one could use

---

[15] St. Augustine, *De Quantitate Animae*, Bk. XXIII, 41; Bk. XXV, 48. Cf. Vernon Bourke, *Augustine's Quest for Wisdom* (Milwaukee, WI: Bruce, 1945), 111–112; Rene Descartes, *Meditations on First Philosophy, Meditation II*, in *Philosophical Works*, vol. 1, translated by Elizabeth S. Haldane and G. R. T. Ross (New York: Dover, 1931), 149–157.

[16] Cf. Richard Swinburne, *The Evolution of the Soul* (New York: Oxford University Press, 1986); Charles Taliaferro, *Consciousness and the Mind of God* (New York: Cambridge University Press, 1994).

[17] Rene Descartes, *Discourse on Method*, Part 5, in *Philosophical Works*, vol. 1, op. cit., 106–118; *Replies to Objections*, Part 4, #1, in *Philosophical Works*, vol. 2, op. cit., 79–96.

[18] Richard Swinburne, *The Evolution of the Soul*, revised edition (New York: Oxford University Press, 1997), 18–196.

the analogy of the sailor and the ship: the sailor guides the movements of the ship and yet the sailor is distinct from the ship and the information by which the sailor guides the ship is in the sailor (as conscious information), not in the ship. However, the ship is merely an artifact, *extrinsically* designed to be steered by some sailor or other, and the sailor has his primary being (as a human) independently of his sailing the ship. By contrast, the relation between the locus of the animal's sensations and the animal as a whole is obviously quite different. In the dog's case the sense organs *naturally* function as instruments of sensation, and the animal's consciousness seems to be in every way dependent on the bodily parts of the animal organism. Thus, it is more natural to suppose that sensation is a *complex action*, with the changes in the sense organs, nervous system, and brain, being *parts* of that conscious, sensitive action, rather than being merely extrinsic (or preparatory) to it.

Moreover, if sensation in nonhuman animals were purely nonmaterial, existing only in their minds, then the functional unity discussed earlier (in Section II) in the bodily parts of the dog would be unintelligible. The running in determined directions by the bodily dog, which is partly why we rightly understand the dog as a unit to begin with, is intelligible only if it includes the dog's sensing. Many of the bodily parts of the dog are reasonably understood as unified precisely as instruments or organs for acts (or states) of sensation. Thus, the parts of the dog seem to be unified as *participating* in the act of sensing an external object and reacting to it – only in this way is the scene we understand as a dog chasing a rabbit actually coherent.

If sensation were not an organic act, then the dog's *movement* as well as *sensation* would have to be viewed as performed by the dog mind as a distinct agent – we would have to say that the dog's nonmaterial thoughts and desires caused his body to move this way and then that way. The dog's body would be merely an extrinsic instrument, somewhat as chalk is an extrinsic instrument used by a teacher to write with on a blackboard. But then, how would the dog's *body* be a unity (for its mind would be extrinsic to it)? What intrinsic unity would the bodily parts have? The answer, we believe, is that the bodily parts would not be intrinsically unified at all. These bodily parts would be like the chalk dust of a sentence written on a blackboard, since the chalk dust is really an aggregate rather than something with intrinsic unity. If sensing and perceiving were nonbodily episodes, then the canine body would have only an extrinsic unity imposed from outside. But that seems incorrect. There does seem to be an intelligible unity *within* the canine body prior to consciousness, a unity that involves the animal's whole way of life, and a way of life whose unity essentially depends on the animal's sensations and bodily desires following such sensations.

Again, it is hard to see how the nonhuman animal's body could be an extrinsic instrument for the animal's mind. An extrinsic instrument is used by a principal agent for a purpose devised by the principal agent for *its* good, not for the good of the instrument (consider again the example of the chalk used by the teacher). Indeed, this is what distinguishes the relation between an extrinsic instrument and a principal cause from the relation between two (or more) co-causes, or the relations between two (or more) parts of a whole. The idea that the body is an extrinsic instrument could have some *initial* plausibility as an account of sensation in human beings (though at the end of the day it cannot be sustained), because humans have a rich mental life; one could therefore abstract from various aspects of human living and think of sensation in human beings as serving *only* their mental life. But this view is quite implausible when presented as an account of the sensations in nonhuman animals. If it were true, the animal's mental life would have to be the end or goal and its body would be an extrinsic instrument serving the animal-mind's needs. The animal mind would have to have a life of its own, to which its body was an extrinsic instrument. But all of the evidence about nonhuman animals goes against this. In nonhuman animals, sensations are subordinated to the survival and flourishing of the bodily organism, rather than vice versa. Their cognitive life has no appearance of being contemplative. Rather, the mental life of dogs, for example, is regularly oriented toward obtaining food or mates or prey, actions which clearly serve the survival and flourishing of the bodily organism as such.

It is usually only when considering sensation in human beings that anyone is tempted to say that it is a purely spiritual act occasioned by changes in the body. And the reason why, as mentioned earlier, is that in human beings sensation often is subordinated to speculative understanding, that is, understanding pursued for its own sake. This is why we thought it helpful to begin with sensation in nonhuman animals. But once one grants that there really is sensation in nonhuman animals, it becomes clear that sensation in human beings is the same type of act as sensation in nonhuman animals (despite their sometimes ulterior goals). There are similar bodily structures functioning as sense organs, and the same type of nerve cells and organization in the brain relevant to sensory impulses. Moreover, there are similar types of complex behavior, leading one to say that in both nonhuman animals and human beings behavior is often specified by sensory information in basically the same manner. Human beings do not usually chase rabbits, but they do sometimes chase dogs. It would be very odd if the turning this way and that way by the dog while he is chasing a rabbit was an entirely different kind of act than the turning this way and that way of the boy who is chasing the dog chasing the rabbit. Clearly, the chasing of a dog by a human is the same sort of act as the dog's chasing of a rabbit. Hence the sensation, an essential component in that behavior, must be of the same type. Sensing is a bodily act, not the act of a distinct consciousness, considered as a reality independent of the body (whether of a dog or of a human), which putatively performs the act of sensing at the end of some sort of bodily process, or as the effect of such a process. Sensing is a hybrid act – an act that is both conscious and bodily at the same time.[19]

A second argument for the proposition that sensation is a bodily act is as follows. The most reasonable interpretation of sensation and perception, we submit, is that the direct object of sensation is not a mental sense datum, but the external stimulus on a sense organ. For one thing, positing mental sensations as intermediaries between the knower and the aspects or qualities of the things acting on one's sense organs prompts insuperable skeptical challenges – if what I directly sense or perceive is always only a mental state, then how could I ever have a good reason to believe that there even is an external cause of these mental states?[20]

Moreover, sensation is passive. Sensation is quite unlike understanding in this regard. Conceptual thought or understanding is active. It requires a mental effort performed by the agent, which is why when two people view the same sensory data, one may understand and the other not. By contrast, in order to sense, all one needs to do is open one's eyes to see or contact an external body to touch, and similarly with the other senses. Also, at the same time that one senses external objects, one is immediately – and without effort – aware of the position and various conditions of one's own body. Even though *perception* involves an active selection and interpretation of what is sensed, sensation itself (as a component in perception) seems to be a direct *reception* of the influence or stimulus from a bodily entity acting on one's sense organs (or a being sensitively *affected* or *moved* by one's own bodily state). Sensation, as Aristotle insisted, is a passion, a being moved by the sensible object.

If that is so, then it is hard to understand how sensation could be a purely mental, nonmaterial event. We would have to say that a material

---

[19] The term "hybrid act" was coined by David Braine, *The Human Person: Animal and Spirit* (Notre Dame: University of Notre Dame Press, 1992), 29ff.

[20] On this point, see, for example: Robert Audi, *Epistemology, A Contemporary Introduction to the Theory of Knowledge* (New York: Routledge, 2003).

force directly produces an effect in a nonmaterial entity. Some claim that there is a mystery here that we simply must live with, that cognition and consciousness will on any theory be shrouded somewhat in mystery.[21] However, the problem is not just that it is difficult to conceive how things of very different sorts could interact, but rather, on this view (that is, that sensation is a purely immaterial state), one must say that a material entity is by itself producing an effect in a nonmaterial, spiritual entity. This seems to be not just a mystery, but a self-contradiction. If one holds, instead, in an Aristotelian manner, that the sensible object acts on (or informs) the enlivened (or ensouled) sensed organ, the problem disappears.[22] Even though sensation is essentially a bodily act, because it is conscious, it may have a nonmaterial aspect as well.

A third argument for the bodiliness of sensation is as follows. This argument moves from the object of the act to the nature of the act. What is sensed is never just a quality or quantity as it is in itself, but always a quality as it appears from this or that direction. For example, one does not simply see red or blue but a surface from this or that angle, that is, from the perspective of one's eyes. The visual scene which one obtains of a house, for example, is necessarily from this or that perspective. Perspective is different from position. One can understand position mathematically, through coordinates, but perspective is something one can directly grasp only by perceptually experiencing it. Someone may know something about a perspective without actually seeing from it, but it is significant that a person can do so only by imagining what it would look like to someone seeing it from that individual place.[23]

---

[21] Colin McGinn holds this, though he himself adopts a materialist position; see his *The Mysterious Flame: Conscious Minds in a Material World* (New York: Basic Books, 1999). Our position, as we explain more fully in the next chapter, is not materialist, but a hylomorphist conception of the human being.

[22] The problem does not arise for the relationship between conceptual understanding – which in the next chapter we argue *is* a nonbodily act – and bodily sense experiences, since conceptual thought essentially involves effort and deliberate selective focusing. Thus, one can hold, as did Thomas Aquinas, that the sense experience is the *instrumental cause* of the conceptual thought; that is, one can hold that the intellect (more precisely, the person with his intellect) makes use of the sense experience to form appropriate concepts and propositions. An instrumental cause produces an effect greater than itself since it acts in cooperation with a principal cause. It will, however, have a specifying influence on the effect. For example, the pen with which one writes (an instrumental cause) specifies the color of the sentence the writer (the principal cause) produces on the paper. Similarly, the sense experience, although only an instrumental cause of conceptual thought, is a specifying cause.

[23] John Campbell, *Past, Space, and Self* (Cambridge, MA: MIT Press, 1994), Chapter 1.

So, what is seen – and the same is true analogously with the other senses – is internally characterized by spatial location. It is not just that what is known is a spatial location. Rather, what is known is the physical effect that the object has on the physical subject. That is, the very act of knowing seems to be characterized by spatial location. So, the facts about perspective are best explained by supposing that what we sense is neither a quality as it is in itself, nor something purely subjective, but something relative in this sense, namely, the thing in its physical action on ourselves. So sensation is a bodily act, and the subject who has the sensation, the agent that performs the act of sensing, is a bodily entity. The agent that senses is not properly understood or characterized as a mind somehow associated with or inhabiting a body, but rather as an animal.

It is worth noting that nothing we have said presupposes a particular answer to the question about the relationship between *qualia* (the phenomenal aspects of sensation and perception) and the bodily organs in sensation and perception, other than to rule out a substance dualist position – that is, in this context, the claim that sensible qualia must be perceived by minds substantially distinct from bodies. Qualia, for all we have said, may be irreducible to physical entities and physical laws.[24] Our argument would not be cast into doubt by that claim, nor by its opposite. Our claim is only that the act of sensation is essentially bodily in nature: if this act also has aspects belonging to it that are not identical with, or completely explainable by, physical properties, this in no way vitiates our argument.

IV. In Human Beings the Agent that Performs the Act of Sensing Is Identical with the Agent that Performs the Act of Understanding

The second premise in the main argument is as follows: in our case, that is, in human beings, that which senses is the same agent as that which understands. That is, in human beings the agent that performs the act of sensing is the same agent that performs the act of understanding, though the agent performs these distinct acts by exercising different capacities or powers. Evidence for this proposition can be found by analyzing singular judgments. When one affirms, for example, that *That is a tree*, it is by

---

[24] On this issue, see, for example, David Chalmers, *The Conscious Mind* (Oxford: Oxford University Press, 1996); Michael Tye, "A Theory of Phenomenal Concepts," in *Minds and Persons, Royal Institute of Philosophy Supplement 53*, ed. Anthony O'Hare (Cambridge, UK: Cambridge University Press), 91–105.

understanding – an intellectual act – that one apprehends what is meant by "tree" and apprehends such objects as unitary, living things. Viewing such an affirmation or judgment as having a subject–predicate structure, we can say that the predicate of the judgment expressed here is grasped by one's understanding (that is, one's capacity to understand, one's *intellect*). The subject of the judgment, however – what one refers to by the word "That" – is apprehended by sensation or perception. What one means by "That" is precisely that which is perceptually present to one.[25] But, clearly, it must be the same thing, the same agent, that apprehends the predicate and the subject of a single judgment. So, it is the same thing, the same agent, which understands and which senses or perceives.

From these two points, the conclusion follows that the agent that understands (and is self-aware) – what everyone agrees that one refers to as "I" – is an animal.

In sum:

1. Sensation in human beings is an organic act.
2. If sensation is an organic act, then the agent that performs the act of sensing is a bodily, organic being.
3. The agent that senses is a bodily, organic being (from 1 and 2).
4. The agent that senses is identical to the agent that understands.
5. The word "I" refers to the thing or agent that understands.
6. Therefore, the word "I" (in the case of human beings) refers to a bodily, organic being (from 4 and 5).

Since organisms that sense (i.e., perform acts of sensing) are classified as animals, it follows that human beings are animals.

V. An Argument from the Nature of Human Intelligence

So far we have argued that substance dualism is incompatible with the nature of sensation. However, substance dualism is also incompatible with the nature of human conceptual thought. That is, there is a strong argument against substance dualism based on the natural dependence of human intelligence on sense experience. Some philosophers view understanding and even willing as so independent of sensation and the body that the result is that the principle of understanding and willing, the soul, must be conceived as complete of itself and without any intrinsic orientation

---

[25] The word "that" signifies a singular thing by means of a concept, but the concept is demonstrative, and so its reference is dependent on sensation or perception.

to matter or the body. However, there is an abundance of evidence to show that human conceptual thought naturally requires sense experience or imagination, and thus operations of the brain. Hence it can be shown that human intelligence has an intrinsic need and functional orientation to matter or the body. This point will provide an additional argument for the position that human beings are animals; for if the most spiritual of human actions (supposing, for the moment, that some human actions are spiritual) still require as prerequisites distinct bodily acts, then the principle of these actions (the soul) must be understood as by nature incomplete and as part of the whole body–soul composite.

The basic argument is again from Aquinas. "What a thing is" is revealed in its actions. But the distinctive actions of which the human soul (the organizing principle or form of the human being) is a principle,[26] such as conceptual thought or understanding, have an intrinsic need for the actions essentially performed with the bodily parts such as the sense organs and the brain. So, the principle of understanding (and willing), the human soul, is by nature a part or incomplete.

Moreover, although (as we shall argue more fully in the next chapter) it is not contradictory to think that the act of understanding could occur in some instance without sense presentations, say, after death, we cannot really conceive of what that would be like. What we directly understand is always an intelligible content or pattern in a sense presentation. What we understand is not just occasioned by sense presentations, but is specified by them. This is shown by the fact that some sense presentations are appropriate for understanding a particular point or issue while others are completely unhelpful. For example, if one wishes to understand a triangle, one immediately reaches for pencil and paper and draws a specific type of diagram. And if one is seeking to understand the nature of circles, one draws a very different type of diagram. This indicates that the sense presentation is more than a mere occasion for one's act of understanding, which might then be informed or specified by something else. If the sense experience were a mere stimulus for the act of understanding but

---

[26] It is important to see that if human understanding is a spiritual act, it still should not be thought of as an act "performed by the soul." Rather, the human being performs the acts of understanding, as it is the human being that performs the acts of sensing or walking. The difference is that sensing and walking are done with bodily organs and understanding is not. See especially Peter Geach's careful way of phrasing the question in his "What Do We Think with," in *God and the Soul* (New York: Schocken, 1969), 3–41. The soul is the *formal source* or principle, enabling the agent to perform such actions; it is not itself the agent.

the act was specified or received its intelligible content elsewhere (as Platonists and innatists hold), then there would be no reason why the sense experience of one thing could not be just as easily the occasion for understanding something quite different – a diagram of a circle could be just as easily the occasion for understanding a triangle as it is for understanding a circle. But this is not the case. Rather, we intellectually grasp the point – when we do so directly – *in* the presentation of sense.[27] After direct understandings, perhaps we can (as we hold is the case) move on to understand by relation and analogy objects for which we do not have sense presentations. Also, while directly understanding an external, physical object, we are concomitantly (or reflexively) aware of our act of understanding. However, knowledge of our mental acts cannot be primary, but only concomitant to the primary and direct knowledge of material things. Our acts of understanding are always into sense presentations or concomitant to, or by comparison or contrast with, what we first understand in sense presentations.

So, in the first place, this means that our intellect (or mind) is by its nature oriented to sense presentations. The human intellect is not designed to turn away from matter in order to obtain its information elsewhere, as Platonists and Cartesians hold. There is intelligibility *in* the material world, and it is that intelligibility which is proportionate to our human minds; our minds are not designed to turn away from or bypass the material world. So, the human intellect cannot naturally perform its function without the aid of the body – a need which manifests an incompleteness in what it is. The principle of human understanding is an incomplete nature.

Secondly, the human act of understanding is incomplete in that it is abstract. By understanding, one directly grasps only a feature held in common by many things, abstracted from other features with which it is one in reality. For example, one directly understands such features as *animal*, *human*, or *triangular*, whereas to know concrete animals, human beings, and triangular things, one must exercise one's perception or imagination, as well as one's intellect. One must grasp those features as concretized in things; but to do that requires bodily perceptions, not just intellectual acts. All the human intellect by itself can grasp is an intelligible aspect of some thing. But to understand an abstract intelligible aspect of a thing just by itself is not to understand the thing in the manner in which it exists. To understand a thing in the manner in which it exists is to understand an intelligible aspect precisely as an aspect of a thing. But this involves

[27] Cf. Bernard Lonergan, *Insight*, 3rd ed. (New York: Philosophical Library, 1970), 3–19.

a reference back to sense experience. For it is by sense experience that we are initially aware of the whole of which the intelligible aspect understood is an aspect. This occurs, of course, in intellectual acts of judgment (affirming or denying a propositional content).

This is not to say that every judgment is singular or that its evidence is narrowly perceptual. There are universal judgments and necessary ones for which the evidence is not just a perceptual link. Still, the abstract intelligible aspect must be conceived as joined to a thing or things, and the notion of a thing is dependent on our initial perceptual experience. Even when we refer to, and infer truths about, immaterial things (as, we hold, is possible), we do so by analogy with material things, and we conceive of them in the manner that is really only fitting to material things. (Thus, we hold that, as Aquinas pointed out, our understanding and language about God are in certain respects unsuited to his nonmaterial nature; the abstractive mode of our understanding fits material things, which exist as composites, not God who is not a composite.[28])

So, even though the act of understanding is done without a bodily organ (as we show in Chapter 2), the human mind cannot complete its act – in the sense that it cannot succeed in understanding a thing in the manner in which that thing exists – by itself alone. This is an important point, because one cannot hold that the soul and the body constitute a single substance and, at the same time, that the soul is complete in its nature.[29] So, although it can survive without the body (since it is possible for it to perform some type of act without the body), it is intrinsically oriented to the body because its operations cannot naturally occur without the aid of the body.

VI. On Privileged Access and the Modal Argument for Substance Dualism

An argument that is often presented to defend a substance dualist view starts from the privileged access or privacy of our mental acts. How can

---

[28] Aquinas, op. cit., Pt. I, q. 13, aa. 1 and 2. See also Patrick Lee, "Does God Have Emotions," in *God Under Fire: Modern Scholarship Reinvents God*, ed. Douglas Huffman and Eric Johnson (Grand Rapids, MI: Zondervan, 2002), 211–230.

[29] To his credit, Descartes wanted to hold that the body and the soul together make up one substance. However, he also held, and emphasized, a position incompatible with that, namely, that the soul is complete in its nature. For discussion and texts: Daisie Radner, "Descartes' Notion of the Unity of Mind and Body," *Journal of the History of Philosophy* 9 (1971), 159–170; Paul Hoffman, "The Unity of Descartes' Man," *Philosophical Review* 95 (1986), 339–392.

sensory acts be bodily events when bodily events are open to public inspec-
tion, at least in principle, whereas my sensory acts are directly known or
observed only by me? Other people can perhaps in some way observe me
having a sensation but they cannot have my sensation. The essential argument would be: that to which one has privileged access is not identical
with that to which there is public access; we have privileged access to our
sensations as well as our thoughts and desires, while there is public access
to bodily acts; therefore sensations are not bodily or organic acts.[30]

The problem with this argument is in the first premise. It is often the
case that the same thing can be known in various ways. If A is known in
one way and B is known in another, this does not mean that A is really
distinct from B.

This is, in essence, the mistake Descartes made in his argument to
identify the self with the mind, where he said that the fact that I can doubt
the existence of the body but not the existence of the mind shows that the
mind and the body are different things.[31] But as Peter Geach pointed out,
using a slightly different counterexample: a boy may doubt the existence
of the postman while being certain of the existence of his father even
though the two are identical.[32] The moral is that the same reality may
be apprehended in different ways; the diversity of apprehensions in no
way proves the diversity of what is apprehended. One may apprehend
a sensation from the standpoint of the one who is having the sensation,
and one may apprehend the sensation from the standpoint of an external
observer. The apprehensions differ, but only one thing (that is, only one
act) is apprehended.

This point is related to another important argument which has been
presented to defend substance dualism, an argument often called the
modal argument for substance dualism.[33] The argument has basically
three steps:

1. I can conceive of existing without my body.
2. Therefore it is possible, metaphysically, that I exist without my
   body.
3. Therefore I am distinct from my body.

[30] Cf. Richard Swinburne, *The Evolution of the Soul* (Oxford: Oxford University Press,
1986), 45–61; Jerome Shaffer, *Philosophy of Mind* (Englewood Cliffs, NJ: Prentice-Hall,
1968), 39–60.
[31] Descartes, *Meditations on First Philosophy.*
[32] Geach, *God and the Soul*, 8.
[33] See, for example, Swinburne, *Evolution of the Soul*, loc. cit.; Taliaferro, loc. cit.

We reject the move from #1 to #2. We concede that because one can conceive of oneself simply as the entity that has this first-person perspective (what things seem like to me), one *can*, in a way, conceive of oneself existing without a body; that is, one can conceive, or even imagine, a first-person perspective without imagining or conceiving of one's body, or any body.[34] But, as we have just explained, one can conceive of the same thing under different aspects or, as Frege expressed it, under different modes of presentation.[35] There is no reason to think that one's concomitant awareness of oneself as a subject of mental acts is an awareness *of one's whole essence*. That is, in one's mental acts (acts of understanding, willing, etc.) one is first of all directly aware of some object distinct from oneself, whatever it is that one is thinking about or choosing. And one is concomitantly aware of oneself as subject of that mental act. But that awareness is very limited: it reveals to one that one exists and that one is a subject of these types of acts, but *what* this subject is essentially and specifically – in particular whether this subject is or is not identical with a bodily being – this concomitant awareness need not reveal anything one way or the other. It is true that I can conceive of a subject of mental acts existing without a body (that is, conceive one without conceiving the other), but from that it simply does not follow that *the particular kind of subject of mental acts that I am* can in fact exist without the body.

So, the conceivability here is based on the limited nature of what is known when one knows oneself from a first-person perspective. Hence the modal argument seems to us to make the same mistake as the Cartesian argument, but from a different starting point. The parallel is as follows: I can conceive of the mailman existing while my father does not (for example, I could conceive of the mailman existing after my father dies) but it does not follow that it is *really possible* for the mailman to exist while my father does not (since in fact they could be identical); similarly, from the fact that I can conceive of myself (this entity having this first-person perspective) existing without my body, it does not follow that its existing in that way is actually possible.[36]

---

[34] This could be challenged: Does one perhaps *implicitly* imagine or conceive a determinate position as "zero-point" in one's perspective on the world? If so, then it seems one is *not* imagining or conceiving of oneself outside the body. But we will not challenge the matter here but concede #1 for the sake of argument.

[35] Cf. Gotlob Frege, "Thought," reprinted in *The Frege Reader*, ed. Michael Beaney (Oxford: Blackwell Publishers, 1997).

[36] Colin McGinn articulates an objection to the modal argument for dualism that is close to the objection we have just presented, though McGinn himself speaks of *consciousness*

VII. Human and Personal Identity: The Psychological Continuity View

So far we have concentrated on the question of what a human being is. We have concentrated on the issue of synchronic identity – what *is* a human being at any given time? There is a vast body of literature, however, on the question of the *diachronic* identity of a human person; that is, what makes a person at one time to be the same entity as one that exists at another time? Some answers to this question challenge our claim that you and I are animal organisms (of a rational nature). In the next two sections, we consider these challenges.

Answers to the question about *personal* identity are not replies (at least directly) to the question, what is a person, or what is a human being? Rather, they answer the question, what does it take for a person to persist, or to survive? That is, under what conditions is a person at one time the same entity as an entity that existed at some earlier time? We say that we exist today, but that we also existed yesterday, two years ago, ten years ago, and so on. The position we argued for earlier implies that each of us can truly say that *I* came to be exactly when the animal organism that I now am came to be, and that I will not cease to be until this animal organism ceases to be. There are various positions, however, which claim that *psychological continuity* is what constitutes the persistence or survival of the person, and so imply that I did not come to be until consciousness or self-consciousness began.[37] Moreover, if psychological continuity is necessary for the persistence or survival of a person, then I

and the body. In discussing McGinn's position, Taliaferro considers this argument: might the person be identical with the body and yet be unaware of the connection between himself and the body? One's ignorance of the connection, or of the connecting property, would enable one to conceive of one as existing without the other and yet it is not strong evidence for their real difference (see Colin McGinn, *The Problem of Consciousness* (Oxford; Basil Blackwell, 1990), 20; Taliaferro, op. cit., 173–217). To this objection, Taliaferro distinguishes between weakly conceiving a contingent relation or distinction (namely, failing to apprehend their identity) and strongly conceiving a distinction (namely, a positive grasp of the properties involved that leads one to see one as possibly existing without the other). He then holds that the distinction between the person and the body is strongly conceived, that is, based on a positive grasp of the properties of person and body, rather than weakly conceived. However, it seems that such a reply in effect grants that the modal argument is by itself insufficient to support its conclusion, which is our contention in this section. For a critical discussion of Taliaferro's defense of the modal argument, see Stewart Goetz, "Modal Dualism: A Critique," in *Soul, Body, and Survival*, ed. Kevin Corcoran (Ithaca, NY: Cornell University Press, 2001), 89–104, at 94.

37 Others claim that psychological continuity is necessary, though not sufficient, for personal identity across time. In either case, tying personal identity to psychological continuity poses an objection to our position.

could cease to be before this animal organism (the animal organism I am now, or coincide with now) ceases to be.

The main argument for the psychological continuity view is based on a consideration of possible "body-swappings" and brain transplants. Suppose a device has been invented which could record the state of one brain and impose that state on a second brain by restructuring it so that it was exactly like the state of the first brain, and that this process involved the destruction of the first brain. The device could be called a "brain state transfer device"[38] or simply a teletransporter. Would the operation be person-preserving? That is, would the person with the new body be identical with the original person? In discussing this case, Sydney Shoemaker admits that many people would be inclined at first to say that the first person was killed and that merely a psychological duplicate of him was created. But he argues further that we can tell a story that would enhance the plausibility of thinking of teletransportation as, on the contrary, a persisting person who swaps bodies:

Imagine a society living in an environment in which an increase in some sort of radiation has made it impossible for a human body to remain healthy for more than a few years. Being highly advanced technologically, the society has developed the following procedure for dealing with this. For each person there is a stock of duplicate bodies, cloned from cells taken from that person and grown by an accelerated process in a radiation-proof vault, where they are then stored. Periodically a person goes into the hospital for a "body-change." This consists in his total brain-state being transferred to the brain of one of his duplicate bodies. At the end of the procedure the original body is incinerated. We are to imagine that in this society going in for a body-change is as routine an occurrence as going to have one's teeth cleaned is in ours.[39]

---

[38] Discussion of such devices is standard fare in the literature on personal identity. Locke first hypothesized that the memories and personality of a prince might be transferred to the body of a cobbler and claimed that in that case the prince would survive but with the cobbler's body (John Locke, *An Essay Concerning Human Understanding* (Amherst, NY: Prometheus Books, 1995), Chapter 27, Subsection 15, 250–251.) A brain-state transfer device was discussed by Bernard Williams, "The Self and the Future," *The Philosophical Review* 79 (1970), 161–180, though Williams strongly disagreed with Locke; see also Robert Nozick, *Philosophical Explanations* (Cambridge, MA: Harvard University Press, 1981), 39; Sydney Shoemaker, "Survival and the Importance of Identity," in *Self and Identity, Contemporary Philosophical Issues*, ed. Daniel Kolak and Raymond Martin (New York: Macmillan, 1991), 267–273. A general discussion is found in Harold Noonan, *Personal Identity* (London: Routledge, 1989). Articles with various viewpoints are reprinted in *Person Identity*, ed. Raymond Martin and John Barresi (Malden, MA: Blackwell Publishers, 2003); Martin and Barresi, eds., *Personal Identity* (Oxford: Blackwell Publishers, 2003).

[39] Shoemaker, op. cit., 267–268. A scenario very much like this was depicted in the Arnold Schwarzenegger movie in 2000, "The Sixth Day."

Shoemaker argues that in such a society what *they* would mean by the word "person" would be such that the teletransportation would be person-preserving. But their meaning of "person" would in every other way be the same as what we in our society mean by "person," since they would call the same kinds of things as we do "persons" and would make the same types of inferences and consequences from their notion of person as we do. So, Shoemaker claims, *we* in our society ought also to regard teletransportation as person-preserving. And it follows that psychological continuity (in the strong sense explained by Shoemaker, for example) constitutes personal identity.[40]

A similar argument can be made considering a "cerebrum transplant." Suppose that the cerebrum of a prince (named "Prince") is transplanted into the body of a cobbler (named "Cobbler"), whose own cerebrum has been removed and destroyed. After the operation the living body with Prince's cerebrum has the thoughts, memories, intentions, and personality of Prince, while the other living body is in a persistent vegetative state (has periods of waking and sleeping, responds to stimuli, but is not conscious). Where is Prince after the operation? Many people are inclined to say that Prince survives or persists but acquires a new body, namely Cobbler's body. If that is right, then it means that personal identity is constituted by psychological continuity. For, one is not likely to say that we are cerebra and that in such an operation the human organism that was Prince survived but acquired new arms, legs, and so on. Rather – the argument continues – it seems that the organism that was Cobbler survives, since his biological life is not interrupted, and the *personal* survival of Prince is due to the persistence of what makes him who he is, namely, his thoughts, character, and so on.

It is usually claimed that this view of personal identity is consistent with either an immaterialist or a materialist view of what a human person is. Immaterialists (such as Locke) hold that the person could be transferred to a distinct immaterial soul. Materialists hold that a person's thoughts and character are necessarily realized in, or supervenient upon, some material; and yet many materialists also hold that a person's thought and character could be transferred to a distinct human animal and that the person would thereby be (or be realized in) the new animal.

It is true that the problem of the diachronic identity of the human person is logically distinct from the problem of the synchronic identity of

---

[40] Many of the examples seem to presuppose physicalism, namely, that the dispositions of the brain are sufficient to determine all psychological states. We disagree, but will not argue the issue in this chapter. See Chapter 2.

the human person. Still, the problems are obviously tied together. We hold that the alleged intuitions appealed to by scenarios of brain-state transfers or cerebrum transfers are in fact logically dependent on an anterior, even if implicit, view of what the human person *is* (the issue of synchronic identity).[41] In other words, we hold that the thought that a particular person persists both before and after the destruction of a human animal logically *presupposes* that the person is not a (particular kind of) animal. And so we suggest that what must be said about diachronic personal identity during extraordinary, and often technically impossible, events is less clear than the proposition that we are rational animals.

As Jennifer Whiting points out, the problem of personal identity has its special character "due largely to the fact that persons view their own existence and persistence over time from different points of view."[42] That is, viewed from the outside, we do appear to be animals of a specific type, rational animals. But viewing ourselves from the inside, we may be inclined to think of our persisting as requiring only a psychological continuity. This inclination is brought to surface by various thought experiments. However, the prima facie view of oneself from the inside (one's first-person perspective of oneself) is necessarily partial. And the idea that one's identity is constituted by psychological continuity, we submit, is initially due to forgetting the limitations or partiality of the first-person point of view.[43]

In other words, one's consciousness of oneself from the inside is susceptible – if one believes it reveals to one the *whole* essence of the self – to an *illusory* sense of oneself as a subject distinct from what is known from the outside. And so there is an inclination to think that the survival of one's thoughts and personality, or, more correctly, of an entity with the same *type of* thoughts and personality as oneself, *is* oneself.

So such an inclination to have such thoughts does not provide strong warrant for them. For suppose there is psychological continuity after one of these fictional brain-state-transfer procedures (or teletransportations). And suppose that the thinker thinks that *he* exists, *he* now seems to have a new body, and, as a consequence, *he* is identical with the person he remembers himself as being. Such an inference would be without foundation. While the thinker with the transferred brain states, or transplanted

---

[41] The position that in effect denies any synchronic identity for substances – sometimes called "four dimensionalism" or "perdurantism" – is examined later, see pp. 29–31.

[42] Jennifer Whiting, "Personal Identity: The Non-Branching Form of 'What Matters,'" in *The Blackwell Guide to Metaphysics*, ed. Richard Gale (Malden, MA: Blackwell Publishers, 2002), 190.

[43] This is not to say there are no limitations on the third-person perspective.

cerebrum, does (we imagine) think that *he* exists, it is *not* clear that "he" or the "he" whom he thinks about is the same entity as the one from whom the brain states or cerebrum were transplanted. Only if one *first* identifies the referent of "he" with the memories, character, basic intentions, and so on, does the thought make any sense. We, on the contrary, would say simply that in such cases the first person became severely impaired, and that the second person simply acquired new memories, thoughts, intentions, and so on, that are *qualitatively similar* to the memories, thoughts, and so on, of the first person. But these memories, thoughts, and so on, are not *numerically* identical with the memories, thoughts, and so on, of the first person.

Moreover, the duplication objection to the psychological continuity view of personal identity has never been adequately answered. Suppose one says that personal identity consists in (rather than just is evidenced by) continuities of beliefs, memory, character, and basic intentions. In other words, person A is identical with person B if person B has the same beliefs, memories, character, and basic intentions as person A – even though person A and person B (at different times) have different and noncontinuous bodies (or animal organisms). Then it would be possible for the teletransporter to transfer the state of a person A's brain to two (or more) brains rather than to just one. The two copies (B and C) would go on to lead their lives, having different experiences, facing different challenges and opportunities, and undoubtedly developing different beliefs and at least slightly different characters, memories, and intentions. But both have the psychological continuity with A such that on the psychological continuity view each is identical with A. Yet, after a time, they have significantly different properties, and so they cannot be identical with each other. Nor are there different respects of identity in question here, so that one could say that B is identical with A in one respect but is different in a different respect.[44]

In such a case it would seem perfectly reasonable to hold that the teletransportation procedure produces *replicas* of the original self rather than literally transporting the self. For, B and C are each psychologically continuous with A. On the psychological continuity view, it follows that B is identical with A and C is identical with A; but, by the transitivity of

---

[44] The same issue is presented by the imagined scenario of an individual whose brain hemispheres are equally capable and one hemisphere is transplanted into a second (very similar) body and the other hemisphere is placed in a third (similar) body. See Derek Parfit, "The Unimportance of Identity," in Martin and Barresi, *Personal Identity*, 292–318.

identity, it would also follow that B is identical with C. But since B now has different properties from C, it would also follow that B is *not* identical with C. Hence the psychological continuity view of personal identity leads to a self-contradiction, and so must be false.

Attempts to respond to this difficulty do not seem successful. One response is to say that the person survives the teletransportation procedure only if there is a unique survivor.[45] On this position, what is required for personal survival is *nonbranching* psychological continuity. That is, A would survive as B if and only if C did not survive – or A would survive as C if and only if B did not survive. But the difficulty here is that it does not seem coherent to hold that whether B is identical with A should depend upon facts which are *extrinsic* to A and B.[46] Viewing this point from the first-person perspective, one must ask: how can whether I survive, whether I am the same person as was lying on a particular operating room yesterday, depend upon the existence or nonexistence of someone very much like me in another room several yards away?[47]

Another attempt to respond to the duplication problem proceeds by attempting to weaken the identity relation. Derek Parfit has argued that the identity relation is not an all or nothing affair. Rather, according to Parfit, *A is identical with B*, in the broad sense, means only that B has a large degree of the relevant type of continuity with A, and that, among the beings that exist, B has the highest degree of the relevant continuity with A. This relation – identity, in the broad sense, as opposed to the strict sense, in which it would imply an all or nothing relation – is, according to Parfit, *all that matters* when speaking about persons.[48] We criticize this position later, see pp. 30–38. If this attempt to weaken the identity relation is unsuccessful (as we argue later), then the duplication objection against the psychological continuity view of personal identity provides decisive evidence against it.

Peter van Inwagen and Trenton Merricks have identified a second major problem with the psychological continuity view. They have shown that it is incompatible with the position that persons are enduring subjects. That is, the psychological continuity view requires one to hold that persons

---

[45] Shoemaker, loc. cit.; Whiting, loc. cit.

[46] Harold Noonan refers to this point as "the only x and y principle," Noonan, *Personal Identity*.

[47] This objection has been pressed by, among others, Bernard Williams, loc. cit., and David Wiggins, *Sameness and Substance* (London: Oxford Press, 1980), 95–96.

[48] See Derek Parfit, "Personal Identity," *The Philosophical Review* 80 (1971); Whiting, loc. cit.

perdure rather than endure (that is, they do not exist all at once, but are extended in time – instead of being substances that endure, they are like baseball games or concrete songs, where an extension in time is part of what they are).

Here is the argument. Suppose that on January 1, 2000, I suffer a major trauma to my brain such that all of my memories and character are wiped out. When I say "I did this" or "I did that," what does "I" refer to? If I endure through time (rather than being a time-worm, or a perdurer) then "I" refers to some substance – whether it is material or immaterial does not matter for this argument. Suppose for a moment that Locke is right and that "I" refers to an immaterial soul. Then, if the psychological continuity view of personal identity were true, the following three propositions would follow, using the name "Anima" to refer to the substance referred to by the word "I":

1. The referent of the pretraumatic utterances of "I" that were uttered by the lips of the body connected to Anima is identical with Anima (this follows from the endurantist position).

2. Anima is identical with the referent of the *post*-traumatic utterances of "I" uttered by the lips of the body connected to Anima (this also follows from the endurantist position)

3. The referent of the pretraumatic utterances of "I" proceeding from the lips of the body connected to Anima is *not* identical with the referent of the post-traumatic utterances of "I" that proceed from those lips (this follows from the psychological continuity view of personal identity, together with the supposition of the pervasive trauma).

Plainly, however, propositions 1 through 3 are logically incoherent. Thus, the psychological continuity view is incompatible with the position that "I" refers to an enduring substance.

The argument can be reconstructed if one holds, as we do, that "I" refers to a rational animal. In other words, suppose that "I" refers to an enduring substance that is a rational animal. Suppose again that a terrible accident causes all of the psychological information involved in personal psychological continuity to be subtracted from that substance but that the substance continues to exist. Then, "I" refers to the same substance both before and after the loss of memory, character, and so on, and so *I* did survive the unfortunate incident. But on the psychological continuity view, I do *not* survive – since x and y are the same person only if there is some sufficient degree of sameness of memories, character, and so on.

Thus, as van Inwagen and Merricks show, the psychological continuity view is incompatible with the endurantist position, namely, with the view that "I" refers to an enduring substance.

The only way to save the psychological continuity view is to deny that "I" refers to an enduring entity and embrace perdurantism, that is, to hold that "I" refers to a *series of events* (suitably connected in some psychological way) or to a "person-stage" of the whole series suitably connected; in either case, one says that persons perdure rather than endure. So, the only way out of the difficulty is to adopt perdurantism. But perdurantism also has grave difficulties.

Perdurantism is usually presented as a specific position regarding human persons or personal identity. The position we briefly examined and criticized earlier which we called "eventism" (Section I) and associated with process philosophy is a more general doctrine – that is, it holds that *all* apparent substances are series of events. So, the arguments we presented against eventism also cast doubt on perdurantism.

In addition, there are two further difficulties specifically for perdurantism. A first additional difficulty for perdurantism concerns temporal extent. According to perdurantism, the person is the sum of person-stages suitably connected. But what is a person-stage, and, more importantly, how could person-stages give rise to a person's temporal extent? If the person-stage does *not* have temporal extent, then the addition of no matter how many person-stages to each other will never give rise to a temporally extended series – just as the addition of no matter how many unextended points will never produce an extended line. On the other hand, if the person-stage *does* have temporal extent, then what explanatory gain has been achieved by denying an enduring substance? In other words, one must posit a temporally enduring something at some stage, to get a temporally extended series. Perdurance presupposes endurance at some lower level.[49] But if one must admit endurantism at one level, why not admit it at the level that common sense and explanatory practice seem to demand? We conclude that perdurantism should not be accepted. Since the psychological continuity view of personal identity logically implies perdurantism, we conclude that the psychological continuity view of persons should also be rejected.

[49] This is very close to the argument against perdurantism presented by Roderick Chisholm in *Person and Object*. Aristotle argues in the same way for the existence of a continuing subject in every change – whether a substance or matter – depending on the type of change involved, in *Physics*, Bk. I. Also see Chappell, *Understanding Human Goods*.

The second problem with perdurantism is that, as has been argued by several philosophers, it in effect denies the existence of change altogether. On the perdurantist position an object, such as a human being, is not wholly present at any given time. Rather, just as an object has spatial parts, so that at small portions of space only part of it is present, so each object has temporal parts. An object, for example an apple, has a part that is present at one time, say on Monday, and another part of the apple that is present at another time, say, on Tuesday (it does not matter how small or large the parts selected). The apple is composed of different temporal parts or stages. Thus, the apple is green at one temporal stage (say, Monday) and red at another temporal stage (say, Tuesday). But on this view it follows that in the strict sense there is no change: just as a flagpole that is green at one spatial part and red at another part does not involve any change, so an apple that is green at one temporal part and red at another part involves no change.[50] For real change to occur, the same subject must first be characterized in one way and then in another way. However, that change does occur, both in external things and in ourselves is, we take it, obvious. The *changing* of the apple from green to red and myriad other changes are evident to our senses and prompt us to ask why and to formulate hypotheses or theories to provide explanation for such changes. And we obviously undergo and bring about changes in ourselves – the reader right now is experiencing some type of change, whether pleasant or unpleasant, enlightening or disappointing. Thus, the perdurance theory, or temporal parts theory, has grave difficulties. But the psychological continuity view requires the perdurance theory, and so its serious difficulties are also grave problems for the psychological continuity view.

Still another attempt to place central importance on psychological continuity rather than on substantial endurance is to concede that personal identity in the strict sense cannot be constituted by psychological continuity, but to insist nevertheless that only psychological continuity is practically important. Parfit is among those who argue that personal identity is often indeterminate – for example, in the duplication cases, there just is no fact of the matter (says Parfit) about whether either offshoot, or

---

[50] This point is argued at length by David Oderberg, "Temporal Parts and the Possibility of Change," *Philosophy and Phenomenological Research* 69 (2004), 686–708; also see Sally Haslanger, "Persistence through Time," in *Oxford Handbook of Metaphysics*, ed. Michael Loux and Dean Zimmerman (New York: Oxford University Press, 2003); E. J. Lowe, *A Survey of Metaphysics* (New York: Oxford University Press, 2002).

which one, is identical with the original.[51] But, according to Parfit, all that is really important to us is psychological continuity. The only thing important for me when considering my "self-interest" is whether someone survives who is psychologically continuous with me in such a way that this later self would think of himself as me. Suppose the teletransporter does not transport *me* to another place, but that it merely produces a *replica* of me and that, meanwhile, *I* die. That is, suppose (just as we argued earlier) that teletransportation does not ensure *identity*, but ensures only that there will be a literally distinct individual psychologically continuous with me. Parfit insists that this should not matter to me in the least if I am deliberating whether to make use of such a device. Psychological continuity may not be the same as strict identity (he refers to it as identity in the broad sense), but it is all that matters.

Parfit's strongest argument for this position begins by considering brain bisection cases. Suppose that the left hemisphere of my brain is extracted and implanted into another body very similar to my body and (what is not now possible) the nerves of the left hemisphere of my brain are connected to the new body. Meanwhile the right hemisphere of my brain is transplanted into a third body quite similar to my present body. Both individuals survive, call them A and B, and both are, let us suppose, psychologically continuous with me. In fact, says Parfit, if B had not survived, we would not hesitate to say that A *was me*. Similar events (Parfit reminds us) occur with stroke victims; that is, stroke victims can at times lose the entire functioning of one of the hemispheres of their brains and yet survive. Parfit then argues as follows. Neither A nor B can be strictly identical with me, since (as we saw earlier) this would entail that A and B are identical with each other when they obviously are not. Yet if only the transplant to A had been attempted, and the brain hemisphere left behind had been destroyed in the process, we would not hesitate to say that I was identical with A and that the operation was a success (and the same if the transplant was made into the body of B) – for these cases would be relevantly similar (says Parfit) to the stroke victim cases. So, a

---

[51] Parfit, *Reasons and Person*, Chapters 10–13; Jeff McMahan takes a position similar to Parfit's and shows in detail the implications of this view for the moral assessment of abortion and euthanasia, in Jeff McMahan, *The Ethics of Killing, Problems at the Margins of Life* (New York: Oxford University Press, 2002). McMahan adds, however, that to be of "egoistic concern," the psychological continuity must be grounded in the physical parts of the brain that are the substrate for consciousness and mental activity. See ibid., 55–59. This addition does not affect the basic difficulties we raise for the Parfitian theory.

single success would involve my identity and – the decisive point – would entail the *survival or persistence* of what is important to me. But then, asks Parfit, how could a double success (the survival of both A and B) mean a failure? His answer, of course, is that it could not. And so Parfit concludes that if both A and B survived, then neither would be strictly identical with me, but still, everything that is important to me *would survive*, indeed, would be present twice over.

To see what is wrong with Parfit's argument, it is important to notice that it is based on his claim that personal identity is not a determinate, all or nothing fact. His position is that only psychological continuity is practically important rests on his prior *reductionism* concerning personal identity. That is, according to Parfit, personal identity consists in a set of other facts, such as facts about memory, intentions, and character.[52] If A is psychologically continuous with B, then there is no further *fact* to ask about; there is no further fact, such as A *is* B, or A *is not* B. Whereas a nonreductionist about personal identity will say that these other facts are, typically but not always, evidence or manifestations of an underlying real identity across time.

Yet his argument for his reductionist claim is not convincing. Parfit argues that personal identity does depend in some way on the persistence of either psychological traits or physical components, such as brain cells, or on a combination of both. He then asks us to imagine a spectrum of cases in which at the near end of the spectrum only 1 percent of those components and traits are replaced (say, only 1 percent of my brain cells and connected psychological traits are replaced), while at the far end of the spectrum 90 percent of those components and traits are replaced. He then says that most of us would agree that at the near end of the spectrum I survive, and that at the far end of the spectrum I do not survive (note, this is his *combined* spectrum case – both psychological traits and physical components such as one's cells are replaced). He then he adds:

If we do not yet accept the Reductionist View, and continue to believe that our identity must be determinate, what should we claim about these cases? If we continue to assume that my Replica would not be me, we are forced to the following conclusion. There must be some critical percentage which is such that, if the surgeons replace less than this percent, it will be me who wakes up, but if they replace more then this percent, it will *not* be me but only someone else, who is merely like me. . . . Such a view is not incoherent. But it is hard to believe.[53]

---

[52] Parfit, *Reasons and Persons*, 231–243.
[53] Ibid., 235

A few pages later he states his argument more fully:

These claims are hard to believe. It is hard to believe (1) that the difference between life and death could just consist in any of the very small differences described above. We are inclined to believe that there is always a difference between some future person's being me, and his being someone else. And we are inclined to believe that this is a deep difference. But between neighbouring cases in this Spectrum the differences are trivial. It is therefore hard to believe that, in one of these cases, the resulting person would quite straightforwardly be me, and that, in the next case, he would quite straightforwardly be someone else.[54]

We agree with Parfit that the sharp difference between someone being me and someone not being me must be, if it exists, a "deep" fact. The difference cannot *consist in* a difference of more or less of some other stuff or components, but it must be a substantial difference. Parfit's argument is that if there were such a difference (a deep fact), then it could not occur with the addition of a trivial fact (say, the subtraction of one brain cell). Yet Parfit's argument ignores the fact that in many cases a substantial change is *caused by* a small change in the addition or subtraction of some stuff or components. For example, a certain degree of heat is required to effect many significant chemical changes, such as explosions, water arising from hydrogen and oxygen, where just a little less heat would not enable that substantial change.[55] In other words, *very slight changes can give rise to, or prevent, the generation of new substances.* The generation of a new substance is a radical, an all or nothing event; but it is disposed to, or prevented by, slight changes, that is, changes in which there are spectra or continua of more or less degrees of change. The same is true with the ceasing to be of substances (in Aristotelian language, corruption of substances). If a human person is an animal organism, as we have argued, then there is no surprise at all that this organism will survive a continuum of slight changes right up to the point at which the proverbial last straw is reached, that is, where a further slight change removes the possibility of any central integration at all of the various organs and tissues, and that is the death – an abrupt, noncontinuous change – of the organism.

---

[54] Ibid., 239.

[55] We are here supposing that the formation of water is a substantial change, in the Aristotelian sense, that is, the generation of a new substance. If that is not so, a similar example could be drawn from organisms: a spermatozoon can penetrate an ovum only if the chemical composition is just right in the vaginal tract of the female; if the chemical composition is changed very slightly, penetration by the spermatozoon of the ovum will be rendered impossible and thus a new substance will not come to be.

Thus, Parfit's spectrum argument rests on ignoring the distinction between a spectrum of continuous changes and what such a spectrum might cause. And since his argument for the position that psychological continuity is all that matters rests on the reductionist view of personal identity – for if there really is a simple fact that I do or do not survive a certain event, then it *is* crucially important to me which fact is the case – it follows that his case for the exclusive practical importance of psychological continuity is also undermined. So, we submit that genuine survival or persistence of a rational animal across time requires *numerical identity of the psychophysical substance*, not just some degree of psychological continuity together with some degree of biological continuity. And we submit that in some instances of real diachronic personal identity, psychological continuity is actually entirely lacking – as in comas or severe amnesia.

Parfit introduced the fission scenario by comparing it to a stroke victim, where a person loses the entire functioning of one of the hemispheres of his brain and yet is surely identical with his former self. Next, Parfit describes a case in which one brain hemisphere of person A is transplanted into a body similar to A's body (in fact, into the body of A's twin), and he concludes that, even if we hold the physical criterion of personal identity, we would have to say that in this case A did survive, that the person after the surgery was identical with A before the surgery. And from there it is easy for Parfit to conclude that if *both* brain hemispheres are successfully transplanted, what was important for A in the first transplant has occurred twice over (even though the two resulting individuals could not be "strictly identical" with A). But the mistake here is in supposing that transplanting A's brain hemisphere into his twin's body would result in a person identical with A. Suppose A has not suffered a stroke, and suppose that the transplant takes place, but that the brain hemisphere left behind in A's body continues to integrate, or help integrate, the various bodily systems in A. In that case, we submit that A survives, but that his extracted brain hemisphere either aids another individual to survive or, when joined to the other bodily parts, generates a new human organism and thus a new human person.

Neither psychological nor biological continuity is sufficient to constitute diachronic identity. When a cell divides into two cells (in mitotic division, half of its chromosomes going to one daughter cell and the other half to another daughter cell), we rightly say that cell A has ceased to exist and produced two new "daughter cells."[56] Thus, biological *continuity* is

---

[56] This case is discussed by David Oderberg, *The Metaphysics of Identity Over Time* (New York: St. Martin's Press, 1993).

not sufficient for the identity across time of an organism. Similarly, if the teletransporter produced personalities *psychologically* continuous with S (without destroying or hardly altering the original person) we should simply say that the two psychological replicas of S were quite distinct from S. The question to ask in a case of a brain hemisphere transplant from A into another body is the same question that should be asked in any other life-threatening surgery performed on a human individual; namely, has the animal organism continued to exist?

Suppose that I enter a machine that makes an exact replica of me, but that I remain fully conscious throughout the whole procedure, in fact, suppose I hardly feel a thing. It seems clear that it would be me that walked out of the machine. And it seems clear that what I hope *for myself* would be completely unaffected, except indirectly (the possibility of meeting my replica or his being mistaken for me, etc.) by the creation of a duplicate. Were such a duplicate made of me, *I myself*, and not he, would be bound by my promises and vows, liable for my debts and offenses, and so on. If my duplicate without my permission withdrew money from my bank account or took my automobile, that clearly would be theft. But if these things are true, then there *is* a numerical identity across time, and it *does* matter. In other words, *there is some fact of the matter*, not just psychological continuity or the lack thereof.[57] Parfit can say that psychological connectedness is the only thing practically important because he has already denied determinate identity. But, given that a person in the future either will or will not be identical with me, given that whether a person at one time is identical with a person at some earlier time is a matter of truth and not just a matter of decision, then (in teletransportation or brain bisection cases) whether A will be me, or B will be me, or neither will be me, is enormously important to me and to anyone who cares about me.

Christopher Tollefsen has recently showed this point by comparing teletransportation (and other such devices that preserve only psychological continuity) with the thought experiment about the experience machine made famous by Robert Nozick's argument against hedonism in *Anarchy, State and Utopia*.[58] Suppose, said Nozick, that you could plug yourself into an experience machine that would give you *the experience* of having a fully meaningful life – the experience of creating great art, having

---

[57] Note that the further fact is not a Cartesian ego (as Parfit seems to think is necessary for the view that personal identity is determinate) but the persistence of a psychophysical substance.

[58] Robert Nozick, *Anarchy, State and Utopia* (Oxford: Blackwell Publishers, 1968), 43–45.

wonderful relationships, thinking great thoughts, and so on – but once plugged in you could not get unplugged. Most people agree that they would not choose to plug into the experience machine. And what this shows, Nozick points out, is that we value, or recognize as inherently worthwhile, not just experience, but reality, really acting and forming our lives. Tollefsen argues that the experience machine argument also shows that whether a person in the past was *really* me, or a person in the future will *really* be me, is profoundly important. What one undergoes in the experience machine is a mere experience or appearance, not a reality. And what we desire – what we recognize as inherently worthwhile – is not mere appearance, but "what is available to us through genuine human action."[59] Moreover, this point is especially important when considering acts of will: an act of will, or an act of consent, registers morally and socially only if there is a real act as opposed to the mere experience of one. What a person is morally responsible for, what he is actually committed to, and (where a duty arises from a past promise, choice, or agreement) what he owes to people, must all be based on what he has *in reality* willed and done, not what he merely had the experience of doing or the appearance of having done.

It follows that – supposing now that someone could get plugged into the experience machine and then later get unplugged – if someone had *the experience* of having consented to marriage with someone, he would not thereby be married. He would no more be married than if he had dreamed he had married someone. If he had the experience of making certain promises or borrowing money in the experience machine, he would not be bound by those promises or have those debts: what matters morally and socially are *real* acts of will, not the mere experience or appearance of such acts.

These points about the experience machine and dreams apply to processes, such as teletransportation or cerebrum transplants, that merely produce replicas of a person. Suppose that A's psychological states – his memories, intentions, and so on – are transferred to B and A dies in the process. According to Parfit, it may be true that B is not, strictly speaking, identical with A, but even so, A has what matters in survival. We should not even ask whether B really is A or not; A has all that matters in survival or continued living. If A is told of the prospect before the procedure, he should not be afraid since, although *he* may not, strictly speaking, be alive

---

[59] Christopher Tollefsen, "Experience Machines, Dreams, and What Matters," *The Journal of Value Inquiry* 37 (2003), 153–164, at 157.

later, what happens will be just as good as his remaining alive. However, what is transferred to B are not A's numerically identical memories and intentions and psychological states. What is transferred are psychological states that are *qualitatively similar*, not numerically identical, to A's psychological states.[60] So, if A was married, then B will not be married to Mrs. A. And whatever promises A made, B will not be bound by them. For B did not give the actual consent to be married to Mrs. A, and B himself did not make the promises that A made – B has only the experiences of having been married, making promises, and so on. So, just as a person who has only the experience of getting married and of making promises in an experience machine is not really married, and is not bound by the mere experience of having made promises, just so, B's false memories of having been married and of having made promises do not give him the relevant obligations and rights.

Moreover, if B learns that the memories he has are actually results of transfer or transplant from A's brain and actual life, he will rightly feel that his autonomy has been violated. The plans and commitments he thought were his, that is, of his own making, he discovers are actually the product of someone else's (A's) choices. They would no more be his plans and commitments than if he had been induced to have them through hypnosis. Because it is the acts of will themselves that produce obligations and rights, rather than the experiences of them, and because who we are is shaped by our actual choices, not by dreams or experiences not grounded in reality, it follows that it is vitally important whether I really am the person I think I was a year ago, two years ago, and so on. So, *numerical identity* across time is a real and determinate relation, and it matters whether persona A at one time really is or is not numerically identical with person B at another time.[61]

---

[60] Ibid., 160.

[61] As Harold Noonan pointed out, our different attitudes toward persons and toward things confirm that numerical identity across time is both determinate and important. We distinguish quite easily the question whether the self-same substantial entity will survive from the question whether something just like the original will survive. We generally regard this distinction as unimportant with regard to things, but as crucial with regard to persons. That is, we value persons *themselves* and desire that good things happen to *those persons*. But we value our computers, for example, merely as loci of useful characteristics and would have them replaced by others (and often do) of equal or better utility. What is more, we find no difficulty in distinguishing our differing attitudes to persons and to things. Noonan, op. cit., 199.

Lynne Rudder Baker also expresses this point well: "Moreover, speaking for myself, psychological continuity without identity is not what concerns me in matters of survival. I want to know: Will I be around? Not: Will someone just like me be around? . . . . In fact,

We conclude that psychological continuity cannot be the criterion for determining when we come to be and cease to be. Rather, we are human animals and we came to be when the animal organisms that we are came to be, and we will cease to be only when these animal organisms cease to be.

VIII. Against Constitutionalism

Let us consider still another objection to the position that human beings, human persons, are animals. This objection is based on "constitutionalism," which has also been called the "new dualism." This view claims that we *are* animal organisms, but not in the sense of strict identity. Rather we are only derivatively animal organisms, in the sense of being *constituted* by animal organisms.

In the argument presented against dualism (Sections II–III), the key premises were (as we numbered them) (1) sensation is a bodily act and (2) it is the same agent that performs the act of sensing and which performs the act of understanding or conceptual thought. We argued further that since the agent that performs a bodily act is a bodily entity, the agent that understands also is a bodily entity, an animal organism. Constitutionalists admit that we can say, "I sense," taking the word "sense" as denoting an organic or bodily action, but precisely because it is an organic action, they would add that "is" in this case has a different meaning than when one says, "I understand" or "I choose." The properties or actions that directly belong to the organism or animal, they argue, are directly attributable to the person that the animal or organism constitutes, but those properties or actions do not actually directly characterize him.[62]

Their key idea is that persons are not identical with animals, but they are constituted by them. Constitution is a general relation, one that is weaker than identity but stronger than composition (for example, being composed of certain elements). Consider Michelangelo's statue *David* and

regardless of how many psychological replicas of me there are, I would not have the same concern for any of my psychological replicas as I have for myself. I would not care about those replicas as much as I care for my family and friends. We are interested in identity because we are interested in particular individuals (*de re*), and not just in whoever fits a particular description (*de dicto*)" (Lynne Rudder Baker, *Persons and Bodies* (New York: Cambridge University Press, 2000), 129–130).

[62] Baker, *Persons and Bodies*, 130.; also see E. J. Lowe, "Identity, Composition, and the Simplicity of the Self," in *Soul, Body, and Survival*, 139–158; Frederick Doepke, "Spatially Coinciding Objects," in *Material Constitution: A Reader*, ed. Michael C. Rea (New York: Rowman and Littlefield, 1997), 10–24; Mark Johnston, "Constitution Is Not Identity," ibid., 44–62.

the piece of marble *David* is constituted by. Let us name the piece of marble "lumpl." The two are not identical, for the statue could be melted down and so cease to exist even though the piece of marble (lumpl) would continue to be. Also, the particles composing lumpl could gradually all be replaced and yet *David* would survive. In that case lumpl would cease to be but *David* would persist. That is (the constitutionalists hold) since the *persistence conditions* of *David* are distinct from those of lumpl, it follows that *David* and lumpl are not identical. On the other hand, all of the particles that compose lumpl also compose *David*. And so *David* and lumpl, while not identical, do occupy the same space; they are spatially coincident objects.

Applying the idea of constitutionalism to the question of personal identity, one gets the following results. On this view I am not identical with my body but I am constituted by my body. Also, I am not identical with this animal but I am constituted by this animal. To be a person is to be an entity that, as Locke said, is conscious of itself or, as Lynne Rudder Baker puts it, has a first-person perspective – is aware of himself as himself.[63] This position is distinct from Cartesian dualism; indeed Baker has classified it as a type of materialism.[64] For, unlike Cartesian dualism, constitutionalism does hold that the person is necessarily constituted by a body, though it need not be the body one presently has, and indeed may, by way of gradual replacement of parts with artificial ones, be entirely artificial rather than organic.[65]

In virtue of the constitution relation, the higher entity (for example, the statue *David* or a person) inherits certain of the properties of the lower entity. And the lower entity (for example, the piece of marble or the animal) inherits certain of the properties of the higher entity. So one can say, for example, that I weigh 185 pounds and that I worry about getting out of debt. But the first predication is an indirect one. What it really means is "The body that constitutes me, or the *animal* that constitutes me, weighs 185 pounds." The second predication, however, is direct: the property, worrying about such and such, belongs nonderivatively to the person, the referent of "I."

If this view were correct, then we would not be *identical with* animals, as we argued earlier. Also, if this view were correct, then one might hold

[63] Ibid.
[64] Lynne Baker, "Materialism with a Human Face," in *Soul, Body, and Survival*, 159–180.
[65] Lynne Rudder Baker, *Persons and Bodies: A Constitution View* (Cambridge, UK: Cambridge University Press, 2000), 108ff.

that this organism that constitutes me came to be at one time, but that *I* came to be at a later time. Thus, Lynne Rudder Baker denies that we ever were fetuses.[66] Moreover, on this view one could say that I cease to be long before the time that the organism that now constitutes me ceases to be; for example, if the animal that constitutes me entered into an irreversible coma or (perhaps) a so-called persistent vegetative state.

As we saw, the principal argument for constitutionalism is based on the claim that there obviously are different persistence conditions for the entity that constitutes the higher entity and the higher entity itself. Isn't it obvious, so the argument goes, that *David* is distinct from lumpl since *David* could survive the gradual ceasing to be of lumpl? And lumpl could survive the demise of *David* – for example, if vandals melted down the famed statue. Similarly, Baker argues that I could survive the demise of the animal that now constitutes me – each of my organs could be replaced, one by one, by an artificial device, until at some point I cease to be constituted by a living organism at all, but retain my first-person perspective, and so remain a person.[67]

But we submit that to argue in this fashion is to put the cart before the horse, or in other words, to beg the question. Different persistence conditions cannot be evidence for the real distinction between A and B. Rather, the real distinction between A and B must be known (or perhaps implicitly assumed) before one knows (or holds) that A has different persistence conditions than B. In the important case: if a human person and the human animal are really identical, then, though at times a human animal person may not be able to exercise all of his basic natural capacities (for example, before he has actively developed such immediately exercisable capacities in himself, or when he is in a coma), still the substantial entity that is the person continues to be. Whether this is indeed the case depends, of course, on whether the human person *is* identical with the human animal.[68]

---

[66] Ibid., 204ff.

[67] Ibid., 108.

[68] Eric Olson, in "Material Coincidence and the Indiscernibility Problem," *The Philosophical Quarterly* 51 (2001), 353, after presenting several arguments against constitutionalism, suggests this point when he writes: "As I see it, the constitutionalist must say something like this: the differences between Person [a person] and Animal [the animal that constitutes that person] all follow from the fact that Person is a person and Animal is an animal. Being a person entails having 'personal' identity-conditions (incompatible with those of animals), not being alive in the biological sense, and being able to think and experience. Being an animal entails having 'animal' identity-conditions (incompatible with those of people), and being unable to think."

The constitutionalist proposal has further and more serious difficulties as well. Setting aside the possibility that A and B are simply two distinct but somehow interacting substances, we need to consider three possibilities for a unified relation between A and B, for example, for the relation between the human person and the human animal. First, A may be related to B as stuff, or parts, related to a whole. Second, A may be related to B as the constitutionalists claim, namely, as two distinct substances, though colocated and standing in the constitution relation. Or, third, A and B may be related as the less determinate concept of a substance to the more determinate concept of that self-same substance. We maintain that there is good evidence to indicate that the human animal and the human person are related in the third way, not in either of the first two ways.[69] That is, there is substantial evidence to indicate that the human person and the human animal are the same substance, not two, colocated substances.

Consider a substance with three parts, x, y, and z. x–y–z constitute one substantial entity if there is a single self-integration among them, together they regularly perform characteristic actions and reactions, and this self-integration and regular unity of the parts comes from within rather than being imposed from outside (as in artifacts). Now, could x–y–z together make up one substance, say, an animal, and also a distinct substance, say, a person? What would be the evidence for the substantial distinction of the lower entity (in this case the animal) from the higher entity (the person)? We have already said that different persistence conditions is not an allowable answer, since we must first know the real distinction between the substances before we know that they have different persistence conditions.

On the other hand, there *is* clear evidence for their real identity, in other words, that the distinction (between the human animal and the human person) is only a distinction between more and less general concepts. If the various parts of the *animal* are regularly arranged or ordered from within in such a way as to participate in the action that characterizes the person, then this is evidence of substantial unity, as opposed to colocation of distinct substances. But this is precisely what we find in the case of the human person, that is, the concrete rational animal.[70] The individual

---

[69] The term "human person" denotes more than what is denoted by "rational animal." *Human person* denotes, in addition to *rational animal*, the proposition that this rational animal is the ultimate, morally responsible *subject of acting*. This additional denotation is important for certain purposes, notably in theology, but need not concern us here.

[70] This is close to the argument against constitutionalism that Eric Olson calls "the indiscernibility problem." Olson, "Material Coincidence and the Indiscernibility Problem,"

human organism from conception forward is programmed, by his DNA, (and epigenetic state), to develop himself to full physical maturity[71]; but this physical maturity includes the possession of a highly complex brain.[72] And the human brain is internally oriented to providing the sort of sensory and perceptual experience that can serve as the content in which a human being understands and performs acts of understanding and self-reflection, adopting an objective standpoint and a first-person perspective. The human organism is internally structured to participate in those actions which distinguish the human animal from other animals. The organic life of a human being does not develop in a distinct or neutral direction in relation to the rational and voluntary actions of the human person – those actions which move us to call the human animal a person. Rather, the human animal's biological structure is internally oriented to developing the organs necessary for actions characteristic of persons.

Moreover, viewing the internal coordination from the standpoint of the personal side, one can see that the human being's mode of being an animal is specifically rational or personal. Typically, his animal functions are modified or specified by rationality. Thus, humans seek nourishment, shelter, sexual union, bearing and raising of children – all animal acts – in a specifically rational manner. Hence being rational, which enables one to have a first-person perspective and allows one to view oneself from an objective standpoint,[73] is, as Aristotle insisted, the specifically human manner of being an animal, that is, being an animal in a rational and self-conscious way, not the actuation of a distinct, even if colocated, substance.[74] Where A and B are internally oriented to each other, such that

---

337–355. He there cites similar arguments by Michael Burke, "Copper Statues and Pieces of Copper," *Analysis* 52 (1992), 12–17; id., "Person and Bodies: How to Avoid the New Dualism," *American Philosophical Quarterly* 34 (1997), 451–467; Dean Zimmerman, "Theories of Masses and Problems of Constitution," *Philosophical Review* 104 (1995), 53–110; and see also Olson's earlier work, *The Human Animal: Personal Identity without Psychology* (New York: Oxford University Press, 1997), 97–102.

[71] For the evidence of this, see, for example: Scott Gilbert, *Developmental Biology*, 7th ed. (Sunderland, MA: Sinnauer Associates, 2003), Chapters 7–12; Keith Moore and T. V. N. Persaud, *The Developing Human, Clinically Oriented Embryology*, 7th ed. (New York: W.B. Saunders, 2003), Chapters 2–5.

[72] R. Joseph reviews the recent literature on fetal brain and cognitive development: "Fetal Brain and Cognitive Development," *Developmental Review* 20 (1999), 81–98.

[73] Campbell, op. cit., 73–154; Baker, "Materialism with a Human Face," in *Persons and Bodies*, 59–88.

[74] This argument does not depend on holding to a doctrine of the supervenience of the mental upon the physical. See Olson, "Material Coincidence and the Indiscernibility Problem," 345. He puts the point as follows: "The indiscernibility need not involve

they are naturally incomplete without each other (they can perform no actions in which the other does not participate), and they cannot perform opposed actions, then A and B cannot be distinct whole substances.[75] Rather, either they are parts of a single whole substance or simply distinct aspects (concepts) of a single substance. The latter obtains in the case of the relation between the human animal and the human person. *Human animal* is just the less determinate, or more abstract, concept of the self-same substance apprehended more fully in the concept *human person*.

What of the analogy so often used of a statue to the marble (or copper) which constitutes it? Might one argue that the human animal seems to be related to the person as the piece of marble is related to the statue, and since marble and the statue are distinct, so must be the human animal and the human person? The difficulty here is that a statue is an artifact, not a natural substance. So, strictly speaking, the statue is an aggregate of substances viewed as having a unity because of the use to which we will or may put them. There is a spatiotemporal continuity in aggregates (some particles falling away and being replaced by others, but not all of the particles being replaced at once), and so *this aggregate*, which has its unity from its relation to our use, persists but only in a loose sense. The aggregate persists, in some sense, even if the particles that constitute it are rearranged so that it (the aggregate) is no longer subject to the use we had been making of it (its shape is changed so that it can no longer be called a statue). So, the argument by analogy does not get off the ground. It is not the case that there are two substances, the piece of marble and the statue,

---

supervenience at all. What the critics want to know is *why* Person can think. They doubt whether any satisfactory answer is compatible with the claim that Animal, which has the same microstructure, the same surroundings and the same evolutionary history as Person cannot think. Likewise, they want to know why Animal is an animal, and they doubt whether any satisfactory answer is compatible with the claim that Person, despite being made entirely of living tissues arranged just as Animal's are, is not an animal. The real issue is not supervenience but explanation." Our point is that the specific way in which human organisms perform many strictly organic functions – such as brain development – is determined by the organism's personal capacities. *That* is a problem of explanation.

[75] Conjoined twins, of various sorts, are all in some sense incomplete without each other (they share at least parts of some organs with each other, most of the time many whole organs). But each can perform actions, including perceiving, imagining, talking, etc., that are fundamentally independent of actions performed by the other twin. Moreover, each is internally oriented to being distinct and independent, but an anomaly prevents their full separation. Thus, a conjoined twin is a distinct substance from his or her twin and also has an organic, not just spatial, unity (of some degree) with his or her twin, but this is an *overlapping* or only a partial organic union. For more on conjoined twins, see pp. 44–49.

having different persistence conditions. Rather, there is an aggregate of substances (elements making up the marble) arranged to form a statue (an artifact) and then later perhaps not so arranged.[76] There is nothing here to suggest that it is a common occurrence for two really distinct substances to be colocated.

Baker's argument that the human person is not identical with an organism because he or she could cease to be (derivatively) an organism but continue to exist, through gradual replacement of all his or her organic parts by artificial parts is mistaken. First, the argument falsely supposes that memories, intentions, and thought transferred to an artificial cerebrum would be numerically and not just qualitatively the same. Memories, intentions, and thoughts are individuated by the subject in which they inhere, and so if such experiences could be "transferred" to another material agent, they would not be numerically identical. Second, it seems more reasonable to believe that at some point in the process the organization necessary for the numerically same being to continue to exist would break down and so that individual would perish, even though (supposing the "transfer" is really possible) qualitatively similar memories and other experiences could be induced in another mechanism.[77]

IX. Conjoined Twins and Organic Unity and Distinctness

Finally, another argument against the position that we are animal organisms has been presented by Jeff McMahan and is based on a consideration of dicephalic conjoined twins. Conjoined twins are monozygotic twins[78] that share organs and so are joined in their body (either at their chest or at their back) or sometimes at the tops of their heads. In dicephalic twins the union includes the abdomen, pelvis, and thorax. Thus dicephalic twins have one trunk and two heads, though they do not share all of their organs. The famous Hensel Twins (Abigail and Brittany) each has a heart and a stomach but they share three lungs and all of the organs in the lower

---

[76] Burke, "Copper Statues and Pieces of Copper," 12–17; and ibid., "Preserving the Principle of One Object to a Place: A Novel Account of the Relations among Objects, Sorts, Sortals, and Persistence Conditions," in *Material Constitution*, 236–272.

[77] Since conceptual thoughts, as distinct from sense experiences or sense memories, are spiritual acts or states (as we argue in Chapter 2), we do not see how these could be induced or copied into material devices.

[78] That is, twins that occur by the division of one zygote (sometimes also called "identical twins") rather than by the fertilization of two different ova by two different spermatozoa (referred to as "dizygotic" twins).

part of their body. McMahan argues that with dicephalic twins there are two persons but only one organism.

Decephalic twins such as the Hensel girls constitute a single integrally functioning set of organs wrapped in a single skin, sustained by a single coordinated system of metabolism, served by a single blood-stream, protected by a single immune system.... These systems and the processes they sustain together constitute a single biological life, despite the fact that various aspects of this life are somehow jointly governed by two brains.[79]

On the other hand, McMahan continues, each is a distinct person since each has her own private thoughts, emotions, and expressions, and is a separate center of consciousness.[80] Since dicephalic twins are not different types of beings from you or me, McMahan concludes that the human person is not identical with the human organism.

Thus, according to McMahan, human persons are not organisms, though they are related to organisms. Moreover, eschewing substance dualism and constitutionalism, McMahan argues that a human person – every human person – is an embodied mind, that is, a functioning brain, related to the organism as a part to the whole.[81]

The first point to notice is that some conjoined twins (though not dicephalic ones) can be separated. when this occurs there are no grounds for saying a new organism comes to be (as there are, for example, with cuttings in plants or monozygotic twins in mammals); so it is clear that there were two organisms all along, growing and functioning in distinct directions, at least with respect to most functions. It is possible for two distinct organisms to share organs. And, since that is so, there is no principled reason why two organisms could not have intertwined circulatory and immune systems and share very many (though not all) organs.

Second, McMahan assumes that being one organism and being two organisms are exclusive in all respects. That is, he assumes that conjoined twins must be *either* one organism *or* two but that they cannot be *both* one and two, although in different respects. His argument is that since they are one organism, they cannot be, at the same time, two organisms. But this is a mistake. Conjoined twins *are* distinct organisms (as we show in a moment), but they also have a real organic unity. The conjoined twins are one organism in many respects (with respect to many organic functions) but two organisms with respect to other functions (such as sensations and

---

[79] McMahan, op. cit., 37.
[80] Ibid., 38.
[81] Ibid., 66–94.

many movements, since one twin typically has direct control over only one side).

To this one might object that similar disunity occurs in human beings who have undergone callosotomy (or commissurotomy) – a severing of the corpus callosum so that there appear to be two "centers of consciousness." In such cases, literally the left side is sometimes not aware of what the right side is doing.[82] Plainly, however, there is only one organism in the callosotomy case, and so (it may be objected) functions in some respects independent of one another do not prove that there are distinct organisms.

In reply, the decisive point showing that the conjoined twins are two organisms (while at the same time having some degree of organic unity) is that each has her own brain, including brainstem – the organ responsible for much of the central organization of the animal. This fact indicates that from the beginning, whether twinning occurs by incomplete fission or by a partial fusion of twins initially completely separate,[83] each is *internally oriented to* being organically complete and independent but that some anomalous occurrence (anomalous, since conjoined twins are extremely rare) prevents that. By contrast, with the individual who has undergone a split-brain procedure (callosotomy), it is clear that there is an internal organic orientation toward full integration but a partial breakdown in that integration occurs.[84]

---

[82] For example, a patient having undergone such a procedure, when presented with a blue spot on the left field of his vision and a red spot on the right field of his vision will claim he sees only one color, and if he can write with each hand, his right hand will write that the spot is red while his left hand will write that it is blue. For a discussion of such cases, see Thomas Nagel, "Brain Bisection and the Unity of Consciousness," *Synthese* 22 (1971), 396–413; Parfit, *Reasons and Persons*, 245–280.

[83] These are the two theories on how conjoined twins occur. See Ronan O'Rahilly and Fabiola Mueller, *General Embryology and Teratology* (New York: Wiley-Liss, 2000), 53–55.

[84] Moreover – though it is not essential for our argument – it does not seem accurate to describe such patients as "having two centers of consciousness," as is often claimed. As John Robinson pointed out, these same patients invariably at other times *can* compare what is seen on the left side of their visual field with what is seen on the right side. From this fact Robinson concludes that "It seems that we must regard the commissurotomy patient as a single subject of experience and action who has perceptual experiences localized in each of his two hemispheres" (John Robinson, "Personal Identity and Survival," *Journal of Philosophy* 85 (1988), 319–328, at 327. See also D. M. MacKay, "Conscious Agency and Unsplit and Split Brains," in *Consciousness and the Physical World*, ed. B. Josephson and V. Raamachandran (London: Pergamon, 1980), 108ff). Robinson further suggests what seems to us the most natural interpretation of the facts, namely, "that the commissurotomy patient may have perceptual experiences located in each hemisphere but that these experiences are not conscious ones – there is nothing it is like to have these experiences. The experimental evidence suggests that the unattended hemisphere

McMahan considers the argument that since the dicephalic twins have two brains, they must be distinct organisms. To this he replies, "It is rather (though not exactly) like the claim that a plane with duplicate control mechanisms for a pilot and a copilot is really two distinct but overlapping planes."[85] But these cases are very dissimilar. First, though there is a high degree of integration between the twins, this integration is not *complete* (being established only by the organs which they do share in common). Second, the plane's duplicate control mechanism is designed to do the same thing the first control mechanism does. In the twins' case, however, there are not just different brains, there are other different organs (eyes, ears, etc.), and there are different and sometimes (in varying degrees) opposite functions or actions. This is evidence of distinct organisms, albeit with some overlapping organs.

The third difficulty in McMahan's argument concerning dicephalic twins is that if his interpretation of their situation were correct, then none of the organs in the twins could be assigned to one individual rather than the other. Each set of eyes, each set of ears, and so on, would not belong biologically more to one girl than to the other. Each of these organs would have to be a part of a single larger organism, subservient to the survival and functioning of this one organism. But this plainly is not the case. It is indisputable that each one *biologically* has not only her own brain, but also her own skull, eyes, ears, and many organs, while sharing many other organs.

McMahan's proposal that we are embodied minds or functioning brains, parts of whole human organisms, also is not tenable. He rejects identifying the self with consciousness and he rejects the psychological continuity theory of diachronic personal identity. He also rejects constitutionalism, though, like the constitutionalists, he wishes to distinguish one's self from one's organism. He proposes, then, that what I am is a *part* of a human organism, namely, the brain when it is capable of being conscious.

There are several difficulties with this proposal. First, the brain is itself a complex whole and gradually emerges in the self-development of the embryo. The brain as a whole organ is clearly present in rudimentary form, with much differentiation, as early as ten weeks. Before that, the

---

supports nonconscious experiences (of which, in normal circumstances, a normal subject could ordinarily become conscious) and not an independent stream of consciousness" (Robinson, op. cit., 326).

[85] McMahan, op. cit., 37.

epigenetic precursor of the brain is visibly present from the thirteenth day, with the appearance of the primitive streak, and even before that its epigenetic primordium is present in the embryo from day one which has the information and inherent active disposition to develop a brain.[86] The human child's brain does not develop sufficiently to support *conceptual* thought until between six months and a year after birth. McMahan, however, locates the beginning of the self with the beginning of bare consciousness, which he locates between the twentieth and twenty-eighth week of gestation.[87] But the selection of this point along a continuum of self-integrated development of the human embryo as the point at which the self comes to be seems arbitrary. McMahan sees some of the real difficulties in requiring psychological continuity for personal identity (some of which we have already discussed). But, once one rightly rejects the requirement of psychological continuity, it is hard to see how the beginning of the immediately exercisable capacity for sensation and perception should be necessary for the coming to be of you or me.

Second, and most serious, the difficulties we mentioned about substance dualism are also problems for this view. I cannot be simply a brain any more than I can be simply a soul. For, as we argued earlier, it is clear that it is the same substantial entity referred to by the word "I" that senses (an action performed with the eyes, the skin, the ears, etc., as well as with the brain), and which imagines (an action performed with the brain). But the agent that senses is clearly the whole animal organism, not just the brain. And so "I" must refer to the whole animal organism. Also, it must be the same whole animal organism that walks, runs, talks, makes love, and which thinks and is self-conscious. Hence in each of these actions, it is the whole animal organism that performs the action, though he or she performs these various actions *with* different organs. The *I*, or *self*, cannot be identified with a part or an organ, but only with the whole to which each of these actions is ultimately attributable.

In sum, there is strong evidence that human beings are animals. The actions of sensing and perceiving, and the strong connections that human rationality and self-consciousness have to sensation and perception, show that human beings are bodily, organic beings. The natural dependence of the human intellect on sensation and the body shows that the principle of human conceptual thought (the human soul) is by nature incomplete, a

---

[86] See Chapter 4.
[87] McMahan, op. cit., 267–268.

part of the body–soul composite. The various objections to this position – the modal argument for substance dualism, the psychological continuity view of personal identity, reductionism in regard to personal identity, constitutionalism, and dicephalic twins – do not provide compelling counterevidence to that position.

2

Human Beings Are Persons

We argued in Chapter 1 that human beings are bodily beings, animal organisms, and that therefore they come to be when the human physical organism comes to be, do not cease to be until the human physical organism ceases to be, and so we cannot accurately regard our bodies as mere extrinsic tools. It may seem from this, however, that we are committed to physicalism – the view that human beings are purely physical entities (in the sense that there is no aspect of them that is not, or does not supervene upon, physical, material entities).[1] It may seem that we are committed to the view that human beings are not different in kind from other animals, and that all animals, humans included, are simply the by-products of the blind shuffling of the simpler physical entities and forces.

But if this were true – that is, if human beings were only different in degree and not in kind from other animals, plants, molecules, and so on – then it would be hard to see any justification for holding that they are the kind of beings to whom we have any serious moral obligation to treat with full moral respect, for example, to treat as ends and never as mere means.

Moreover, some theists, in particular some philosophers of the Jewish, Christian, or Muslim heritages, may worry that the position defended in Chapter 1 closes the door to accepting such theologically based key

---

[1] On the definition of physicalism, see, for example, Jaegwon Kim, *Philosophy of Mind* (Boulder, CO: Westview Press, 1998), 1–24, 104–113. Eleanore Stump, *Aquinas* (New York: Routledge, 2003), 212–216; William Haskers, *Emergent Dualism* (Ithaca, NY: Cornell University Press, 1999), 27–57.

propositions: man is created in the image of God, the human soul is immortal, and there is a resurrection of the body at the end of the world.

In this chapter we address these questions. We will argue that while human beings are animals, they are a specific kind of animal, and that there is a radical difference in kind between human beings and other animals.[2] Secondly, we will show that the position that human beings are animals is not in any way incompatible with holding that an aspect of the human being, that is, the human soul, transcends matter. That is, we will show that the animalist position defended in Chapter 1 is fully compatible with the position that the human being could not simply be the product of the interaction of purely physical beings and forces, and we will offer evidence for that point. We will also show that the position defended in Chapter 1 is compatible with the position that the human soul is the sort of principle or being that could survive death.[3] And we will show (briefly) that our position is fully compatible with the belief, held by Christians by faith, that there is a resurrection of the body at the end of the world.

Finally, we will also argue that this difference in kind grounds a moral obligation on our part to treat human beings in a way that is radically different from the way we may (morally) treat other beings – indeed, that we are morally obligated to give full moral respect to the lives and intrinsic basic goods of all human beings, and treat them as ends and never as mere means. So, Section I defends the proposition that human beings are radically different in kind from other animals because human beings have a nature which includes the basic natural capacities for conceptual thought and free choice. Section II shows the compatibility of our animalist position with the immortality of the soul and the resurrection of the body, and Section III shows how possessing a nature with the basic natural capacities of conceptual thought and free choice grounds full moral worth or rights.

---

[2] See the important work of Mortimer Adler, *The Difference of Man and the Difference It Makes* (New York: Holt, Rineholt & Wilson, 1967) and his *Intellect: Mind Over Matter* (New York: Macmillan Publishing Co., 1990). Adler makes the following important clarification. Two things are different in degree if each has a property but one has more of it than the other. Two things differ in kind if one has a property that the other simply lacks. The difference in kind is *superficial* if it emerges from some other difference in degree (for example, the difference between water as liquid and water as ice). The difference is *radical* if it does not emerge from some other difference in degree.

[3] In fact, we hold by faith (Catholic faith) that the human soul actually *is* immortal and we think there is a good philosophical argument to show this point. However, for purposes of the arguments defended in this book, we need only defend the position that belief in the immortality of the soul is *compatible* with what we argue for here.

I. The Difference in Kind between Human Beings and Other Animals

A. *Conceptual Thought*

We know what a thing is like through its actions. For example, we discover what a metal is or that a thing is alive through its distinctive actions. The actions of a thing are just the unfolding or fulfillment of what it is, and so, as the scholastic slogan put it, action follows being (*agere sequitur esse*). Our argument will be that human beings fundamentally differ from other animals because they perform actions which manifest a transcendence of matter not possessed by other animals. Human beings perform spiritual actions, that is, actions performed without bodily organs. From this it follows that an aspect of the human being, the human soul, transcends matter, and as a consequence cannot simply be the product of purely physical forces. From these points we conclude that human beings are radically different in kind, not just in degree, from other animals.

A first step in the argument is the claim that human beings perform *acts of understanding*, or conceptual thought, and that such acts are fundamentally different kinds of acts than acts of sensing, perceiving, or imagination. An act of understanding is the grasping of, or awareness of, a nature shared in common by many things. In Aristotle's memorable phrase, to understand is not just to know water (by sensing or perceiving this water), but to know what it is to be water.[4] By our senses and perceptual abilities, we know the individual qualities and quantities that modify, or have modified, our sense organs – this color or this shape, for example. But by understanding (conceptual thought), we apprehend a nature held in common by many – not this or that water, but what it is to be water. The object of the sensory powers, including imagination, is always an individual, a *this* at a particular place and a particular time, a characteristic, such as this red, this shape, this tone, which is thoroughly conditioned by space and time.

The contrast is evident upon examination of language. Proper names refer to individuals or groups of individuals that can be designated in a determinate time and place. Thus, "Winston Churchill" is a name that refers to a determinate individual, whereas the nouns "human," "horse," "atom," and "organism" are common names. Common names do not designate determinate individuals or determinate groups of individuals (such as "those five people in the corner"). Rather, they designate *classes*.

---

[4] Aristotle, *De Anima*, Bk. III, Chapter 4.

Thus, if we say, "Organisms are composed of organs, tissues and cells," the word "organisms" designates the whole class of organisms, a class that extends indefinitely into the past and indefinitely into the future. All syntactical languages distinguish between proper names and common names.

But a class is not an arbitrary collection of individuals. It is a collection of individuals that have something in common. There is always some feature, some nature or property, that is the criterion of membership for the class. Thus, the class of organisms is all, and only those, that have the nature of *living, bodily substance*. And so, to understand the class as such, and not just be able to pick out individuals belonging to that class, one must understand the nature held in common. And to understand the class as a class (as we clearly do in reasoning), one must mentally apprehend the nature or property held in common by the members of the class and compare this to those individual members. Thus, to understand a proposition such as, "All organisms require nutrition for survival," one must understand a nature or universal content designated by the term "organisms": the term designates the nature or feature that entities must have in them in order to belong to that class.

Human beings quite obviously are aware of classes as classes. That is, they do more than group individuals into a class based on a perceived similarity; they are aware of pluralities as holding natures or properties in common.[5] For example, one can perceive, without a concept, the similarity between two square shapes or two triangular shapes, something which other animals do as well as human beings. But human beings also grasp the criterion, the universal property or nature, by which the similars are grouped together.[6]

There are several indications that this is so. First, many universal judgments require an understanding of the nature of the things belonging to a class. If I understand, for example, that every organism is mortal, because every composite living thing is mortal, this is possible only if I mentally

---

[5] See Joel Wallman, *Aping Language* (Cambridge, UK: Cambridge University Press, 1992), especially Chapters 5 and 6.

[6] Cf. Richard J. Connell, *Logical Analysis: An Introduction to Systematic Learning* (Edina, MN: Bellwether Press, 1981), 87–93; John Haldane, "The Source and Destination of Thought," in *Referring to God: Jewish and Christian Philosophical and Theological Perspectives*, ed. Paul Helm (New York: St. Martin's Press, 2000). Mortimer Adler, *Intellect*; Russell Pannier and Thomas D. Sullivan, "The Mind-Marker," in *Theos, Anthropos, Christos: A Compendium of Modern Philosophical Theology*, ed. Roy Abraham Varghese (New York: P. Lang, 2000); James F. Ross, "Immaterial Aspects of Thought," *Journal of Philosophy* 89 (1992), 136–150.

compare the nature, *organism*, with the nature, *composite living thing*, and see that the former entails the latter. That is, my judgment that every composite living thing can be decomposed and thus dies is based on my insight into the nature of a composite living thing. I have understood that the one nature, *subject to death*, is entailed by the other nature, *composite living being*, and *from* that knowledge I then advert to the thought of the individuals which possess those natures. In other words, I judge that individual composite living beings must be included within the class of individuals that are subject to death, but I judge that only in virtue of my seeing that the nature, *being subject to death*, is necessitated by the nature, *composite living being*. This point is also evident from the fact that I judge that a composite living being is *necessarily* capable of death.[7] By the senses, one can grasp only an individual datum. Only by a distinct capacity, an intellect, and only by apprehending *the nature* of a thing can one grasp that a thing is *necessarily* thus or so.

Another example will illustrate this point. When children arrive at the age at which they can study logic, they provide evidence of the ability to grasp a nature or property held in common by many. They obviously do something qualitatively distinct from perceiving a concrete similarity. For example, when studying elementary logic, the child (or young man or woman) grasps the common pattern found in the following arguments:

A   A If it rains then the grass is wet.
     The grass is not wet.
     Therefore, it is not raining.
B   If I had known you were coming, I would have baked you a cake.
     But I did not bake you a cake.
     So (you can see that) I did not know you were coming.

We understand the difference between this type of argument, a *modus tollens* argument, and one that is similar but invalid, namely, the fallacy of affirming the consequent (If A, then B; B, therefore A). But, what is more, we understand *why* the fallacy of affirming the consequent is invalid – namely, some other cause (or antecedent) could be, or could have been, present to lead to that effect (or consequent). A computer, a mechanical device, can be programmed *to operate according to* the *modus tollens* and to react differently toward (give a different output for) words, or rather

---

[7] True, something extrinsic could preserve it from death, but it is the sort of thing that is, by its nature, subject to death. This is the basis for the major premise in the classic example of a syllogism: all men are mortal; Socrates is a man; therefore, Socrates is mortal.

marks, arranged in the pattern of the fallacy of affirming the consequent. But *understanding* the arguments (which humans do) and merely *operating according to* them because programmed to do so (the actions of computers) are entirely different types of actions. The first does, while the second does not, require the understanding or apprehending of a form or nature as distinct from its instances.[8] That is, the first, but not the second, requires a grasp of the universal or abstract nature.[9]

That event, which we can call an insight, is a mental act that is fundamentally distinct, though obviously related to, sensation, perception, or imagination. The universal nature or form is the object of the act of understanding. But whatever exists as physical is an individual, tied to a particular place and time. So, the term of the intellectual act is a nonphysical content. And the intellectual act is a nonphysical act. When someone understands the point of the difference between *modus tollens* and the fallacy of affirming the consequent, he sees that the conclusion *necessarily* follows in the one case, and is invalid, and does *not* necessarily follow in the other case. But one does not grasp necessities, or the lack of necessities, by one's senses, imagination, or any bodily act.[10] What one senses, perceives, or imagines – what one grasps in *bodily* cognitive acts – is always a *this*, with a particular, albeit sometimes vague, contour. But the *point* or the truth that one grasped in grasping the nature of the *modus tollens* argument equally applies not just to this argument or to that one, but to *every possible* instance of it, whether the argument is about horses, electrons, or argument forms themselves. In short, what one grasps in an insight is a nature, property, or form that can be (and usually is) instantiated in many, innumerable cases and which grounds explanations for why things (or relations, as in logic) are as they are.[11]

[8] This is not to say that the nature exists separately from the individuals instantiating it, or as a universal, outside the mind. We agree with Aquinas, who held that the nature exists in the mind as a universal but in the real as individuated. See his *On Being and Essence*, Chapter 3 and his *Summa Theologiae*, Pt. I, q. 84, a. 1.

[9] This argument against physicalism is based not on consciousness as such – which is not unique to human beings – but on conceptual thought. We are inclined to take the position that sensory and perceptual consciousness is not reducible to lower-level activities, but is, unlike conceptual thought, emergent from lower-level activities. In other words, were it not for conceptual thought and free choice (and acts of will in general), we would be inclined toward nonreductive materialism. The argument here, however, is that conceptual thought is neither reducible to nor emergent from material acts.

[10] Cf. Bernard Lonergan, *Insight*, 3rd ed. (New York: Philosophical Library, 1970), Chapters 1–5.

[11] Thus, the universal nature, property, or form is not just an individual or singular content which one can imagine duplicated in other instances, such as a visual scene or the face

The capacity for conceptual thought in human beings radically distinguishes them from other animals. This capacity is at the root of most of the other distinguishing features of human beings. Thus, syntactical language, art, architecture, variety in social groupings and in other customs,[12] burying the dead, making tools, religion, fear of death (and elaborate defense mechanisms to ease living with that fear), wearing clothes, true courting of the opposite sex,[13] free choice, and morality – all of these and more – stem from the ability to reason and understand. Conceptual thought makes all of these specific acts possible by enabling human beings to escape fundamental limitations of two sorts. First, because of conceptual thought, human beings' actions and consciousness are not restricted to the spatiotemporal present. Their awareness and their concern go beyond what can be perceived or imagined as connected immediately with the present.[14] Second, because of conceptual thought, human beings can reflect back upon themselves and their place in reality; that is, they can attain an objective view, and they can attempt to be objective in their assessments and choices. Other animals give no evidence at all of being able to do either of these things; on the contrary, they seem thoroughly tied to the here and now and are unable to take an objective view of things as they are in themselves, or even attempt to attain an objective view.[15]

Note that if the analysis just given is substantially correct, then the power of conceptual thought is not just different in degree from other

of a twin or doppelganger: it is a nature or property, grasping of which reveals necessary truths or connections, as does the form of the *modus tollens* argument, the nature of a circle, or the nature of a living organism. One visual scene may be exactly similar to another – qualitatively indistinguishable from it. But a conceptual content (such as the conceptual content, *organism*) can be instantiated in things that are extremely diverse with respect to vision or any of the senses (say, in an amoeba and in an elephant). Visual (or auditory, olfactory, tactile) similarities are physical relations; by contrast, instantiation, the reciprocal relation of universality, is a strictly logical, nonphysical relation.

[12] Mortimer Adler noted that, upon extended observation of other animals and of human beings, what would first strike one is the immense uniformity in mode of living among other animals, in contrast with the immense variety in modes of living and customs among human beings. See Adler, *Intellect*, supra, note 6.

[13] Cf. Roger Scruton, *Sexual Desire: A Moral Philosophy of the Erotic* (New York: Free Press, 1986).

[14] This point is developed in James B. Reichmann, *Evolution, Animal "Rights," and the Environment* (Washington, DC: Catholic University of America Press, 2000), Chapter 2; see also John Campbell, *Past, Space, and Self: Representation and Mind* (Cambridge: Massachusetts Institute of Technology, 1994).

[15] Lynne Rudder Baker, *Persons and Bodies: A Constitution View* (Cambridge, UK: Cambridge University Press, 2000), Chapter 3; Campbell, *Past, Space, and Self*, supra, note 14.

capacities (such as perceptual thought and instinct) but is different in kind. This means that a being either has this capacity or not, even though – as we will indicate more fully later – a being may have a basic natural capacity for conceptual thought long before he or she develops that capacity to the point where it is immediately exercisable (so an infant, for example, has the basic natural capacity for conceptual thought even though it will be months before he or she actually has a concept). Thus, every human being, including human infants and unborn human beings, has this natural capacity for conceptual thought, but a horse or a dog simply and altogether lacks this capacity. It is sometimes argued that perhaps some nonhuman animals do have minds like humans do, only at a diminished level. Perhaps, it is speculated, it is only the complexity of the human brain, a difference only in degree, that distinguishes humans from other animals. Perhaps other primates are intelligent but they have lacked the opportunities to manifest their latent intelligence. But such speculation is misguided. While intelligence is not directly observable, it is unreasonable to think that an intelligence of the same type as human intelligence, no matter how diminished, would not manifest itself in at least some of its characteristic effects.[16] If a group of beings possesses a power, and possesses that power over many years (even decades or centuries), it is implausible to think that such a power would not be actualized.

The fundamental difference between human beings and other animals is quite obvious to the unprejudiced eye. Human beings have literally transformed most landscapes on planet Earth by structuring materials according to their intelligent purposes. Other animals, by contrast, have left few lasting effects, and these – fossils – by accident. Some other animals do build structures for protection and warmth, for example, the beaver's dam and the bee's hive. Yet it is obvious that these animals build such quasi-stable structures from instinct rather than from intelligence. This is evident from the fact that their manner of building is invariant among members of the species, and invariant across generations. If they understood and planned what they were doing, as human beings do, inevitably they would begin to devise various and perhaps improved ways of building. Nothing of that sort occurs. This of course is in marked contrast with the variation and improvement through generations in the art of building among human beings. Only human beings have the *art* of building; that is, only human beings conceive the intelligible purpose and design for

---

[16] Cf. Reichmann, supra, note 14; see also Dennis Bonnette, *The Origin of the Human Species* (Atlanta, GA: Rodopi, 2001); Wallman, loc. cit.

what they construct. Only human beings conceive *what* they are doing, as opposed to blindly following a (genetically determined) sequence of acts which, by natural selection or by the creator's extrinsic design (or both), usually produces success.

This points up a more general difference between human beings and nonhuman animals. There is a marked invariance of general pattern of living among nonhuman animals and their societies. Human beings, on the other hand, display great variety, not only in houses and cities, but also in dress, customs, courting practices, and societal arrangements. True, because of their common human nature, there is an underlying sameness among human beings – the different cultures pursue the same basic purposes or goods of life, health, friendship, family, learning, aesthetic experience, and so on. Yet there is great variety in the manners of pursuing these common basic purposes. By contrast, other animals not only pursue the same ends within their species (notably lacking such goods as learning for its own sake, skillful performance as true artistic endeavor, and aesthetic experience, that is, experience of the beautiful for its own sake), but they also pursue these ends in a manner that is uniform among all the members of their species and in the same way from generation to generation.

Again, human beings do, while other animals do not, form political societies. Other animals form societies according to instinct, as evidenced by the specific invariance of the structures of their societies, and by their sameness across generations.[17] Human beings form ideas or concepts of how their societies should be structured, and express these in the form of constitutions (written or unwritten), and then to a certain extent (never fully) live up to those constitutions. Thus, because of the capacity for conceptual thought and reasoning, man is a *political* animal, not just a social animal (many other animals also being social).

Conceptual thought also grounds the human being's unique ability to make tools to be used indefinitely into the future. Nonhuman animals are able to perceive a concrete relation, such as the spatial relation between two sticks and a concrete object they now wish to retrieve, and build a tool on a specific occasion. But human beings fashion tools that they plan to use for a variety of situations in the future. And, what is more, only human beings *mass produce* tools; for, evidently, only they are able to grasp the nature of the tool in abstraction from this or that concrete instance. If nonhuman animals had the capacity for true conceptual thought, then they would make tools based on *concepts* of how they could be used, and

---

[17] Adler, *Intellect*, supra, note 6.

thus they would mass produce them and, by now, would have conceived of replaceable parts for tools. Nothing even approaching this, of course, has been observed.

Again, human beings deliberate about their actions. True, the smell of tasty food spontaneously attracts a healthy human being just as it attracts a nonhuman animal. But the human being goes further. The human being begins to reflect on the different possible actions he could perform in relation to the food. Of each action, he understands both advantages and disadvantages. He is able to *understand* that eating the food (an act that he can understand as well as imagine) is, though good in one respect, bad in another, because it might negatively impact *forms* of fulfillment such as health and religion. Thus, unlike other animals, the human being understands different aspects of the same concrete particular: these are intelligible but not imaginable or perceptible features or aspects. This ability, at least in part, is what enables the human being to make free choices.

Rationality is not merely a capacity whose actualization is isolated from the other activities that a human being performs. Rather, as the logic of definition indicates, "rational" refers not just to the activity or even just the capacity, but to the distinct kind of being of the human species, which involves a fundamentally different way of being an animal. Among organisms, each new specific difference indicates not just a new and isolated capacity, but a distinctive way of being an organism, or a distinctive way of being an animal. Thus the specific difference, *sensing*, as in a sensing organism, that is, an animal, refers not just to the capacity for sensation. Rather, the organism's whole mode of living, principally its mode of obtaining nourishment and reproduction, is affected by its capacity to sense and perceive. Similarly, conceptual thought changes how human beings perform most of their other activities.[18] The rationality of a rational animal, a human being, affects his or her whole mode of life – how he obtains food, reproduces, gathers in groups, seeks shelter. In other words, his rationality specifies his mode of being an organism and of being an animal.

B. Free Choice, Moral Agency

The most important capacity made possible by rationality, and the one that without doubt most profoundly determines how human beings

---

[18] The purely vegetative activities, such as respiration and growth, are not directly changed in the rational animal. But nourishment, sexual reproduction, and social gathering are profoundly changed, and wholly new types of activities appear, such as contemplative understanding (understanding for its own sake) and genuine aesthetic experience.

should be treated, is free choice. In this short space we will not attempt to prove with certainty that human beings make free choices, nor examine all of the arguments and counterarguments in this debate. However, we will present a sketch of an argument for free choice and explain the significance that free choice has for the fundamental difference between human beings and other animals.

Consider a concrete example. One morning, Smith resolves to skip lunch that day, for both religious and heath-conscious purposes. But in the afternoon, taking a walk and passing by a local pizza parlor, Smith smells the aroma of pizza wafting through the air. He immediately desires the pizza, his mouth watering. He begins to deliberate: he could go to the pizza parlor and have some pizza or he could continue to walk, keeping to his fast and diet.

Smith understands that there is something good or attractive in each possible course of action. Eating the pizza would be pleasurable, and, he recalls, he might meet his friends or that cute waitress while waiting for his order. On the other hand, passing up the pizza on this occasion would be good both religiously and for his health. In other words, each course of action offers some distinctive good, some benefit, not offered by the other. He cannot do both, so he must make up his mind: he must decide which course of action to follow. This act of "making up his mind" is an act of the will. If Smith decides to eat the pizza, but slips and falls on the way and never gets to the pizza parlor, he has still willed to do so. And although he does not perform the physical behavior to carry out his choice, he is still morally responsible for his choice.

There is strong evidence that such a choice is *free*, that is, that such a choice is not determined by the events that preceded it, but is determined by the person making the choice in the very act of choosing. Expressed otherwise: the events and realities (including Smith's character) antecedent to some choices are not sufficient to bring it about that he choose (will) this course of action rather than that one (or that he choose rather than not choose). In some choices, a person could have chosen the other option, or not chosen at all, under the very same conditions. Suppose Smith did choose to go eat the pizza. Given everything that happened to him up to the point just prior to his choice – including everything in his environment, everything in his heredity, everything in his understanding, and in his character – it was still possible for him to choose to continue walking. His environment, heredity, and character together were not sufficient to bring it about that he choose this rather than that, or even that he choose rather than not choose. Expressed positively: he himself in the very act of choosing determines his act of willing. Human beings are ultimate authors of their own acts of will and (together with nature and nurture) their own character.[19]

How, then, does a person finally will one course of action rather another? The person by his own act of will directs his will toward this option rather than toward that one, and in such a way that he could, in those very same circumstances, have chosen otherwise.[20]

A good case can be made to support this position.[21] First, objectively, when, for example, Smith deliberates about which possible action to

---

[19] Cf. Robert Kane, *The Significance of Free Will* (Oxford: Oxford University Press, 1998). This point does not contradict the position that God causes free choices, only that God *determines* them. On this point, see Germain Grisez, *Beyond the New Theism* (Notre Dame, IN: University of Notre Dame Press, 1975), Chapter 18.

[20] Hence the position we are proposing is an incompatibilist view of free choice. Having alternate possibilities, that is, the ability to will otherwise, is essential to free choice and moral responsibility. It seems to us that the Frankfurt-alleged counterexamples (proposed to disprove the principle of alternate possibilities) are not genuine counterexamples. On these alleged counterexamples, there is a first agent who deliberates and decides, but there is a second, more powerful agent who in some way monitors the first agent and is ready and able to cause the first agent to do the act desired by the second agent if the first agent begins to will or perform otherwise than the desired outcome. It turns out, however (on the imagined scenario), that the first agent decides on his own to do the act which the second agent was ready to compel him to do. So, according to advocates of Frankfurt examples, the first agent acted freely, was morally responsible, and yet could not have willed or acted otherwise. See Harry Frankfurt, "Alternate Possibilities and Moral Responsibilities," *Journal of Philosophy* 66 (1969), 829–839. For a recent defense of this approach, see John Martin Fischer and Mark Ravizza, *Responsibility and Control: A Theory of Moral Responsibility* (Cambridge, UK: Cambridge University Press, 1998). The problem is that the monitoring device, however it is imagined, will be unable to alert the second agent that the first agent is about to, or has begun to, act otherwise than the second agent plans. The act of willing is not determinate prior to its occurrence and so cannot be known before it occurs. And once it has occurred, it is too late to prevent it. (This was the ground for Aquinas's position that not even God can know a future contingent precisely as future, that is, as it exists in its causes, but he can know it only as it is in act – yet, since God is not in time, what is future with respect to us is not future with respect to God. See St. Thomas Aquinas, *Summa Theologiae*, Pt. I, q. 14, a. 13.) The second agent could prevent the physical, external action carrying out the choice, but the act of will is free and undetermined even if the external behavior executing the choice is prevented. Although his argument against the Frankfurt examples is not precisely the one presented here, an article that overlaps somewhat with this argument is P. A. Woodward, "Why Frankfurt Examples Beg the Question," *Journal of Social Philosophy* 33 (2002), 540–547.

[21] A more extended argument can be seen in Joseph M. Boyle, Jr., Germain Grisez, and Olaf Tollefsen, *Free Choice: A Self-Referential Argument* (Notre Dame, IN: University of Notre Dame Press, 1976); see also Peter van Inwagen, *An Essay on Free Will* (Oxford: Oxford University Press, 1986); and Peter van Inwagen, "Free Will Remains a Mystery," in *The Oxford Handbook of Free Will*, ed. Robert Kane (Oxford: Oxford University Press, 2002), 158–170.

perform, each option has in it what it takes to be a possible object of choice. When persons deliberate, and find some distinctive good in different, incompatible possible actions, they are free, for: (a) they have the capacity to understand the distinct types of good or fulfillment found (directly or indirectly) in the different possible courses of action and (b) they are capable of willing whatever they understand to be good (fulfilling) in some way or other.[22] That is, each alternative offers a distinct type of good or benefit, and it is up to the person deliberating which type of good he will choose.

In the example mentioned, both eating the pizza and continuing to walk have a distinctive sort of goodness or attractiveness. Each offers some benefit the other one does not offer. So, since each alternative has some goodness in it (some goodness that is understood), it seems that each one *can* be willed. And, secondly, while each is good, to a certain extent, neither alternative (at least in many situations) is good, or better, in *every respect*. Here the role of conceptual thought, or intellect, becomes clear. The person deliberating is able to see, that is, to *understand*, that each alternative is good, but that none is best absolutely speaking, that is, according to every consideration, or in every respect. And so, neither the content of the option nor the strength of one or another desire determines the choice. Hence there are acts of will in which one directs one's will toward this or that option without one's act of will being determined by antecedent events or causes.

The principal case for the opposite position, determinism, has traditionally been the claim that determinism is suggested, even if not entailed, by the scientific worldview. Science progresses by finding the causes which explain why an event or property is as it is; it seeks to uncover causes which determine, at least on the macrolevel, the events and properties to occur, and to occur in the manner they do. This of course does not by itself prove universal determinism. But one might adopt universal determinism as a hypothesis. One might then argue that the progress of science, gradually uncovering hitherto unknown determining causes, *confirms*, or *suggests*, the idea that *all* events, including choices, are determined by antecedent events.[23]

---

[22] The argument here is indebted to Thomas Aquinas. See, e.g., *Summa Theologiae*, I–II, q. 10, aa. 1–2.

[23] See Henry Sidgwick, *Methods of Ethics* (London: Macmillan Publishing Co., 1901); Daniel C. Dennett, *Brainstorms: Philosophical Essays on Mind and Psychology* (Cambridge, MA: MIT Press, 1978).

However, the idea that science will uncover the *determining* causes of *every* event already has been refuted by science itself. Part of quantum mechanics is the idea that some events – at the microlevel – are *not* determined, or at least not fully determined, by their antecedent events. Some philosophers have argued that this indeterminacy at the microlevel leaves room for free choice. We do not make that claim, since the laws of quantum mechanics still determine *sets of events*. And, more importantly, whatever one says about acts of will, the physical actions that carry out acts of will are macrolevel events and so do not fall within the indeterminacy described by quantum mechanics. Still, quantum physics does show that the determinist thesis is not universal, that there are exceptions to it. And if there are exceptions of one type (microlevel events) why could there not be exceptions of another type (free choices) as well? That is, for the universal determinists' case from scientific methodology to work, these determinists would have to show that microlevel events are the only exception to the determinist thesis, something which no one has even attempted to do.[24]

Moreover, let us suppose for the sake of argument that the empirical sciences do assume as a methodological practice that events have determining causes. Still, libertarians can simply say that the scientific method is limited, that it does not extend to every entity which exists. In fact, renowned scientists such as Werner Heisenberg held this very position.[25] Further, any claim that the scientific method should be seen as the exclusive method used to study any dimension of the real is itself a nonscientific thesis. The position that the scientific method must apply to every entity, and to every inference, is self-inconsistent, since this assertion is not itself an application of the scientific method. Thus, the success of the scientific method cannot be used to justify excluding the possibility of other types of inquiry suited to entities (or aspects of entities) to which the scientific method is not fully adequate.[26] Free choices and thoughts, we submit, are entities of this sort.

The principal objection against the libertarian position we have presented has been the claim that if choices are not determined by antecedent events then they are mere random or chance events, and thus not under the agent's control – a conclusion exactly opposite the result intended by

---

[24] Joseph Boyle, Germain Grisez, and and Olaf Tollefsen, *Free Choice*, supra, note 21.

[25] Werner Heisenberg, *Physics and Philosophy: The Revolution in Modern Science* (New York: Harper & Row, 1958).

[26] Of course, the empirical sciences are helpful in understanding some aspects of human behavior and choice.

libertarians. Richard Double has expressed this argument quite clearly. He first proposes what he calls "The Principle of Rational Explanation":

Citing a person's reasoning process R rationally explains a choice C only if the probability of C given R is greater than the probability of not C given R.[27]

He then argues that either the choice C is rationally explained by rational process R or not. If R does *not* explain C, then C is not rational; that is, free human decisions are not rational. But if R *does* explain C, then C *is* determined, at least to a certain extent (R renders C more probable). What is more, Double argues, our decisions (C) are ours just to the extent that they stem from, are determined by, our rational processes (R).[28] So, contrary to the libertarians' claim, indeterminacy is inversely proportional to rationality and autonomous control.[29]

This argument assumes, however, that being rational and having an explanation (where the *explanans* renders the *explanandum* more probable than its opposite) are one and the same. The libertarian notion of freedom requires that free choice is rational (not necessarily morally right, but that there are reasons for the choice); but this does not entail that those reasons make this choice more probable than that one. The point could be expressed this way: in deliberating between action A and action B, where one sees some distinctive benefit in each, there is a rational explanation why one *could* choose A, and a rational explanation why one *could* choose B. So, either choice would be rational, in the sense that either choice would be responsive to some benefit understood to be realized or promoted by the action.

The determinist might at this point, however, demand that more is needed. The determinist supposes that in order for the choice to be rational or intelligible, there must also be an explanation (in Double's sense, at least) why the person chose A *rather than* B. But it is just here that the indeterminacy is located.[30] So we admit that there is no explanation for why a person freely chooses A *rather than* B, but it does not follow, for the reasons just stated, that the person acted irrationally or that his

---

[27] Richard Double, "Libertarianism and Rationality," in *Agents, Causes, Events: Essays on Indeterminism and Free Will*, ed. Timothy O'Connor (Oxford: Oxford University Press, 1995), 57–65, at 60.

[28] Ibid., 63.

[29] A similar objection has been pressed by Galen Strawson, *The Bounds of Freedom* (Oxford: Oxford University Press, 2002).

[30] Thus we disagree with Dennett, who, in *Brainstorms*, supra, note 23, locates the indeterminacy in the randomness of the remembrances and thoughts that occur to one.

act is unintelligible, random, or a mere chance event. Moreover, Double's claim that our choices are our own just to the extent that they are *determined* by reasons, and that rationality and indeterminacy are inversely proportional, again assumes that rationality is operative by determining. We have shown, however, that *each* option deliberated about in a free choice would be in some way rational (even if not morally right, or *fully* rational) and so rationality applies to the decision process as a whole, not to an alleged determining *part* of it.

This point also partly answers another objection to the idea of libertarian free choice. It may seem that when we deliberate, one action, for whatever reason, will appear to be best. But if that is so, then it seems that we are determined – in the sense that the opposite is not possible – to choose the option that appears best.

But as indicated earlier, in some cases (that is, in those situations where there is a free choice) no option is best (or appears best) in every respect or according to every consideration. It is true that if one option really does offer as much benefit as the other option, plus more, and one knows it, then one cannot choose the option offering less, and one does not make a free choice. This sometimes happens: when house hunting, for example, one may see that one house has every good feature that another one has, plus more. In that situation, the second house cannot be chosen, since it has no distinctive attractiveness. It simply drops out of consideration. Thus, not every choice is free. In other situations, however, one option offers one type of benefit or good, and the other option offers a different type: eating pizza versus keeping one's diet, going to law school versus going to medical school, and so on. In such situations, neither option is better in every respect. Rather, each offers a distinct and incommensurable[31] benefit. In those kinds of situations, there is free choice.

In sum, in Section I.A, we argued that human beings are radically different in kind from other animals because they have (as entailed by their nature, from the moment they come to be) the basic, natural capacity for conceptual thought. In Section I.B, we have argued that human beings are different in kind from other animals because they have (as a basic natural capacity) the power to make free choices. Human beings are animals, but they are animals of a fundamentally different sort.

---

[31] That is, the benefits (and harms) offered by one option cannot be simply measured against those offered by another option, since the totality of benefits (and harms) lacks a single common measuring standard, or covering value.

II. Survival after Death

A. *The Human Soul after Death*

The aim of this chapter is to show that the bodiliness of the human being – the fact that a human being is an animal organism that comes to be when that organism comes to be and does not cease to be until that organism ceases to be – is fully compatible with the claim that human beings are in many respects fundamentally different from other material entities. In this section, we wish to show that the bodiliness of the human being does not preclude holding that an aspect of the human being, the human soul, transcends matter and indeed survives the human being's death.

One might argue that one cannot hold that the human being is an animal, but at the same time a person with a spiritual soul, and that the soul persists after the human being's death. Many philosophers hold that there are only two alternatives in the question of what a human being is: physicalism (the human being is nothing but a material being) or substance dualism (the human being is a spiritual entity inhabiting or associated with a body that is not himself or herself).

However, there is indeed a third possibility, a via media between the extremes of physicalism and substance dualism. It is true *both* that the human being is an animal *and* that the human being has a spiritual soul that could not have emerged from lower beings, so that the human being is radically different in kind, and not just in degree, from lower animals. As a matter of historical fact, Thomas Aquinas presented a third alternative, different both from physicalism and from substance dualism (which he encountered in Platonism). We submit that Aquinas's position on this issue, or a position close to it, is correct. We will present the case for this point in three steps.

1. Like other organisms, the human being has a matter-form composition. The various cells, tissues, organs, and so on, must be organized or unified so as to make up one being. The ultimate principle of unity cannot be a material organ, since this would only give rise to an aggregate of this organ with other bodies (and so the unity of this organ with others would remain unexplained), but it must be a *form* or *order* determining the components to be one substantial entity.[32] In a living being, this form or principle of unity can

---

[32] This is not as contentious as it may at first seem. If one holds that an organism or, in particular, a human being, is genuinely one thing, then *some type* of matter-form composition is a logical consequence, given the facts of generation, nutrition, and death. Animal

be referred to as a soul, since the soul is (philosophically) defined as the first principle of life in an organized body.[33] The soul is the formal source (as opposed to the efficient cause) of the living operations of a living being, such operations as growth, nourishment, perception, and, in the human being, understanding and willing. The efficient cause of these operations, in the sense of the subject that performs these operations, is the living organism as a whole. Thus, the human being is not a soul using or inhabiting a body, but a composite of soul *and* body (if by "body" one refers to the material components in the makeup of a human being).

2. And yet the human soul is spiritual. Unlike the souls of other animals, it is the sort of thing that could survive death[34] and could not have emerged from lower animals. Human beings perform actions, such as understanding (conceptual thought), that are not physical actions, as we showed earlier in this chapter. That is, acts of understanding and willing are actions performed by the human being, but the actions themselves are performed without bodily organs. The act of understanding is an action that terminates in a universal feature. But every bodily action has as its term an individual body (or part of a body), in a particular space and particular time.

   The character of an action reveals the character of its principle or source. So if there are actions that are independent of matter (in the sense of being performed without a material organ), then the source of these actions must in some way *be* or *exist* independently of matter. This is not to say that the subject of these actions – which is the human being as a whole – has its existence independently of matter, but that the formal source of these actions, the human soul, has its actuality or existence independently of matter. This means

---

organisms consume food and convert it into parts of themselves. Animal organisms die and some are consumed by other animals. It is obvious that some of the matter-energy that once went into the makeup of one animal ends up in the makeup of another. In fact *all* of the matter-energy within an animal *could* end up in the makeup of another animal. And so now there must be within the animal a formal principle, a principle of unity, determining the matter-energy in its makeup to be of this kind rather than of another kind. Exactly how the material and formal principles are related we need not commit to for our argument; we need not, for example, commit to the whole theory of matter held by Aquinas or Aristotle, only that there is a distinction between the matter-energy in an animal (including a human animal) and the formal principle.

[33] Aristotle, loc. cit.

[34] We believe that the human soul *does* survive death, but for the purposes here it is important to show only the *compatibility* of belief in its survival with the position that the human being is an animal organism.

that the human soul has its actuality or existence through itself, rather than through the actuality of the whole composite, the whole human nature.

The meaning of this conclusion can be clarified by contrasting it with what one can reasonably infer about the souls of other animals.[35] Since all of the actions of nonrational animals are physical actions, it follows that such an animal's soul will not have its actuality through itself, but it will have its actuality only through the actuality of the whole. In this respect, the nonrational animal's soul is like other parts of a substantial whole: it comes to be as what it is, only with, or after, the coming to be of the substantial whole of which it is a part, and it ceases to be with the ceasing to be of that substantial whole. Since the nonrational animal's soul is *only* the unity or form of the animal's living body, when the nonrational animal dies, its soul ceases to be, for there is nothing of which it can be a form or unity. However, the human soul is the formal source of functions which are not functions of bodily parts of the human being; so, the human soul *does not* depend for its existence on the whole of which it is a part. And if this is so, then it can survive, and it would not be self-contradictory for it to function after the death of the whole human being and the disintegration of his or her body.

3. But the human soul, while spiritual, and capable of surviving death, is not the whole human being. The human being is the subject of bodily actions, and that which performs living bodily actions *is* a living body, an organism.

Another point that shows this is the human intellect's natural orientation to cooperation with bodily powers. Human intelligence has a natural need and functional orientation to matter or the body. Human understanding is itself a spiritual act, an act performed without a bodily organ. Nevertheless, it is naturally dependent[36] on sensation and thus is by nature incomplete. So, although the human soul can survive without the body (since it is not inconceivable that it could perform some type of act without

---

[35] If by "soul" one means the unity or form of an organized living body, or the first principle of life in a living body, then all living things have souls – plants, nonrational animals, as well as rational animals.

[36] The qualification "naturally" is necessary. What may happen through special divine intervention is another matter, and one that is important for considerations about the human soul existing after death, without being substantially united with a body.

the body), it is intrinsically oriented to the body because its operations cannot naturally attain their end without the aid of the body.

From this it follows that the human soul's spiritual capacities are naturally oriented to cooperation with the material capacities (those capacities whose actuation includes use of a bodily organ). And so the principle of these capacities, the human soul, is by nature proportioned to union with the body. As a heart naturally belongs together with other bodily parts, as a key is incomplete without a lock, so the human soul is naturally only a part of the whole human nature, which includes both soul and body.[37] On the one hand, the human soul transcends matter and can survive the death of the whole human being (though when it does so, it exists in a highly unnatural and diminished condition); on the other hand, the human soul is naturally incomplete. It is, according to what it is, oriented to informing a body (matter).

The following objection might be raised against this position. We have tried to be precise in stating that the evidence shows that conceptual thought is an act performed without a bodily organ, and yet the subject of this act is the whole human being, who is composed of body and soul. One might object that the idea that the soul transcends matter, and could survive in separation from matter, depends upon confusing the aforementioned claim with a different and unwarranted one; namely, the human soul is actually the *subject* of acts of conceptual thought. Indeed, Aquinas's formulation of the argument for this point (that the human soul does not depend for its existence on the body) seems to invite that objection:

Therefore the intellectual principle itself, which is called the mind or the intellect, has an operation *per se*, in which it does not communicate with the body. But nothing can operate *per se*, unless it subsists *per se*. For an entity does not operate unless it is in act: hence a thing operates in the manner in which it exists. Thus, we do not say that *heat* heats, but that the hot thing heats.[38]

Thus, the claim that the soul transcends matter, or exists independently of matter, seems to rest on the mistaken idea that it is the human soul that performs the act of understanding (and willing).[39]

---

[37] The analogy is not complete because the soul can continue to exist without the body after death, but even then it would be in an unnatural condition.

[38] Aquinas, op. cit., Pt. I, q. 75, a. 2, corpus.

[39] This problem was clearly presented by Gregory Coulter, "Mental and Bodily Relations: Is There a Mind-Body Problem?" *Proceedings of the American Catholic Philosophical Association* 66 (1992), 251–266.

Yet, Aquinas insists that, strictly speaking, it is the human being who understands *with his intellect* rather than the soul being the subject of the act. The powers of the soul, including the intellect and the will, he insists, are in the soul as their principle, not as in a subject.[40] So, the key premise in the argument is *not that the soul* acts independently of matter. Rather, the key premise is that the *act of understanding* (conceptual thought) is an act that is itself performed without a bodily organ (though bodily operations are, given the natural condition of the human being, needed as prerequisites to that act). The *subject* of the act is the whole human being. Still, the inference remains valid: if the *act* is independent of matter, then the *principle* or *source* of that act must be independent of matter. The seventeenth-century Thomist John Poinsot, better known as John of St. Thomas, expressed this point quite clearly:

It remains therefore to prove the major of this first syllogism, that no principle of intellectual operation is dependent on a body. And it is proved, because the intellectual operation, as we saw, is spiritual and exceeding all corporeal entities. Therefore it is necessary that that which is the root and principle, from which it proceeds, is a spiritual substance, if indeed operation does not have any existence except that which it receives from the principle from which it proceeds. Therefore if it has a spiritual existence [*esse*], it receives this from its principle. Therefore this principle cannot be corporeal, since it cannot give an existence exceeding itself.[41]

The action (conceptual thought) is independent of matter; therefore, the principle of this action must be in some way independent of matter. Its capacities cannot be restricted to the potentialities inherent in matter.[42] This does not mean that the subject of the action must be wholly without matter. Rather, it means that some part or aspect of the subject of this action must be independent of and transcending matter. If this were not so, as John Poinsot points out, there would be a higher degree of perfection in the action than there is in the principle or formal source of the action. In short, there is a factor in us, an aspect of us, whereby we transcend the limitations of matter, but that factor or aspect is not the whole of us but only a part. As a consequence, this factor, the soul, could not have emerged from lower forces, and this factor can survive death. These points are fully compatible with the fact that we are animals.

[40] Aquinas, op. cit., Pt. I, q. 75, a. 2, reply to obj. 2; q. 77, a. 5.
[41] John of St. Thomas, *Cursus Philosophicus Thomisticus*, Tomus III, *Naturalis Philosophiae*, ed. B. Reiser (Turin, Italy: Marietti, 1948–1950).
[42] John calls the soul a spiritual *substance* since it has its existence through itself, but it is not a *complete* substance.

William Hasker holds that the mind is a spiritual substance that emerges from material forces.[43] It is true that an effect that is more perfect than any of its causes can emerge from the convergence of several causes.[44] However, a bodily act (such as reproduction) must terminate immediately in a body – a thing whose form or configuration comes to be only through the coming to be of that composite. The new form (whether accidental or substantial) can come to be only through the modification or coming to be of a material entity formed in a certain way. And so bodies, even several acting in convergence, could not produce a soul whose existence is not dependent on the whole of which it is a part. As Aquinas points out, an entity can *come to be* only in the manner in which it *exists*; if it exists through itself (not dependent on the whole of which it is a part), then it can only come to be through itself (though caused by another), that is, directly, not through the coming to be of another.[45] Hence the human soul must be directly caused to be, not produced through the coming to be of the whole (the human being) of which it is a part.

Another objection might be presented as follows. In this life the subject of mental actions (understanding and willing) is the whole human being. Christians believe that in the next life, before the resurrection of the body (which we will discuss in a moment), the subject of the mental actions (supposing God does intervene) is the soul. What is more, the capacities to understand and will in this life are possessed by the whole human being – you or I can understand and will just as you and I can sit or walk. But in the next life, it seems that the same capacities will remain but will inhere in the soul rather than in the whole human being. Is there not, one might object, an incoherence here?

Our reply is that it is a difficulty but not a contradiction. The soul is a part of the whole human being. Every action and capacity belongs to the whole: parts do not act, only whole substances act and capacities are on the same level as their corresponding acts. Because human understanding (conceptual thought) is performed without a bodily organ (even though it naturally requires sense presentations for its specification), then such an act is in itself possible without any bodily component. So, the subject of the acts of understanding and willing before death (the whole human being) will not be, in the strict sense, the same substance as the subject of acts of

---

[43] William Hasker, *The Emergent Self* (Ithaca, NY: Cornell University Press, 1999).
[44] See O. P. Benedict Ashley, *Theologies of the Body* (St. Louis, MO: Pope John Center, 1985), 256–260.
[45] Aquinas, op. cit., Pt. I, q. 75.

understanding and willing after death (the separated soul). Speaking of this situation, John Haldane compares the human soul to elements which are virtually present in the compound, as, for example, carbon is virtually present in a living organism:

> For want of an existing term let me introduce the expression "residual substance" to introduce the idea of a something to which are transferred certain powers hitherto possessed and exercised by a more extensive and more potent substance.[46]

While the whole human being is alive, the soul is not a complete substance, but is an aspect of the one substance, the human being, that exists. Still, it is present *virtually* or, more precisely, *in power*. Suppose A and B are aspects of a unitary substance (and so they are not present fully or actually as substances, else there would not be one substance but an aggregate of many). A is present in power inasmuch as some of the properties of the whole A/B are the result of the contribution of A; but A is not present in act (is not a distinct substance) since the properties and powers of A/B are new in the sense that they are not just the results of the natures of A, B, and their causal interactions.[47] In this manner the elements carbon and nitrogen, for example, are present by power, and not in act, within an organism, which has powers belonging to the whole which are not reducible to or fully explainable by the properties and powers of its parts – for example, the powers of reproduction and self-nourishment. And yet some of the properties possessed by the organism are the result of contributions of carbon and nitrogen. Haldane's suggestion is not that the soul's presence is exactly like elements in an organism – it is not – but that such a virtual presence can serve as a *model* for the postmortem existence of the human soul:

> Now the question is whether in the case that A/B ceases to exist, certain of its powers might be transferred to A, which, though hitherto merely virtual, might now emerge as actual. To fix this idea think of compound pigment colours such as brown, and the claim that red, say, exists virtually, but not actually, in this compound. What that means is that, certain conditions obtaining, the brown pigment might be destroyed but red pigment is precipitated out.[48]

---

[46] John J. Haldane, "The Examined Death and Hope of the Future," *Proceedings of the American Catholic Philosophical Association* 74 (2000), 245–257 and 254.

[47] William Wallace, *The Modeling of Nature* (Washington, DC: Catholic University of America Press, 1996), 35–53; Christopher Decaen, "Elemental Virtual Presence in St. Thomas," *The Thomist* 64 (2000), 271–300; Peter Hoenen, *The Philosophical Nature of Physical Bodies* (West Baden Springs, IN: West Baden College, 1955).

[48] Haldane, supra, note 46.

For this model to work, the powers transferred from A/B to A must naturally depend on B. But given that the human act of understanding is not itself an act performed with a bodily organ, though it is naturally oriented to being performed in cooperation with acts of bodily organs, it follows that the model could apply. The powers of understanding (conceptual thought) and willing *could* be transferred to a nonphysical substance that "precipitated out" at death, namely, the separated human soul. So, while it is not, strictly speaking, the same substance that understands and wills before death and after death (before the resurrection), this anomaly is not an impossibility or self-contradiction.

Still, a further objection might be raised. Since we are human beings, soul–matter composites, animals of a particular sort, it is fair to ask: how could the survival of just an aspect of us be important for religion or be of any solace to us? Moreover, it is hard to see just what such a soul would do. We have said that the human soul is naturally oriented to union with the body and that all of the actions of a human being – including conceptual thought and choice – belong (in this life) not to the soul, but to the whole human being, the soul being the formal source but not the agent of these actions.

Here, we think, one must frankly admit the limitations of our understanding. Philosophy can provide strong evidence for the conclusion that the soul, in fact, does survive death, but just what happens after death continues to be, especially with respect to reason unaided by faith, a mystery, and gives rise to some perplexity. The human intellect is naturally apt to grasp intelligible features in sense presentations (with a concomitant awareness of its acts, and inferences and analogies from what it does directly know). So, if the soul is not united with the body, then it is in an unnatural condition and is, absent a special divine intervention, literally unable to do anything.

Lest these remarks seem incompatible with what Christianity promises about eternal life, allow us to note that these are exactly the positions that Thomas Aquinas also held. Aquinas held that the separated human soul is in an unnatural condition, can operate only by means of a special divine intervention (God infusing ideas into it), and that even then its mode of understanding will be, because unnatural, less clear or luminous than desirable.[49] But these are not actually difficulties for the position set out in this book. Rather, our only point is that the fact that human beings are animals, rather than souls inhabiting bodies, is fully compatible with

---

[49] Aquinas, op. cit., Pt. I, q. 89, a. 1.

the teachings of biblical faiths (Judaism, Christianity, and Islam) on the immortality of the soul.

B. Resurrection of the Body

Another worry is that the theory presented here may collide with religiously based belief in the resurrection of the body. The argument would be that if we simply *were* souls or minds, then it would be easier to believe that the mind could be reattached, as it were, to a reconstituted body. Since we have argued that the body is part of the self and have also rejected the psychological theory of personal identity, then (so the argument might go) it is hard to see how after the destruction of the bodily self even God could do anything that would constitute a resurrection of that bodily self.

A detailed discussion of the philosophical issues raised by belief in the resurrection is obviously not possible here, but a few points can be made. First, we believe that the animalist position coheres with belief in the resurrection while substance dualism does not. There are two difficulties regarding resurrection for the substance dualist position: first, substance dualism has a much more difficult time explaining the centrality of the belief in the resurrection, at least in Christian faith. Writing to the Corinthians, who had denied the resurrection, St. Paul reasoned as follows:

Now if Christ is preached as raised from the dead, how can some of you say that there is no resurrection of the dead?... For if the dead are not raised, then Christ has not been raised. If Christ has not been raised, your faith is futile and you are still in your sins. Then those also who have fallen asleep in Christ have perished. If for this life only we have hoped in Christ, we are of all men most to be pitied (1 Cor. 15: 12, 16–19).

In the Gospels, we see that the resurrection of the body is central to Christ's promise. As the *Catechism of the Catholic Church* summarizes:

Jesus links faith in the resurrection to his own person: "I am the Resurrection and the life" (Jn 11: 25). It is Jesus himself who on the last day will raise up those who have believed in him, who have eaten his body and drunk his blood (Cf. Jn 5:24–25; 6:40, 54). Already now in this present life he gives a sign and pledge of this by restoring some of the dead to life, (Cf. Mk 5:21–42; Lk 7:11–17; Jn 11) announcing thereby his own Resurrection, though it was to be of another order. He speaks of this unique event as the "sign of Jonah," (Mt 12:39) the sign of the temple: he announces that he will be put to death but rise thereafter on the third day (Cf. Mk 10:34; Jn 2:19–22).

To be a witness to Christ is to be a "witness to his Resurrection," to "[have eaten and drunk] with him after he rose from the dead." (Act 1:22; 10:41; cf. 4:33)

Encounters with the risen Christ characterize the Christian hope of resurrection. We shall rise like Christ, with him, and through him.[50]

There may be a way of reconciling with substance dualism the teaching that the resurrection is needed for our complete salvation,[51] but the doctrine that a human being *is* just a living body (with a rational, spiritual soul) makes sense of this doctrine much more easily and more fully. If I just *were* a soul, even though I had a natural orientation to union with my body, then the nonexistence of the resurrection might be disappointing, but it is hard to see how it would render the faith *futile* (as St. Paul argues). And it would be difficult to explain why bodily resurrection would be at the center, rather than, say, "icing on the cake," for the central teaching about life with Christ.

A second difficulty for substance dualism's coherence with belief in the resurrection is that it implies that, strictly speaking, the person does not die – that is, does not *die* in the sense that, for example, horses and rabbits die.[52] Strictly speaking, one would always have to say (as a Christian), not that Christ rose from the dead but that his body was raised, not that the dead rise again but that their bodies are raised.

But how does the position defended here cohere with belief in the resurrection? "Resurrection" means *rising again*, so what rises must be numerically the same body as the one that died. This prompts the question, what is necessary for numerical identity of the body? Basically, four views on how resurrection is possible have been proposed. We think the first two (van Inwagen's simulacrum theory and the fission theory) are not tenable. The third (the soul alone providing continuity) we think is doubtful. And so we favor the more traditional position (the reassembly position).

Van Inwagen, a Christian materialist (on the nature of the human person) who believes in the resurrection, presents several arguments against the reassembly view (we examine these later in some detail). Still, van Inwagen holds that resurrection does require the biological continuity of the resurrected body with the dead one.[53] He argues that identity requires

---

[50] *Catechism of the Catholic Church*, 2nd ed., #995 (New York: Doubleday, 1997), 281., nos. 994–995.

[51] Charles Taliaferro's "integrative dualism" is an example. See his *Consciousness and the Mind of God* (Oxford: Oxford University Press, 1994).

[52] Steven Davis points this out but accepts it as a nonfatal difficulty (no pun intended). Stephen T. Davis, *Risen Indeed: Making Sense of the Resurrection* (Grand Rapids, MI: Wm. B. Eerdmans, 1993).

[53] Van Inwagen, *The Possibility of Resurrection and Other Essays in Apologetics* (Boulder, CO: Westview Press, 1998), 45–51.

that the life processes of the earlier organism immanently cause those of the later one.[54] So, van Inwagen proposes that at death, God replaces the newly dead body with a simulacrum, and stores the preserved body somewhere for resurrection. In this way the state of the human organism at the later time will be due to the biological processes of that organism. But this view has a very serious problem. Indeed, it is sometimes referred to as "the body snatching view." On this view, it seems that God is causing a massive deception.[55]

The second proposal also requires that the later human being be connected by biological processes to the earlier human being. For an organism at one time to be the same organism as one at an earlier time, an immanent-causal connection seems required. Kevin Corcoran articulates this requirement as follows:

A human body B that exists at t2 is the same as a human body A that exists at t1 just in case the temporal stages leading up to B at t2 are immanent-causally connected to the temporal stage of A at t1.[56]

Given this, the second proposal is that at death there is an immediate resurrection. On this view, at the instant of death, God brings about a fission of all of the constituents (the atoms perhaps) making up the human being. The corpse remains and is spatiotemporally connected but not immanent-causally connected to the living body at the previous moment; the corpse is not actually a single entity but an aggregate of cells and tissues. The living body God produces by fission is the resurrected person. The advantages of this interpretation are that it avoids the objections raised against the reassembly view (to be examined in a moment) but there is an immanent-causal connection between the person at the instant before death and the living body produced by fission, the resurrected living body, at the

---

[54] "Immanent" cause here means an agent's action on itself rather than on an external effect.

[55] Another difficulty is that Christians believe our resurrection is patterned after (and in a mysterious sense a sharing in) Christ's resurrection. On the New Testament account and the belief of traditional Christians, Christ's tomb was empty, but van Inwagen's account does not provide an empty tomb. Van Inwagen could reply that since Christ's resurrection occurs very shortly after death, no simulacrum was created and that the same would be so for any other bodies that rose shortly after their death. Still, this difference between Christ's resurrection and that of most of us is somewhat of a difficulty. Peter van Inwagen, "The Possibility of Resurrection," in *The Possibility of Resurrection and Other Essays in Christian Apologetics* (Boulder, CO: Westview Press, 1997).

[56] Kevin Corcoran, "Physical Persons and Postmortem Survival without Temporal Gaps," in *Soul, Body, and Survival: Essays on the Metaphysics of the Human Person*, ed. Kevin Corcoran (Ithaca, NY: Cornell University Press, 2001), 201–217, at 210.

instant after death. Even though Christians have traditionally thought of and imagined a time intervening between death and resurrection, it is argued that time is bound up with the motion of objects in a given spatial framework, and so temporal comparisons between what is occurring in the "next" life and this one are perhaps inscrutable.[57]

However, we believe that this position is not tenable (though one of us thought otherwise very recently).[58] First, theologically (and our discussion now is about the compatibility of animalism with traditional theological belief in resurrection), the New Testament and the teachings of the Church seem to presuppose an interim (not "time" exactly in our sense but a duration of some sort) between death and resurrection. Second, Catholics believe in the Assumption of Mary into heaven; that is, Mary's body did not suffer corruption but she was assumed body and soul into heaven. Part of this belief, at least tacitly, is that this was a singular privilege, not something that occurs with every human being – which *would* be the case if everyone's resurrection were immediate.

The third difficulty is that this proposal is not really that different from van Inwagen's proposal. On van Inwagen's proposal, God creates from nothing a simulacrum of the corpse, a simulacrum composed of many of the same molecules that once were in the dead person's makeup. As we indicated earlier, this seems to involve God in a massive deception. However, the only difference between van Inwagen's view and the fission proposal is that on the latter view God produces a simulacrum of the corpse by way of fission rather than from nothing. So the central difficulty in van Inwagen's position is equally a difficulty for this view.[59]

---

[57] Cf. James F. Ross, "Together with the Body I Love," *Proceedings of the American Catholic Philosophical Association* 75 (Bronx, NY: ACPA, 2001), 1–18. Dean Zimmerman, "The Compatibility of Materialism and Survival: The 'Falling Elevator' Model," *Faith and Philosophy* 16 (1999), 194–212.

[58] See Patrick Lee, "Soul, Body and Personhood," *American Journal of Jurisprudence* 49 (2005), 122–123.

[59] Another difficulty (for both van Inwagen's view and the fission view) is pointed out in an excellent article by David Hershenov. If one holds that immanent biological causation is required for the identity of the organism, then this biological connection will have to include more than just bare immanent causal connection. Human organisms gradually replace all of their matter over time, but this replacement occurs by gradual assimilation. Matter is taken in from food and air and other matter is lost through exhalation, excretion, and perspiration (see David Hershenov, "Van Inwagen, Zimmerman, and the Materialist Conception of Resurrection," *Religious Studies* 38 (2002), 451–469, at 462). This *gradual* replacement and assimilation of the new by the old enables the new matter to be caught up in the same life processes as the matter already existing in the organism. But neither on van Inwagen's proposal nor on the fission proposal is there room for the

The third interpretation is simply that the human soul continues to exist during a succession of acts and that subsequently God joins this soul to some matter, and the soul configures that matter so that once again the human being, the human person, is alive. In other words, the soul exists for a period as separate from the body. During this interim, the human being does not exist, since the human being is essentially an animal (rational animal), but the soul performs acts of thought, will, memory, and so on (but not acts of sensation, perception, imagination, or any bodily acts). Still, between the human being at the instant before death and the human being at the resurrection, there *will* be an immanent-causal connection, because the human soul persists. Of course, in this life the immanent-causal connection between the organism at one time and the organism at a later time is always a fully *bodily* one.

On this interpretation, however, the immanent-causal connection between the living body at the instant before death and the resurrected body is by way of the persistence of the human soul. The immanent-causal connection (in this life) could, in principle, be quite tenuous, being located perhaps in only a few of the bodily organs (plus the soul). We think that in this special and inevitably obscure case, namely, after death, the immanent-causal connection *perhaps* could be located in the formal principle alone. In other words, we think this proposal is not impossible (though we express doubts about it in a moment). One must remember that the formal principle, or the soul, is not an abstract blueprint, but a particular, an individualized active source or principle. On this interpretation, unlike for substance dualism, death is really the destruction of the human individual. There is a period or interim time (of some sort) during which the human being, the human person, does not exist, even though his soul does exist. Still, there is an immanent-causal connection between the dying human being and the resurrected human being, by way of the human soul.

The difficulty with this view is that, again, one must (if one accepts the teaching of the New Testament and the Church) say that our resurrection is significantly different from Christ's resurrection, in that in Christ's case the soul was *not* the only principle of continuity. In the case of Christ and in those who are raised from the dead before their bodies corrupt, one would have to say (to make the proposal compatible with faith) that

proper assimilation of the new matter by the old. Since the new matter or particles are never properly assimilated, it follows that there is not the biological immanent causal connection typically found in persisting organisms. Hershenov, op. cit., 463.

the same matter is raised up again, so Christ's tomb was empty and the tombs of others perhaps will be empty. If one believes that our resurrection is patterned on Christ's resurrection, this is a serious difficulty for this view.

The fourth interpretation is also the most traditional, and it is the one we favor (though we think that the third view – with the proviso for exceptions for those whose bodies do not corrupt in their tombs or otherwise – is not impossible). This is the reassembly view. On this proposal, God simply reassembles the matter, or much of the matter, that was in the human being at the point of his death and restores it to life by rejoining his immortal soul to it. There are three standard objections to this proposal, but none seems to constitute a serious difficulty for this belief.

The first objection is from van Inwagen. Van Inwagen argues that reassembly of the matter that once constituted the human being would not be sufficient for the identity of the risen individual with the one who died. If, by analogy, a sculpture was destroyed and its atoms scattered throughout the world but then God reassembled it, van Inwagen says that this would not be the same artwork. Its coming from the intentions and actions of this particular sculptor is part of what makes it the artwork that it is. If the new sculpture owes the placement of its material constituents and its configuration to God, or, perhaps to a freak storm, then the original artist could not say that this was *his* sculpture. But its being his artwork is necessary (says van Inwagen) for its being the same sculpture, and so it would not be the same sculpture. Likewise, van Inwagen argues, a human being at one time is identical with a human at later time, only if the human being's parts and configuration are due to the *continual biological processes* of the human organism, rather than to some other cause such as God's miraculous intervention.[60]

Van Inwagen's argument supposes that the identity of a thing is dependent on its causal origin. However, as David Hershenov points out, the particular causal origin of an artwork seems more closely tied to its identity than does the causal origin of an organism.[61] According to van Inwagen, Sculpture B (reassembled by God) cannot be identical with Sculpture A (the original) because they had different causal origins. But Hershenov asks us to suppose that the sculpture had been produced, or that it is re-produced, out of the same materials by the design of the same sculptor, but that this time the sculptor uses apprentices to place each piece

---

[60] Van Inwagen, "The Possibility of Resurrection," loc. cit.
[61] Hershenov, op. cit., 452ff.

of clay into the sculpture. In that case, says Hershenov, it seems that we should perhaps see these sculptures as identical with the first one. So, van Inwagen's analogy with the artwork is not decisive.

Indeed, there is strong reason to believe that the causal origins of a thing, in particular, the causal origins *of an organism*, are not essential to it. Hershenov points out that instead of being conceived when he was, a human being, "could have been conceived later, miraculously produced by God, created in an *in vitro* laboratory, or formed in a freak explosion, as long as these events bring together the same atoms in the same manner as resulted from their father's fertilization of their mother's egg."[62] So the causal origins that bring an organism into existence can vary, and still what is produced be the same organism. If that is so, then there is no reason why God could not *re*-create you after your death, by reassembling at least much of the same or continuous matter that was in you at your death.[63]

The third objection to the traditional reassembly position on resurrection is itself a very old one, namely, the objection from cannibalism. Suppose I die and then much of my body is eaten by a cannibal. Soon after that the cannibal dies. It is impossible then for God to give each of us all of the matter in our bodies just before we died since some of that matter overlaps. So, it is concluded, reassembly is impossible. This argument has been refuted by several classical theologians. As Stephen Davis points out, all that is required to answer this objection is to suppose that God has some principled way of parceling out the shared matter. Davis notes that St. Augustine suggested that God assigns the matter to the one who first possessed it, and that God supplies the missing matter in the cannibals.[64] Aquinas considers this objection in some detail and even considers more complex scenarios, such as a cannibal who ate only

---

[62] Ibid., 452.

[63] Van Inwagen also argues against the reassembly view by claiming that God could reassemble the matter that went into the makeup of van Inwagen when he was ten years old, while the older van Inwagen was still alive. In that case, says van Inwagen, there would be reassembly but not personal identity. But this is not a serious problem for the view, since part of the belief in resurrection is that God would reassemble only the matter (or much of the matter) of the person that was in his makeup just before he died. Of course, God might also cause modifications in the risen human body such as healing, restoring. But both the physical and psychological components re-created would have to be initially from those in the person just before his death.

[64] Stephen T. Davis, "Physicalism and Resurrection," in *Soul, Body and Survival*, 229–248. Davis refers to St. Augustine's *The Enchiridion on Faith, Hope, and Love* (Chicago: Henry Regnery, 1961), Bk. 88 and to his *City of God* (Garden City, NY: Doubleday, 1958), 22.20.

human flesh and a cannibal who developed from semen that was composed from the matter from the flesh of another man. Aquinas begins his treatment by saying that it is not necessary that everything that was in a man materially arise in him at the resurrection. He then says that presumably the one in whom the matter was first will have that matter, unless that matter was, say, in the radical semen from which a man developed; and if that is so, then the matter will be found in him to whose perfection it pertains more.[65] The point is simply that there could be some definite policy (or policies) for assigning overlapping matter, and any needed extra matter could be supplied, as St. Thomas says, by the power of God.[66]

We conclude that the traditional reassembly interpretation of the resurrection is coherent, and the view that only the rational soul provides continuity *might* be coherent (though we have reservations about it). At any rate, the position that human beings are animals is fully compatible with belief in the resurrection (indeed, other theories, such as substance dualism, seem incompatible with that belief). We conclude that the thesis that human beings are animals *is* fully compatible with beliefs that the human soul transcends matter, that the human soul is immortal, and that there is a resurrection of the body.

III. Personhood and Human Dignity

Still, granted that human beings are different in kind (because of the powers of conceptual thought and free choice) from other animals, how

---

[65] St. Thomas, *Summa Contra Gentiles*, Bk. IV, Chapter 80, 13.

[66] One might also object that according to modern physics one cannot, even in principle, trace *the same* particles throughout changes and periods of time. According to modern quantum physics, an electron, for example, is not strictly speaking either here or there and it is meaningless to ask whether this electron in this part of one's body is the same as the electron in that part of the body yesterday. However, the reassembly view need not affirm what modern physics denies (or says is meaningless). The reassembly view only means to affirm a real *material continuity* between the premortem body and the risen body. There is, of course, nothing incoherent in thinking that the same matter (or matter-energy) is first in a carrot, then in a human, and then in an alligator. In the same way, there is nothing incoherent in the idea that some of the same matter that was in a corpse, and became dispersed after its corruption, could at a much later time be reassembled. When someone is cremated, it seems clear that there is a material continuity of some sort between the body before death and the ashes. And this is so even if subatomic and atomic particles are swirling in and out of those ashes. But if there can be such material continuity spanning years and even decades, then it seems that in principle there might be such material continuity retrieved by God for the resurrection.

do these differences show that human beings are entitled to a specific type of respect? Why should having conceptual thought and being moral agents mean that human beings should be treated with a special kind of respect? The general problem can be expressed as follows. It seems that it is morally permissible to *use* some things, to consume them, experiment on them for our benefit (without their consent, or perhaps where they are unable to give or withhold consent), but it is not morally permissible to treat other beings in this way. The question is, where do we draw the line between those two sorts of beings? By what criterion do we draw that line? Or perhaps there just is no such line, and we should always seek to preserve *all* beings, of whatever sort?

But we must eat, we must use some entities for food and shelter, and in doing so we inevitably destroy them. When we eat, we convert entities of one nature into another and thus destroy them. Moreover, no one claims that we should not try to eradicate harmful bacteria (which are forms of life). That is, we should kill harmful bacteria in order to protect ourselves and our children. And it seems clear that we must harvest wheat and rice for food, and trees for shelter. So, plainly it is permissible to kill and use some living things. Given that it is not morally permissible to kill just any type of being, it follows that a line must be drawn: a line between those entities it is morally permissible to use, consume, and destroy and those it is not permissible to use, consume, and destroy. How can the line be drawn in a nonarbitrary way?

Various criteria for where the line should be drawn have been proposed: sentience, consciousness, self-awareness, rationality, or being a moral agent (the last two come to the same thing). We will argue that the criterion is having a rational nature, that is, having the natural capacity to reason and make free choices, a capacity it ordinarily takes months, or even years, to actualize, and which various impediments might prevent from being brought to full actualization, at least in this life. Thus, every human being has full moral worth or dignity, for every human being possesses such a rational nature.

While membership in the species *Homo sapiens* is sufficient for full moral worth, it is not in any direct sense the criterion for moral worth. If we discovered extraterrestrial beings of a rational nature, or that some other terrestrial species did have a rational nature, then we would owe such beings full moral respect. Still, all members of the human species do have full moral worth because all of them do have a rational nature and are moral agents, though many of them are not able immediately to exercise those basic capacities. One could also say that the criterion for full moral worth is *being a person*, since a person is a rational and morally responsible subject.[67]

The other suggestions listed earlier, we believe, are not tenable as criteria of full moral worth and, worse yet, often have the practical effect of leading to the denial that human beings have full moral worth, rather than simply adding other beings to the set of beings deserving full moral respect.[68] Hence it is vital to explain how being a person, that is, being a distinct substance with the basic natural capacities for conceptual thought and free choice, is a basis for the possession of basic rights.

Animal welfarists argue that the criterion of moral worth is simply the ability to experience enjoyment and suffering. Peter Singer, for example, quotes Jeremy Bentham: "The question is not, Can they *reason?* nor Can they *talk?* but, Can they *suffer?*"[69] Singer then presents the following argument for this position:

> The capacity for suffering and enjoyment is *a prerequisite for having interests at all*, a condition that must be satisfied before we can speak of interests in a meaningful way.... A stone does not have interests because it cannot suffer. Nothing that we can do to it could possibly make any difference to its welfare. The capacity for suffering and enjoyment is, however, not only necessary, but also sufficient for us to say that a being has interests – at an absolute minimum, an interest in not suffering.[70]

In short, Singer's argument is: All and only beings which have interests have moral status; but all and only beings that can (now) experience suffering or enjoyment have interests; therefore, all and only beings that can (now) experience suffering or enjoyment have moral status.

The major difficulties with Singer's position all follow from the fact that his proposed criterion for moral status involves the possession of an

---

[67] Boethius's definition, especially as interpreted by St. Thomas Aquinas, is still valid: "An individual substance (that is, a unique substance) of a rational nature." So, neither a nature held in common by many, nor a part is a person. But every whole human being performing its own actions, including actions such as growth toward the mature stage of a human, *is* a person. See Boethius, *De Duobus Naturis* and Aquinas, op. cit., Pt. I, q. 29, a. 1.

[68] See Jenny Teichman, *Social Ethics: A Student's Guide* (Oxford: Blackwell Publishers, 1996).

[69] Peter Singer, "All Animals Are Equal," in *Morality in Practice*, 4th ed., ed. James P. Sterba (Belmont, CA: Wadsworth Publishing Co., 1994) 478, quoting Jeremy Bentham, *Introduction to the Principles of Moral and Legislation*, Chapter 17.

[70] Peter Singer, "All Animals Are Equal," 479. The selection is an excerpt from Peter Singer, *Animal Liberation*, 2nd ed. (New York: The New York Review of Books, 1990).

accidental attribute that varies in degrees. Both the capacity for suffering and the possession of interests are properties which different beings have in different degrees, and the interests themselves are possessed in varying degrees. As we shall show, this feature of Singer's theory leads to untenable conclusions.

Although Singer has made famous the slogan, "All animals are equal," this theory actually leads to *denying* that all animals, including all humans, have equal moral worth or basic rights. Singer means that "All animals are equal" in the sense that all animals would be due "equal consideration." Where the interests of two animals *are* similar in quality and magnitude, then those interests should be counted as equal when deciding what to do, both as individuals and in social policies and actions. However, as Singer himself points out (on this view), some animals can perform actions that others cannot, and thus have interests that those others do not. So the moral status of all animals is not, in fact, equal. One would not be required to extend the right to vote, or to education in reading and arithmetic to pigs, since they are unable to perform such actions. This point leads to several problems when we attempt to compare interests. According to this view, it is the *interests* that matter, not *the kind of being* that is affected by one's actions So, on this view, it would logically follow that if a human child had a toothache and a juvenile rat had a slightly more severe toothache, then we would be morally required to devote our resources to alleviating the rat's toothache rather than the human's.

Moreover, a human newborn infant who will die shortly (and so does not appear to have long-term future interests) or a severely cognitively impaired human will be due *less* consideration than a more mature horse or pig, on the ground that a mature horse or pig will have richer and more developed interests. Since the horse and the pig have higher cognitive and emotional capacities (in the sense of immediately or nearly immediately exercisable capacities) than those newborn infants (that will die shortly) and severely cognitively impaired humans – and it is the interests that directly count morally, not the beings that have those interests – then the interests of the horse and the pig should (on this account) be preferred to the interests of the newborn or the severely cognitively impaired human.[71]

---

[71] Jeff McMahan, whose view is in other respects more complex than Singer's, still holds that only interests are of direct moral concern and explicitly recognizes, and accepts, this logical consequence. See his *The Ethics of Killing, Problems at the Margin of Life* (New York: Oxford University Press, 2002), 205–206.

On the other hand, when we note the differences between types of interests, then Singer's position actually implies an indirect moral elitism. It is true that according to this position no animal is greater than another solely on the ground of its species (that is, according to its substantial nature). Still, one animal will be due more consideration – indirectly – if it has capacities for higher or more complex mental functions. As Singer puts it: "Within these limits we could still hold that, for instance, it is worse to kill a *normal* adult human, with a capacity for self-awareness, and the ability to plan for the future and have meaningful relations with others, than it is to kill a mouse, which presumably does not share all of these characteristics ... " (emphasis supplied).[72] But this difference between degrees of capacity for suffering and enjoyment will also apply to individuals within each species. And so, on this view, while a human will normally have a greater capacity for suffering and enjoyment than other animals, and so will have a higher moral status (indirectly), so too, more intelligent and sophisticated human individuals will have a greater capacity for suffering and enjoyment than less intelligent and less sophisticated human individuals, and so the former will have a higher moral status than the latter. As Richard Arneson expressed this point, "For after all it is just as true that a creative genius has richer and more complex interests than those of an ordinary average Joe as it is true that a human has richer and more complex interests than a baboon."[73]

These difficulties are all due to the selection of a criterion of moral worth that varies in degrees. If the moral status-conferring attribute varies in degrees – whether it be the capacity for enjoyment or suffering, or another attribute that comes in degrees – it will follow that some humans will possess that attribute to a lesser extent than some nonhuman animals, and so inevitably some interests of some nonhuman animals will trump the interests of some humans. Also, it will follow that some humans will possess the attribute in question in a higher degree than other humans, with the result that not all humans will be equal in fundamental moral worth, that is, *dignity*. True, some philosophers bite the bullet on these results. But in our judgment this is too high a price to pay. A sound view of worth and dignity will not entail such difficulties.

---

[72] Singer, "All Animals Are Equal," in *Morality in Practice*, op. cit., 484.
[73] Richard Arneson, "What, if Anything, Renders All Humans Morally Equal?" in *Singer and His Critics*, ed. Dale Jamieson (Malden, MA: Blackwell Publishers, 1999), 103–127, at 105.

On such a view, the criterion of moral worth must be the possession of a property that does not itself vary in degree – it must, that is, be the possession of a nature. Being of moral worth must be grounded in an entity's existence as a substance of a certain sort (we discuss what sort in more detail later) rather than in the possession of a set of accidental or variable properties.

This view explains why our moral concern is for persons, rather than their properties. After all, when dealing with other persons it is clear that the locus of value is the persons themselves. Persons are not mere vehicles for what is intrinsically valuable: one's child, one's neighbor, or even a stranger is not valuable only because of the valuable attributes they possess. If persons were valuable as mere vehicles for something else – some other quality that is regarded as what is *really* of value – then it would follow that the basic moral rule would be simply to maximize those valuable attributes. It would not be morally wrong to kill a child, no matter what age, if doing so enabled one to have two children in the future, and thus to bring it about that there were two vehicles for intrinsic value rather than one.

On the contrary, we are aware that persons themselves – the substantial entities they are – are intrinsically valuable. But if that is so, then what distinguishes those entities that have full moral status (inherent dignity) from those that do not should be the type of substantial entity they are, rather than any accidental attributes they possess. True, it is not self-contradictory to hold that the person himself is valuable, but only in virtue of some accidental attributes he or she possesses. Still, it is more natural, and more theoretically economical, to suppose that *what* has full moral status and that in virtue of which he or she has full moral status are the same.

Moreover, this position more closely tracks the characteristics we find in genuine care or love. Our genuine love for a person remains, or should remain, for as long as that person continues to exist, and is not dependent on his or her possessing further attributes. That is, it seems to be the nature of care or love that it be unconditional and that we continue to desire the well-being or fulfillment of one we love for as long as he or she exists. Of course, this still leaves open the question whether continuing to live is always part of a person's well-being or fulfillment; we do maintain that a person's life always *is* in itself a good, but that is a distinct question from the one being considered just now.

We shall argue later that being a substance *with a rational nature* is the criterion of moral worth. But the point now is that, whatever the specific criterion is, it involves existing as a type of *substance* – being a certain type of thing – rather than possessing a set of accidental or variable properties. In consequence, every substance of that sort will have full moral worth, and any substance of that sort will have a higher and different type of moral worth than entities that are not of that type.[74]

Moreover, the argument for sentience, or the ability to experience suffering and enjoyment, as *the* basic criterion of moral status, supposes that only such beings have interests. However, although rocks do not seem to have interests, the same cannot be said about plants. It is not true that only beings with feelings or some level of consciousness can be reasonably considered to have interests. It is clear that living beings are fulfilled by certain conditions and damaged by others. As Paul Taylor, who defends a biocentrist view (*all* living beings have moral worth), explains:

We can think of the good of an individual nonhuman organism as consisting in the full development of its biological powers. Its good is realized to the extent that it is strong and healthy.[75]

One can then say that what promotes the organism's survival and flourishing is *in its interest* and what diminishes its chances of survival or flourishing is *against its interests*. Further, while it may be initially plausible to think that all animals have rights because they have interests, it is considerably less plausible to think that all living beings (which include wheat, corn, and rice, not to mention weeds and bacteria) have rights. But the interest argument would lead to that position.

Finally, the arguments advanced by Singer and Taylor do not actually attempt to establish that nonhuman animals and other living things have moral rights in the full sense of the term. We think it is true of *every* living being, in some way, that we should not *wantonly* destroy or damage it.[76] With sentient beings, whether their life goes well or badly for them will significantly include their pleasure, comfort, or lack of suffering. And so their flourishing includes pleasure and lack of pain (though it also includes other things such as their life and their activities). Yet it does not follow from these points that they have full basic and inherent dignity (moral

---

[74] This is our solution to what Richard Arneson calls "the Singer problem." Arneson, ibid.

[75] Paul Taylor, "The Ethics of Respect for Nature," in *Morality in Practice*, 488.

[76] Could it be true of every being, living or not? It is hard to see what the good or fulfillment of a nonliving being is, since on that level it is hard to know just what are the basic, substantial entities as opposed to aggregates of entities. Thus, when we breathe we convert oxygen and carbon molecules into carbon dioxide molecules – have we destroyed the oxygen in that process or have we only rearranged the atoms in their constitution? It is hard to say.

worth) or rights.[77] There simply is no conceptual connection between pleasure and pain (enjoyment and suffering), on the one hand, and full moral worth (including genuine rights), on the other hand.[78]

However, almost no one actually argues that these beings have basic dignity or full moral rights. Rather, biocentrists argue that all living things merit *some* consideration, but also hold that human beings are due *more* consideration (though not, apparently, different in kind).[79] In effect, instead of actually holding that all living beings (in the case of biocentrists) or all animals (in the case of animal welfarists) have *rights*, they have simply denied the existence of rights in the full sense of the term.[80] Instead, they hold only that all living beings (or animals or higher mammals) deserve some varying degree of respect or consideration. We agree with this point, but we also maintain that every human being is a subject of rights; that is, every human being should be treated according to the golden rule, and it is absolutely wrong intentionally to kill any innocent human being or intentionally to deprive any innocent human being of any basic, intrinsic good.[81] In other words, we grant that we should take account of the flourishing of living beings and the pleasures and pains of nonhuman animals. But we are not morally related to them in the same way that we are related to other beings who, like ourselves, have a rational nature – beings whom (out of fairness) we should treat as we would have them treat us.

But one might argue for animal rights starting from our natural empathy or affection for them (though most people's natural empathy or affection, notably, does *not* extend to all animals, for example, to spiders or snakes). If one identifies what is to be protected and pursued with what can be felt, that is, enjoyed or suffered in some way, then one might conclude that every entity that can have pleasure or pain deserves (equal?) consideration. If the only intrinsic good were what can be enjoyed and the only intrinsic bad were suffering, then it would not be incoherent to hold that sentience is the criterion of moral standing, that is, that every

---

[77] Cf. Louis G. Lombardi, "Inherent Worth, Respect, and Rights," *Environmental Ethics* 5 (1983), 257–270.

[78] David Oderberg, *Applied Ethics: A Non-Consequentialist Approach* (Oxford: Blackwell Publishers, 2000), 101.

[79] For example, Taylor, "The Ethics of Respect for Nature," supra, note 75.

[80] Peter Singer acknowledges that he is "not convinced that the notion of a moral right is a helpful or meaningful one, except when it is used as a shorthand way of referring to more fundamental considerations."

[81] We are simply abstracting from the issue of capital punishment in this book.

entity with sentience has (some degree of) moral standing. In other words, it seems that one can present an *argument* for animal rights that begins from natural feelings of empathy only by way of a hedonistic value theory. We can think of no other arguments that begin from that natural empathy with, or affection for, other animals.

But hedonism as a general theory of value is mistaken. The good is not exhausted by the experiential aspects of our activity – contrary to a key tenet of hedonism. Real understanding of the way things are, for example, is pleasurable because it is fulfilling or perfective of us, not vice versa. The same is true of life, health, or skillful performance (one enjoys running a good race because it is a genuine accomplishment, a skillful performance, rather than vice versa). So, as Plato and Aristotle pointed out, hedonism places the cart before the horse.

Our desires are not purely arbitrary: we are capable of desiring certain things while other things leave us unmoved, uninterested. So, prior to being desired, the object desired must have something about it which makes it *fitting*, or *suitable*, to be desired. What makes it fitting to us is that it would *fulfill* or *perfect* us in some way or other. Thus, what makes a thing good cannot consist in its being enjoyed or in its satisfying desires or preferences. Rather, desires and preferences are rational only if they are in line with what is genuinely good, that is, genuinely fulfilling.[82] So, hedonism is mistaken. It cannot then provide support for the view that sentience (or the capacity for suffering and enjoyment) is the criterion of full moral worth. While it is wrong to damage or kill a plant wantonly, still it can be morally right to do so for a good reason. Similarly, it is wrong wantonly to damage or kill a nonrational animal, but it can be morally right to do so for a good reason.[83]

---

[82] Thus, the pleasures of the sadist or child molester are *in themselves* bad; it is false to say that such pleasures are bad only because of the harm or pain involved in their total contexts. It is false to say: "It was bad for him to cause so much pain, but at least he enjoyed it." Pleasure is secondary, an aspect of a larger situation or condition (such as health, physical, and emotional); what is central is what is really fulfilling. Pleasure is not a good like understanding or health, which are goods or perfections by themselves, that is, are good in themselves even if in a context that is overall bad or if accompanied by many bads. Rather, pleasure is good (desirable, worthwhile, perfective) if and only if attached to a fulfilling or perfective activity or condition. Pleasure *is* a good: a fulfilling activity or condition is better with it than without it. But pleasure is *unlike* full-fledged goods in that it is not a genuine good apart from some other fulfilling activity or condition. It is a good if and only if attached to another condition or activity that is already good. We examine hedonism in more detail in Chapter 3.

[83] It is worth noting that nonhuman animals themselves not only regularly engage in killing each other, but many of them (lions and tigers, for example) seem to depend for their

Neither sentience nor life itself entails that those who possess them must be respected as ends in themselves or as creatures having full moral worth. Rather, having a rational nature is the ground of full moral worth. The basis of this point can be explained, at least in part, in the following way. When one chooses an action, one chooses it for a reason, that is, for the sake of some good one thinks this action will help to realize. That good may itself be a way of realizing some further good, and that good a means to another, and so on. But the chain of instrumental goods cannot be infinite. So, there must be some ultimate reasons for one's choices: some goods that one recognizes as reasons for choosing, which need no further support and are not mere means to some further good.

Such ultimate reasons for choice are not arbitrarily selected. Intrinsic goods – that is, human goods that as basic aspects of human well-being and fulfillment provide more-than-merely-instrumental reasons for choices and actions – are not just what we happen to desire, perhaps different objects for different people.[84] Rather, the intellectual apprehension that a condition or activity is *really fulfilling* or *perfective* (of me and/or of others like me) is at the same time the apprehension that this condition or activity is a fitting object of pursuit, that is, that it would be worth pursuing.[85] These fundamental human goods are the actualizations of our

whole mode of living (and so their flourishing) on hunting and killing other animals. If nonhuman animals really did have full moral rights, however, we would be morally required to stop them from killing each other. Indeed, we would be morally required to invest considerable resources – economic, military, even – in order to protect zebras and antelopes from lions, sheep and foxes from wolves, and so on.

[84] The Humean notion of practical reason contends that practical reason begins with given ends which are not rationally motivated. However, this view cannot, in the end, make sense of the fact that we seem to make objective value judgments, not contingent on, or merely relative to, what this or that group happens to desire – for example, the judgments that murder or torture is objectively morally wrong. Moreover, the Humean view fails to give an adequate account of how we come to desire certain objects for their own sake to begin with. A perfectionist account, on the contrary, one that identifies the intrinsic goods (the objects desired for their own sake) with objective perfections of the person, is able to give an account of these facts. For criticisms of the Humean notion of practical reason: Joseph Boyle, "Reasons for Action: Evaluative Cognitions that Underlie Motivations," *American Journal of Jurisprudence* 46 (2001), 177–197; R. Jay Wallace, "How to Argue about Practical Reason," *Mind* 99 (1990), 355–387; Christine Korsgaard, "Skepticism about Practical Reason," in her *Creating the Kingdom of Ends* (Cambridge, UK: Cambridge University Press, 1996); David Brink, "Moral Motivation," *Ethics* 107 (1997), 4–32; John Finnis, *Fundamentals of Ethics* (Washington, DC: Georgetown University Press, 1983), 26–79; Joseph Raz, *The Morality of Freedom* (New York: Oxford University Press, 1986), 288–368.

[85] The idea is this: what is to be done is what is perfective. This seems trivial, and perhaps is obvious, but it is the basis for objective, practical reasoning. The question "what is

basic potentialities, the conditions to which we are naturally oriented and which objectively fulfill us, the various aspects of our fulfillment as human persons.[86] They include such fulfillments as human life and health, speculative knowledge or understanding, aesthetic experience, friendship or personal community, harmony among the different aspects of the self.[87]

The conditions or activities understood to be fulfilling and worth pursuing are not individual or particularized objects. I do not apprehend merely that *my* life or knowledge is intrinsically good and to be pursued. I apprehend that life and knowledge, whether instantiated in me or in others, are good and worth pursuing. For example, seeing an infant drowning in a shallow pool of water, I apprehend, without an inference, that a good worth preserving is in danger and so I reach out to save the child. The feature *fulfilling for me or for someone like me* is the feature in a condition or activity that makes it an ultimate reason for action. The question is, in what respect must someone be like me for his or her fulfillment to be correctly viewed as worth pursuing for its own sake in the same way that my good is worth pursuing?

to be done?" is equivalent to the question "what is to be actualized?" But what is to be actualized is what actualizes, that is, what is objectively perfective. For human beings this is life, knowledge of truth, friendship, and so on.

[86] This claim is derived from Thomas Aquinas, and has been developed by Thomists and Aristotelians of various types. It is not necessary here to assume one particular development of that view against others. We need only the point that the basic principles of practical reason come from an insight – which may be interpreted in various ways – that what is to be pursued, what is worth pursuing, is what is fulfilling or perfective of me and others like me. For more on this, see Germain Grisez, Joseph Boyle, and John Finnis, "Practical Principles, Moral Truth and Ultimate Ends," *American Journal of Jurisprudence* 33 (1988), 99–151; John Finnis, Joseph M. Boyle, Jr., Germain Grisez, *Nuclear Deterrence, Morality and Realism* (Oxford: Oxford University Press, 1987), Chapters 9–11. John Finnis, *Fundamentals of Ethics*; John Finnis, *Aquinas, Moral, Political, and Legal Theory* (Oxford: Oxford University Press, 1998); T. D. J. Chappell, *Understanding Human Goods: A Theory of Ethics* (Edinburgh: Edinburgh University Press, 1998); David S. Oderberg, *Moral Theory: A Non-Consequentialist Approach* (Oxford: Blackwell Publishers, 2000); Ralph McInerny, *Aquinas on Human Action: A Theory of Practice* (Washington, DC: Catholic University of America Press, 1992); Mark C. Murphy, *Natural Law and Practical Rationality* (New York: Cambridge University Press, 2002).

[87] Once one apprehends such conditions or activities as really fulfilling and worthy of pursuit, the *moral* norm arises when one has a choice between one option the choice of which is fully compatible with these apprehensions (or judgments) and another option that is not fully compatible with those judgments. The former type of choice is fully reasonable, and respectful of the goods and persons involved, whereas the latter type of choice is not fully reasonable and negates, in one way or another, the intrinsic goodness of one or more instances of the basic goods one has already apprehended as, and recognized to be, intrinsically good.

The answer is not immediately obvious to spontaneous, or first-order, practical reasoning or to first-order moral reasoning. That is, the question of the extension of the fundamental goods genuinely worthy of pursuit and respect needs moral reflection to be answered. By such reflection, we can see that the relevant likeness (to me) is that others too rationally shape their lives, or have the potentiality of doing so. Other likenesses – age, sex, race, appearance, place of origin, and so on – are not relevant to making an entity's fulfillment fundamentally worth pursuing and respecting. But being a rational agent *is* relevant to this issue, for it is an object's being worthy of *rational* pursuit that I apprehend and which makes it an ultimate reason for action, and an intrinsic good.[88] So, I ought primarily to pursue and respect not just life in general, for example, but the life of rational agents – a rational agent being one who either immediately or potentially (with a *radical* potentiality, as part of his or her nature) shapes his or her own life.[89]

Moreover, I understand that the basic goods are not just good for me as an individual, but for me acting in communion – rational cooperation and real friendship – with others. Indeed, communion with others, which includes mutual understanding and self-giving, is itself an irreducible aspect of human well-being and fulfillment – a basic good. But I can act in communion – real communion – only with beings with a rational nature. So, the basic goods are not just goods for me, but goods for me and all those with whom it is possible (in principle, at least) rationally to cooperate. All of the basic goods should be pursued and respected, not just as they are instantiable in me, but as they are instantiable in any being with a rational nature.

In addition, by reflection we see that it would be inconsistent to respect my fulfillment, or my fulfillment plus that of others whom I just happen to like, and *not* respect the fulfillment of other, immediately or potentially, rational agents. For, entailed by rational pursuit of my good (and of the

---

[88] The argument presented here is similar to the approaches found in the following authors: Lombardi, loc. cit.; Michael Goldman, "A Transcendental Defense of Speciesism," *Journal of Value Inquiry* 35 (2001), 59–69; William J. Zanardi, "Why Believe in the Intrinsic Dignity and Equality of Persons?" *Southwest Philosophy Review* 14 (1998), 151–168.

[89] The position that the criterion for full moral worth cannot be an accidental attribute, but is the rational *nature*, that is, being a specific type of substance, is defended in Patrick Lee, "The Pro-Life Argument from Substantial Identity: A Defense," *Bioethics* 18 (2004), 249–263. See also Dean Stretton, "Essential Properties and the Right to Life: A Response to Lee," *Bioethics* 18 (2004), 264–282 and Patrick Lee, "Substantial Identity and the Right to Life: A Rejoinder to Dean Stretton," forthcoming in *Bioethics* 21 (2007), 93–97.

good of others I happen to like) is a demand on my part that others respect my good (and the good of those I like). That is, in pursuing my fulfillment, I am led to appeal to the reason and freedom of others to respect that pursuit and my real fulfillment. But in doing so, consistency, that is reasonableness, demands that I also respect the rational pursuits and real fulfillment of other rational agents – that is, any entity that, immediately or potentially (that is by self-directed development of innate or inherent natural capacities), rationally directs his or her own actions. In other words, the thought of the golden rule, basic fairness, occurs early on in moral reflection. One can *hope* that the weather and other natural forces, including any nonrational agent, will not harm one. But one has a moral *claim* or *right* (one spontaneously makes a moral *demand*) that other mature rational agents respect one's reasonable pursuits and real fulfillment. Consistency, then, demands that one respect reasonable pursuits and real fulfillment of others as well. Thus, having a rational nature, or, being a person, as traditionally defined (a distinct subject or substance with a rational nature), is the criterion for full moral worth.

On this position every human being, of whatever age, size, or degree of development, has inherent and equal fundamental dignity and basic rights. If one holds, on the contrary, that full moral worth or dignity is based on some accidental attribute, then, since the attributes that could be considered to ground basic moral worth (developed consciousness, etc.) vary in degree, one will be led to the conclusion that moral worth also varies in degrees.

It might be objected that the basic natural capacity for rationality also comes in degrees, and so this position (that full moral worth is based on the possession of the basic natural capacity for rationality), if correct, would also lead to the denial of personal equality.[90] However, the criterion for full moral worth is having a nature that entails the capacity (whether existing in root form or developed to the point at which it is immediately exercisable) for conceptual thought and free choice – and not *the development* of that natural basic capacity to some degree or other (and to what degree would necessarily be an arbitrary matter). The criterion for full moral worth and possession of basic rights is not having a capacity for conscious thought and choice which inheres in an entity, but being a certain kind of thing, that is, having a specific type of substantial nature. Thus, possession of full moral worth follows upon being a certain type of entity or substance, namely, a substance with a rational nature, despite the

---

[90] Stretton, op. cit., 264–282.

fact that some persons (substances with a rational nature) have a greater intelligence or are morally superior (exercise their power for free choice in an ethically more excellent way) than others. Since basic rights are grounded in being a certain type of substance, it follows that having such a substantial nature qualifies one as having full moral worth, basic rights, and equal personal dignity.

An analogy may clarify our point. Certain properties follow upon being an animal and so are possessed by every animal, even though in other respects not all animals are equal. For example, every animal has some parts which move other parts and every animal is subject to death (mortal). Because various animals are equally animals – and since being an animal is a type of substance rather than an accidental attribute – then every animal will equally have *those* properties, even though (for example) not every animal equally possesses the property of being able to blend in well to the wooded background. Similarly, possession of full moral worth follows upon being a person (a distinct substance with a rational nature), even though persons are unequal in many respects (intellectually, morally, etc.).

In sum, human beings constitute a special sort of animals. They differ in kind from other animals because they have a rational nature, a nature characterized by having the basic, natural capacities (possessed by each and every human being from the point at which he or she comes to be) for conceptual thought and deliberation and free choice. In virtue of having such a nature, all human beings are persons; and all persons possess the real dignity that is deserving of full moral respect. Thus, every human being deserves full moral respect.

3

Hedonism and Hedonistic Drug-Taking

Our claim in this book is that although human beings are bodily entities, rational *animals*, many of the contemporary, heated ethical controversies arise because some people implicitly (and wrongly) view the self as a pure consciousness (not necessarily substantial), and the body as a mere extrinsic tool. In this chapter we argue that this pattern is exemplified in the ethical theory of hedonism and, in particular, in the practice of hedonistic drug-taking.

I. What Hedonism Is

Traditionally, hedonism is divided into two types: psychological hedonism and ethical hedonism. The psychological hedonist says that as a matter of psychological fact, people are always motivated by the desire for pleasure, either short-term or long-term. The ethical hedonist says two things: first, that the only state of affairs that is good for its own sake is pleasure – nothing is good unless it is itself a pleasure or a means of producing pleasure; second, that one *should* act for the sake of producing maximum pleasure (either for oneself or for people in general).[1]

The two types of hedonism are distinct but obviously related. If pleasure alone is desired and desirable for its own sake (psychological hedonism), then it seems to be the only good (the first tenet of ethical

---

[1] Andrew Moore calls the first type of hedonism "motivational hedonism" and the second "normative hedonism." See Andrew Moore, "Hedonism," *The Stanford Encyclopedia of Philosophy (Summer 2004 Edition)*, ed. Edward N. Zalta, URL: http://plato.stanford. edu/archives/sum2004/entries/hedonism/.

hedonism) – since to say that an object, activity, or state is good is to say *at least* that it is desirable. And if pleasure is the only good, then it also seems natural (though not absolutely necessary) to hold that one ought to produce as much pleasure (for oneself or for people in general) as possible (the second tenet of ethical hedonism).[2] We will argue against psychological hedonism first, and then against ethical hedonism (centering on its first tenet, namely, pleasure is the only intrinsic or final good). But first we must clarify the different types of pleasure.

The first point to notice is that there is no feature or quality held in common by all states or activities called "pleasure." No feature called "pleasure" is held in common by, for example, playing tennis, finishing a difficult job, or tasting an apple. As Aristotle pointed out, there are fundamentally distinct types of pleasure.[3] Aristotle held that pleasure is the experiential aspect of a fulfilling activity or state, and that as there are distinct types of activities or states, so there are distinct types of pleasure. Perhaps it is true that people should pursue pleasure only as an aspect of a fulfilling activity or condition (we argue for this proposition in Section V). Still, people do not always regard pleasure, or a pleasurable sensation, as only an aspect of a fulfilling activity. And so there are other types of pleasure in addition to this type.

Following G. H. von Wright, we can divide pleasures into three types.[4] A first type is illustrated by the pleasure one takes in playing tennis, acquiring philosophical knowledge, listening to a concert, or engaging in a rewarding conversation with a friend. Such pleasures are not bodily sensations, and they cannot be located in specific parts of one's body. Rather, they are, in some way, the experiential aspects of other activities. They are not just the activities, however, for one can perform various fulfilling activities, such as digestion or muscle regeneration, without such activities being pleasant. To be pleasant, an activity must involve one's consciousness of it, and perhaps include attention toward it. However, a

---

[2] On the other hand, the logical connections are not as tight as they might first appear. One could hold that people do desire things other than pleasure, but that they should not, and that to do so is unreasonable. That is, one could be an ethical hedonist without being a psychological hedonist.

[3] Aristotle, *Nicomachean Ethics*, Bk. X, Chapters 4–6.

[4] See Georg Henrik von Wright, *Varieties of Goodness* (London: Routledge and Kegan Paul, 1963), 64–66. Also see William Alston, "Pleasure," in *The Encyclopedia of Philosophy*, ed. Paul Edwards (New York: Macmillan, 1967); William Frankena, *Ethics* (Englewood Cliffs, NJ: Prentice-Hall, 1963), 67–75. David Sobel, "Varieties of Hedonism," *Journal of Social Philosophy* 33 (2002), 240–256. Sobel's division of pleasure into three types does not exactly track ours. We follow, basically, von Wright's and Alston's divisions.

mere awareness of the activity does not seem of itself to be a pleasure: one can be neutrally, or quite indifferently, aware of good things happening to oneself and to others.[5] We can describe this first type of pleasure, then, as the conscious delight in an activity or state.[6] Aristotle's analysis of pleasure applies most aptly to this type. Virtuous persons find morally good actions pleasant; vicious persons take pleasure in revenge or power, as well as other activities or conditions. In this sense, pleasure – as Aristotle pointed out (the Greek is *hedoné*) – refers to the experiential aspect or consequence of an activity, and it is not the (core) good itself, but a consequence of possessing the good or apparent good; though pleasure of this sort *is* a good, when it is a consequence of possessing a real good. We add "apparent good," because we hold that someone can take pleasure in something that is not really good, but merely apparently good (fulfilling). That is, one's conscious delight in participating in a good is one type of pleasure, but we hold that one's delight can be misdirected (and in that case is not a good).[7] We defend this claim in Section V. Let us call this first type of pleasure "conscious enjoyment."

A second type of pleasure is illustrated by the relief the factory worker feels when the five o'clock whistle blows, or the relief one feels when any difficult job is completed. Von Wright describes this type of pleasure as follows:

In addition to passive [our third type] and active [our first type] pleasure there is that which I shall call *pleasure of satisfaction* or *contentedness*. It is the pleasure which we feel at getting that which we desire or need or want – irrespective of whether the desired thing by itself gives us pleasure.[8]

Thus, doing forty push-ups or solving a crossword puzzle may not be in themselves pleasant, but completing those tasks is a distinct type of pleasure. Again, the pleasure does not consist in a particular, localizable

---

[5] Thus, we disagree with Panayot Butchvarov's position that this type of pleasure consists solely in the consciousness of the goodness qua goodness of activities one performs or states one is in. See Panayot Butchvarov, *Skepticism in Ethics* (Bloomington: Indiana University Press, 1989), 92–95. However, our overall argument does not depend on this point; one could agree with Butchvarov and still accept the argument in the rest of this chapter.

[6] This is probably the meaning denoted by the term *delectatio* in Aquinas's ethical treatises. See, for example, *Summa Theologiae*, Pt. I–II, q. 31, aa. 1 and 2.

[7] An example would be delighting in the apparent solution of a problem that turns out to be a mistake, or delighting in the apparent devotion of a friend who turns out to be unfaithful. Aquinas discusses this type of case where he analyzes unnatural pleasures (*delectationes*). *Summa Theologiae*, Pt. I–II, q. 31, a. 7.

[8] Von Wright, op. cit., 65.

sensation, though the experience may be accompanied by some sensations. Nor is the activity itself particularly pleasant, or the cause of pleasure (as in type-one pleasure). Rather, this pleasure consists in the satisfaction of a desire. One might group this type together with the first type of pleasure we explained earlier. For this type of pleasure seems to be a *conscious delight*, not in the activity itself (like the other type-one pleasures) but in its completion. However, it is useful to treat this as a distinct type, since it has figured prominently in debates about psychological hedonism (we return to this point in Section II). Let us call this second type of pleasure "satisfaction of a desire."

A third type of pleasure is a bodily sensation. This is illustrated by the pleasurable experiences of the taste of an apple, the feel of a warm bath, a sexual orgasm, or the "high" experienced as a result of drinking alcohol. One important difference between this type and the others is that, more frequently than in the other types, at times we seem to desire the pleasure itself rather than the activity that the pleasure accompanies. The primary object of desire in the first type (conscious enjoyment) is (usually) the activity one is consciously delighting in; the primary object of desire in the second type (satisfaction of a desire) is the object of another, first-order desire. In this third type (sensation), however, it seems, in many instances, that the primary object of desire is the pleasure itself. For example, one can desire the taste itself of an apple or the sheer feeling of a sexual orgasm.

So, pleasure can be defined as a conscious, agreeable feeling, which is (1) an appetitive reaction to some other activity or condition, (2) a satisfaction of a desire, or (3) a specific sensation. This list may seem expansive. But one should notice that although there is no simple quality common to all pleasures, all are conscious, agreeable feelings.

II. Preliminary Arguments against Psychological and Ethical Hedonism

A first difficulty with ethical hedonism emerges from a consideration of psychological hedonism. Psychological hedonism, again, is the claim that the only things we desire for their own sake are pleasures. However, at least sometimes we desire objects distinct from pleasure (understood in any of the three types mentioned earlier). It is obvious that not all of our actions are for the sake of type-three pleasure (pleasure as a sensation). Almost everyone will grant that at least some of our actions are motivated (in some way) by other experiences or states of affairs.⁹ Consider, for example, someone's choice to work a mathematical problem which has no foreseeable practical use. If asked why he works the mathematical problem, the person might say, "Simply because I enjoy doing it." The psychological hedonist, of course, might welcome such an answer. He might argue that this person works the problem precisely for the sake of the pleasure he gets from it, and so his desire is, after all, simply a desire for pleasure. However, the pleasure he desires is of type-two; that is, it is the pleasure that consists in the satisfaction of a desire. So his desire for this type of pleasure will be a desire to satisfy a desire for something else; it will be a second-order desire, depending on some first-order desire. But this first-order desire is certainly not directed to a pleasure. That is, one could not obtain pleasure from the satisfaction of the desire for the solution of a mathematical problem (the second-order desire) unless one first desired that solution; and *that* desire (the first-order desire for the solution) is a desire for a state which is distinct from pleasure.¹⁰ Therefore, there are objects or states of affairs other than pleasure that are desired for their own sake.

A similar point can be made by examining type-one pleasures (conscious enjoyments of activities). When someone enjoys playing tennis, the pleasure consists in the conscious delight in the performance of an activity one desires for its own sake. One could not obtain pleasure from playing tennis unless one viewed it as, at least in some sense, good. Here Aristotle's point is certainly correct: pleasure, in many instances at least, is consequent to an activity whose object is something other than the pleasure.¹¹ So, psychological hedonism is mistaken.

As von Wright explains, there is a necessary connection between desire and pleasure, but the connection is not that pleasure is desire's object; rather, obtaining what one desires, which is a condition or activity distinct from pleasure, *results in* pleasure. Psychological hedonists confuse these connections. "The error of [psychological] hedonism is that it mistakes the necessary connection which holds between the satisfaction of desire

---

⁹ See Toni Ronnow-Rasmussen, "Hedonism, Preferentialism, and Value Bearers," *The Journal of Value Inquiry* 36 (2002), 463–472.

¹⁰ This point is similar to that made by Joseph Butler against egoism: Joseph Butler, *Fifteen Sermons*, Sermon XI, "Upon the Love of Neighbor," reprinted in *Ethics, History, Theory, and Contemporary Issues*, 3rd ed., ed. Steven M. Cahn and Peter Markie (New York: Oxford University Press, 2006), 237ff.; also see Joel Feinberg, "Psychological Egoism," in ibid., 527–534.

¹¹ Aristotle, op. cit., Bk. X, Chapters 4–6.

and pleasure, for a necessary connection between desire and pleasure *as its object.*"[12] Desire is, of course, intrinsically connected to what is good: while not everything desired is genuinely good, what is genuinely good is the *fitting* object of desire (more on this later). And so the primary object of desire – what one naturally desires on the first level before desiring to satisfy a desire – is, at least in many cases, not pleasure, but a condition or activity the attainment of which is pleasurable.

This argument does not refute *ethical* hedonism. Someone could still hold that when people do act for states other than pleasure for its own sake, they are just mistaken. However, the fact that psychological hedonism is mistaken strongly suggests, or provides strong evidence for, the proposition that ethical hedonism is false; that is, that pleasure is not the only noninstrumental good. The fact that people *do* act for the sake of knowledge, moral uprightness, play, friendship, and other objects and do not treat these objects as means to pleasure is strong evidence that people grasp something intrinsically worthwhile in those objects.

III. An Argument against Hedonism from Qualitative Differences among Pleasures

There is a second difficulty with ethical hedonism. It is often argued that (1) there clearly are qualitative differences among pleasures (that is, qualitatively higher and lower types of pleasures), but (2) such qualitative differences implicitly suppose some criterion other than pleasure itself by which to rank the qualitatively different types, and so (3) pleasure cannot be the only intrinsic good. This argument is often advanced in the context of discussions of J. S. Mill's modification of the hedonism he inherited from Jeremy Bentham. Bentham was a pure and quantitative hedonist: what counts is pleasure and pleasure alone (pure hedonism).[13] If one action will produce a greater amount of pleasure than another, taking into account various factors such as intensity, duration, and number of people experiencing it, then that action should be done (quantitative hedonism). Bentham explicitly denied that the *quality* of a pleasure should be considered; only its *quantity* is important. Famously, he said, "Prejudice apart, the game of push-pin is of equal value with the arts and sciences of music and poetry. If the game of push-pin furnish more pleasure, it is

---

[12] Von Wright, op. cit., 83.
[13] Jeremy Bentham, *Introduction to the Principles of Moral and Legislation*, selections reprinted in Cahn and Markie, op. cit., 309–316.

more valuable than either."[14] Critics then pointed out that according to Bentham's theory, if one person obtained greater pleasure from wallowing in mud than another person obtained in reading Shakespeare, then the former experience would be intrinsically more valuable than the second. Of course, a Benthamite might reply that this could not occur – the experience of reading Shakespeare with understanding will always have a greater quantity of pleasure than an experience of wallowing in mud.

However, suppose we compare the Shakespeare reading with two, three, or some other number of wallowings in mud. If there is only a quantitative difference between pleasures, then some number of mud wallowings will outweigh the Shakespeare reading. Mill rightly recoiled from such a conclusion. It seems clear that the *quality* of the pleasure should be considered, as well as its quantity. And this was Mill's modification:

> It is quite compatible with the principle of utility to recognize the fact, that some kinds of pleasure are more desirable and more valuable than others. It would be absurd that while, in estimating all other things, quality is considered as well as quantity, the estimation of pleasures should be supposed to depend on quantity alone.[15]

Thus, in response to critics of hedonism, Mill was able to say that, according to his position, a dissatisfied Socrates is still better than a satisfied fool.

So, there *are* qualitative differences among pleasures. Yet, it is often argued that this admission is implicitly a denial of hedonism itself. If action A has more, or an equal amount of, pleasure than action B, and yet B is more valuable than A, it cannot be qua pleasure that it is more valuable. B must be better than A with respect to some feature or criterion distinct from pleasure. If one grants that Socrates's understanding is higher than the exquisite pleasures of a gourmand, this can only be on the basis of some criterion other than pleasure.

In his defense of a qualitative hedonism, Rem Edwards replied to the preceding argument by denying that one type of pleasurable experience (e.g., the pleasure of several wallowings in mud) can be meaningfully said to have the same, or a greater, amount of pleasure as another type of pleasurable experience (e.g., a Shakespeare reading).[16] In other words, according to Edwards, two experiences can differ qua pleasure; that is, qua

---

[14] Bentham, op. cit., Bk. III, Chapter I.
[15] John Stuart Mill, *Utilitarianism*, in *Collected Works of John Stuart Mill*, vol. X (London: Routledge and Kegan Paul, 1969), 211.
[16] Rem B. Edwards, *Pleasures and Pains: A Theory of Qualitative Hedonism* (Ithaca, NY: Cornell University Press, 1979), 106–111.

experience or feeling without being *quantifiably* comparable. Edwards still holds that what is intrinsically valuable is a quality of experience – an agreeable feeling – but he holds that there are irreducibly distinct types of agreeable feelings.[17]

Edwards pointed out – rightly we think – that in the way it is usually presented, the argument against hedonism based on qualitative differences among pleasures is unsuccessful. However, the argument can be amended so that, even if it does not strictly demonstrate that hedonism is false, it does cast considerable doubt on it. Edwards's answer to the standard version of the argument is that two pleasures can be qualitatively different, but not on the basis of something other than pleasure. But in order for hedonism to make sense, this claim must not only lack self-contradiction; it must actually be true. The claim does not appear to be self-contradictory (as is usually supposed when the argument is presented); still, it does not seem to fit the facts. It seems that people very often *do* rank different pleasures on the basis of the activities or conditions they are consequent to, rather than only on the pleasures derived from them. The experience one has of knowledge or understanding science or philosophy, for example, certainly *seems* to many people less intense qua pleasure and yet, in some sense, higher than other, more intensely pleasurable experiences. Edwards, of course, could hold that people are just confused when they adopt these views, but he owes us a reason for holding this point – other than simply its not being self-contradictory.

Moreover, although hedonism is not self-contradictory, it seems to be self-inconsistent. A self-inconsistency is distinct from a self-contradiction. A self-contradiction is a conflict between two propositions, such that both cannot be true, or between the subject and the predicate of a single proposition, such that they are incompatible. An example of a self-contradiction is this: "This vacuum cleaner is absolutely and unconditionally guaranteed, except for parts and labor." A self-inconsistency (or performative self-inconsistency) is standardly defined as a conflict between what is said (one or more propositions) and *the act* of affirming it. An example of a

---

[17] Edwards also, at one point, says that feelings cannot be detached from their objects. For example, the pleasure of the sweetness of sugar cannot be detached from the sweetness of sugar; the pleasure of friendship or of philosophical inquiry cannot be detached from the friendship or the philosophical inquiry (p. 91). This position moves him very close to ours. Still, his position remains hedonistic (unlike ours), at least in this sense: he denies that any object is intrinsically good in isolation from feeling or pleasure; thus, it is *the pleasure of* friendship or philosophical inquiry that is good, not the friendship or the inquiry itself.

(performative) self-inconsistency is this: "No one can put words together to form a complete sentence." Or: "There are no true propositions."[18] In each case, some aspect of the *act* of affirming the proposition undermines it.

But the act of affirming hedonism undermines the credibility of that affirmation. Suppose you argue with a hedonist about some matter of fact. Suppose that in a philosophical conversation a hedonist makes a claim about his experience. Should you believe him? If he acts on his hedonism, then whether his claim is true is of itself not relevant to what he should tell you. Of course, he may reason that telling the truth is a policy that will generally lead to the most pleasure (for all concerned, say). But he may very well consider that his telling the truth in this particular case would seem *not* to lead to more pleasure (or less pain) overall, but instead that telling the truth, in this case, would lead to more pain than pleasure. In other words, the hedonist cannot, consistently, have a respect for truth-telling for its own sake. If he is consistent, he must view truth as merely instrumentally valuable. Therefore, if the consistent hedonist did happen to tell you the truth, then he would have to admit that if lying had seemed more productive of pleasure (and less productive of pain) on this occasion, then he would have (or should have) lied to you. But when the hedonist argues with you, isn't he *claiming*, in any case, that this is not his attitude to the truth? Isn't there, implicit in the *act* of speaking to you, a claim that he is saying what he says, not for an ulterior purpose (such as pleasure), but because he thinks it is true? Isn't he *vouching* for its truth? In short, doesn't the hedonist (if he is telling the truth) have to claim: "When I speak to you I might just as well lie to you as not, because I don't care a whit about truth in itself"? And isn't that inconsistent with a serious argument? These considerations suggest that there must be some good – knowledge of truth, for example – that is not confined to pleasurable experience.

IV. Hedonism and Dualism

Although Edwards is a qualitative hedonist, we believe his argument against quantitative hedonism reveals a central problem in hedonism itself, of whatever type. Edwards first distinguishes between quantitative

---

[18] See Joseph M. Boyle, Jr., Germain Grisez, and Olaf Tollefsen, *Free Choice: A Self-Referential Argument* (Notre Dame, IN: University of Notre Dame Press, 1976), Chapter 5.

and qualitative hedonism. The quantitative hedonist, he says, holds that there is only one quality of agreeable feeling called "pleasure" and that any two pleasures differ only quantitatively, that is, in intensity or duration.[19] The qualitative hedonist, on the contrary, denies both these points. The qualitative hedonist holds that although only agreeable feelings are intrinsically good, some are qualitatively better than others; that is, certain pleasurable experiences (for example, the pleasure of philosophical inquiry, married love, or the experience of beauty) cannot be outweighed by any quantity (intensity and duration) of others (for example, food, drink, or sexual orgasms).[20] Arguing against the quantitative hedonist, Edwards first points out that from the quantitative hedonist viewpoint it follows that all goods other than the agreeable feeling referred to as "pleasure," which he refers to as "pluralistic goods," are merely instrumental to pleasure. From this it follows, he says, that all pluralistic goods (such as friendship, knowledge, or beauty) are expendable and replaceable:

There is good reason to suspect that most self-professed quantitative hedonists have not been fully aware of the clear implication of their position, which we shall call "the replaceability thesis," that since all so-called pluralistic goods are merely of instrumental value, and since "pleasure is pleasure" no matter what its source, then each pluralistic good could in principle be replaced by an equally efficient or more efficient source of agreeable feeling without any loss of intrinsic worth.[21]

Edwards then gives a penetrating analysis of Aldous Huxley's description in *Brave New World* of a society in which the standard sources of pleasure have been replaced – by a drug without negative side effects (*soma*), by "movies" involving all the senses (the *feelies*), by trivial sex, and so on. The quantitative hedonist, says Edwards, must conclude (if he is consistent) that Huxley's brave new world is ideal. But, says Edwards, something like this situation – a situation in which efficacious alternate sources of intense pleasure have been found – *is* attainable, at least in principle, not by drugs, free sex, and "feelies," but by well-placed electrodes. By stimulating the pleasure centers of the brain through well-placed electrodes, one can produce an intensely pleasurable and euphoric

---

[19] Edwards, op. cit., 69.
[20] Or a qualitative hedonist could possibly hold that one instance of a pleasure of one type is equal to a certain number of pleasures of another type. However, it is hard to see how such a judgment could be anything but arbitrary.
[21] Edwards, op. cit., 50.

condition.[22] Such a prospect raises a significant question regarding quantitative hedonism:

If the ideal is sustained agreeable feeling during all our wakeful moments with no disagreeable feeling intermixed, we now know that this state is attainable by merely hooking up a set of well-placed electrodes to the "pleasure centers" of the brain and stimulating the brain with mild electric shocks. . . . Suppose that we knew how to sustain life and awareness for years and years with little or no physical exercise. If we had a chance, under those conditions, to consign ourselves to a hospital bed attached to a well-placed set of electrodes for the next fifty or sixty years of our life, but with no other type of human activity, experience, or fulfillment, would we take it?[23]

Most of us would definitely reject such an opportunity, and, according to Edwards, reasonably so.[24] Moreover, we would decline the option not just out of moral considerations, but centrally on the basis of what we consider to be constitutive of what is genuinely worthwhile.[25] These facts show that the sheer quantity of pleasure is not the only rational consideration. After examining this argument, however, Edwards does not draw this conclusion. Instead, he concludes that such facts refute *quantitative* hedonism, but not *qualitative* hedonism, and he adopts the latter.

He rejects electronic happiness as fully adequate, but still embraces a qualitative hedonism, for (he argues) there are important, qualitatively higher experiences that the electrodes cannot produce. Nonlocalized pleasures – the higher pleasures, says Edwards – are normally not obtainable in isolation from the activity or context that causes them:

We are never in a position to contemplate the worth of a *pure* pleasure either in experience, thought, or imagination. There is no one quality of agreeable feeling that would count as pure pleasure, and intentional pleasures are not available to us in total isolation from their objects.[26]

[22] Cf. Robert Nozick, *Anarchy, State and Utopia* (New York: Basic Books, 1974), 42ff.; Germain Grisez and Russell Shaw, *Beyond the New Morality, the Responsibilities of Freedom*, 3rd ed. (Notre Dame, IN: University of Notre Dame Press, 1988), 35ff.; John Finnis, *The Fundamentals of Ethics* (Washington, DC: Georgetown University Press, 1983), 37ff.; Sobel, op. cit., 240–256.

[23] Edwards, op. cit., 60.

[24] Edwards, op. cit., 62–64.

[25] See Sobel's discussion of the argument concerning pleasure machines: Sobel, op. cit., at 243ff.

[26] Ibid., 108. As Edwards later admits (op. cit., 92), however, the intentionality of an act or state does not require the real existence of its object. One's fear of the lion in one's doorway does not entail the real existence of a lion in one's doorway. Similarly, one can

In other words, he rejects electronic happiness (as complete), not because he holds there is some intrinsic good other than pleasure, but because the electrodes cannot provide a specific type of qualitatively superior pleasure.

But suppose that the electrodes *could* offer such experiences. Suppose a set of electrodes could offer us the experience of philosophical creativity, of a happy marriage and family, of beautiful music, and so on. Edwards raises just this possibility, but he retains his hedonistic position:

> Given the prospect of uninterrupted enjoyment of such an electronically simulated universe at least during our leisure time, and the assurance that no one in the "real" world would ever be hurt by our enjoyment of it, might we not be logically constrained to choose the life of the human electrode operator on qualitatively hedonistic grounds? In principle, yes; but in practice, no.[27]

This answer brings to light the dualistic presuppositions of hedonism, qualitative as well as quantitative (and of purely hedonistic choices). For the point that Edwards made about quantitative hedonism applies equally to qualitative hedonism: if the only intrinsic good is an agreeable *feeling*, then whatever the source or object of that feeling is, this source is, in principle, dispensable. And this means that, according to hedonism – qualitative as well as quantitative – every desirable end other than feelings, including knowledge, friendship, and virtue, is replaceable: if another device could produce the *feelings or experience* of such knowledge, friendship, or virtue more efficaciously, then this device would, according to hedonism, be objectively preferable.[28]

have the experience of the taste of an apple without a real apple, and, at least in principle, one could have the pleasurable experience of having a good marriage without the real existence of a good marriage or even the real existence of a marriage at all.

[27] Edwards, op. cit., 67.

[28] Cf. "If by electronic brain stimulation, the phenomenal taste of peppermint ice cream could be richly reproduced, then we would not need to eat real peppermint ice cream to experience just that form of enjoyment. The same thing is true, in principle, of *all* other intentional pleasures (or pains). *Normally*, however, the most efficient way to experience these forms of enjoyment is to stay in touch with the real world" (emphasis added; Edwards, op. cit., 92). If we understand Fred Feldman's "attitudinal hedonism" correctly (namely, the good consists in the *enjoyment* of suitable objects by deserving people), then this criticism applies to his position as well. See Fred Feldman, "The Good Life: A Defense of Attitudinal Hedonism," *Philosophy and Phenomenological Research* 65 (2002), 605–628. That is, if he locates the good in the enjoyment itself, rather than the total state of affairs (for example, a fulfilling activity that is enjoyed), then this criticism applies to it. But if he holds that the good consists in the total state of affairs rather than just in the enjoyment itself, then it does not qualify as genuine hedonism.

These arguments do not absolutely refute hedonism. It does not seem to be internally *self-contradictory*. Yet hedonism presupposes body–self dualism and is self-inconsistent. Moreover, people do, in fact, care for ends other than mere states of consciousness for their own sakes. The genuine hedonist (of whatever type) must, then, hold that people are enthralled by a deep confusion. While we cannot convict the hedonist of self-contradiction for holding that position, it does have serious difficulties and it is denied, in effect, by common sense.

A widely discussed thought experiment similar to Edwards's is proposed by Robert Nozick in his *Anarchy, State and Utopia*. Nozick wrote: "Suppose there were an experience machine that would give you any experience you desired. Super-duper neuropsychologists could stimulate your brain so that you would think and feel you were writing a great novel, or making a friend, or reading an interesting book. All the time you would be floating in a tank, with electrodes attached to your brain. Should you plug into this machine for life, preprogramming your life's experiences?"[29] As Nozick points out, the thought experiment shows that we care about actually *doing* certain things, and actually *being* in certain ways, not just the *experience* of doing or being in certain ways.[30] Such thought experiments not only show (or help to show) that pleasure, or feeling, is not the only intrinsic good; they also suggest that the reason why a thing is good, desirable, or worthwhile is not in the category of pleasure or feeling. The ground or basis for a thing's being desirable is its being *really perfective or fulfilling* (we provide some argument for this in the next section). Thus, pleasure is good, but only if it is part of, or a consequence of, a genuinely fulfilling activity or condition. Sadistic pleasures, for example, are inherently disordered and so are not good.

Moreover, in every hedonistic choice (that is, in every choice to pursue mere experience as detached from the larger real perfection of which it may be a part), this same reduction of real goods (such as knowledge, friendship, life, virtue) to the level of mere expendable and replaceable sources of agreeable feeling is enacted. Hedonistic choices by their very nature detach one from concern, or respect, for what is really worthwhile. A hedonistic choice, by its nature, involves reducing the real

---

[29] Nozick, op. cit., 42.
[30] Around the same time, and independently, Germain Grisez and Russell Shaw proposed the thought experiment of an experience machine. See Grisez and Shaw, op. cit., 37ff. The first edition of this book was published in 1974.

world – including our bodies and others – to the level of replaceable and dispensable means of obtaining an effect in one's consciousness.

V. Pleasures are Good only as Aspects of Real Perfections

If acting for pleasure by itself (instead of as an aspect of a fulfilling activity) presupposes a dualistic conception of the human being, then what is the ethical status of pleasure? Is pleasure a good? The question of what is intrinsically good and worthwhile does not admit of strict demonstration: a recognition of what is intrinsically good is presupposed by all other practical, that is, specifically ethical, reasoning and so cannot be reached through logical deduction or demonstration. However, the points made in the previous sections lend support to the view of practical reason and its basic principles that we sketched earlier.[31] When one chooses an action, one chooses it for a reason. One's reason is a good (or goods) one thinks this action will help realize. That good (or goods) may itself be a way of realizing some further good, and that good a means to another. But the chain of goods cannot be infinite. So, there must be some ultimate reasons for one's choices, and these reasons are goods that one recognizes as *reasons* for choosing, which need no further support and are not mere means to some further good. We hold, then, that there are ultimate *reasons* for action and *ultimate*, or basic, goods. That is, the ultimate motivations for our deliberate actions are not simply given desires or passions. Rather, they are practical judgments that this or that condition would be worthwhile to realize.[32]

What is the character of these ultimate reasons, these ultimate goods? We hold that they are real fulfillments or perfections of oneself and of others. Thus we endorse an objectivist and perfectionist account of human well-being, rejecting preferentialism, or "satisfactionism," as well as hedonism.[33] Difficulties with preferentialism begin to emerge when

---

[31] See Chapter 2, Section III.

[32] Cf., Germain Grisez, John Finnis, and Joseph Boyle, "Practical Principles, Moral Truth and Ultimate Ends," *American Journal of Jurisprudence* 33 (1988), 99–151. Robert P. George, *In Defense of Natural Law* (New York: Oxford University Press, 1999), Chapters 1–3.

[33] Please note, however, that the perfectionism we endorse is pluralistic. It does not include the claim that one type of good, say, contemplation, is the *one* good specific to human nature that should be especially promoted. We hold that there are several, irreducible and incommensurable basic human goods. As a consequence, the good life people are called to fashion will be quite different for different people. The ethical principles we endorse require *respect* for all of the basic goods, both in oneself and in others, rather

one considers desires based on mistaken beliefs: desires for objects that are clearly harmful to the desirer or desires (even long-term ones) for trivial projects (such as memorizing the contents of phone books or knocking down as many icicles in the country as possible).[34] To handle such problematic desires, one must refer not to just any desires or preferences but to *informed* desires or preferences.[35] But one is then faced with the difficulty of specifying what to count as a sufficiently informed desire or preference.

Someone might desire to inflict severe pain on all dogs and cats that came his way, even after he had all the empirical information about such pain that one could have. But such a desire would be inappropriate or unsuitable. Or if someone desired to make it his life's project to knock down as many icicles as possible, and hired crews of workers and fleets of trucks to reach icicles on skyscrapers, even though he had full information about icicles, their effects, and so on, we would say that his life was *not* going well, that he was wasting it.[36] But if human well-being consisted in obtaining what one desired, or obtaining one's preferences, or just those preferences one would have if one were fully informed, then we would have to say that such a person did have well-being. Since that is plainly not true, the preferentialist position must be mistaken.

Preferentialism, in any of its variants, holds that what makes a thing good is that it is desired (or would be desired, given full information, etc.). But this is to put the cart before the horse. It seems that there must be some basis in *what is desired* to distinguish between an informed desire and an uninformed desire. For it is usually possible to ask: "But what is it about these objects, as opposed to those, which makes them such that we should desire them?" Clearly, it is not purely arbitrary which things human beings desire, anymore than it is arbitrary which things

than a promotion or fashioning of one pattern of life or of a life as near that pattern as possible. Thus, criticisms of perfectionism on the grounds that it is hostile to diversity and pluralism, as opposed to relativism (see, for example, L. W. Sumner, "Two Theories of the Good," in *The Good Life and the Human Good*, ed. Steven M. Cahn and Peter Markie (Cambridge, UK: Cambridge University Press, 1992), 1–14), do not apply to the perfectionism we propose.

[34] See Richard Kraut, "Desire and the Human Good," in *Morality and the Good Life*, ed. Thomas L. Carson and Paul K. Moser (New York: Oxford University Press, 1997), 164–176.

[35] For such accounts, see Richard B. Brandt, *Facts, Values, and Morality* (New York: Cambridge University Press, 1996); ibid., *A Theory of the Good and the Right* (Oxford: Clarendon Press, 1979); Thomas L. Carson, *Value and the Good Life* (Notre Dame, IN: University of Notre Dame Press, 2000); James Griffin, *Well-Being, Its Meaning, Measurement and Moral Importance* (Oxford: Clarendon Press, 1986).

[36] This argument is pressed by Richard Kraut, loc. cit.

horses or tigers desire. What, then, in the objects desired makes them stand out from other objects not desired? Such questions show that it is not just a chicken–egg question about which came first: which is logically prior – the desire or that aspect of the object that makes it worthy to be desired? Since there is a difference between suitable and unsuitable desires, even between suitable fully informed desires and unsuitable fully informed desires, it follows that prior to being desired, the object desired must have in it something that makes it suitable to be desired. Thus, what makes a thing good cannot consist in its being the satisfaction of desires or preferences; rather, desires and preferences are rational only if they are in line with what is genuinely worthwhile. And, we submit, what makes an object genuinely worthwhile is that it is really fulfilling or perfective, either for oneself or for someone for whose sake one is prepared to act.[37]

We deliberate about what to do because we recognize that, first, there is some point in acting, and, secondly, not all courses of action would equally realize what we see as worth pursuing. We recognize some point (or points, really) to acting, because we understand on the basis of our own experience and our knowledge of possibilities that some ends or purposes are worth pursuing precisely because they are fulfilling or perfective of human beings in one respect or another. For example, one experiences the condition of health and, its opposite, sickness and naturally prefers being healthy to being sick. But, further, one comes to *understand* that health is a condition that is perfective and, as perfective, is worthy of pursuit; and one *understands* sickness to be a condition opposed to human well-being and thus as something worth taking various measures to avoid. One's understanding that a condition or activity has the feature *perfective* (or *fulfilling*) or *actualizing* is the basis for one's understanding – not just feeling – that the condition or activity is worthy of pursuit.

Thus, what makes something intrinsically valuable cannot be merely that it satisfies desires or preferences; rather, it must be objectively perfective or fulfilling of human persons. The good is what perfects and fulfills us. We should want this or that, but our wanting them is not what makes them good.[38] And since we are rational animals (as we argued in Chapters 1 and 2), what is really fulfilling for us is not just one object or activity, but several. Since we are animals, bodily health and life are components

---

[37] This position, of course, is in line with the classical tradition, stretching from Plato, Aristotle, Aquinas, to contemporary natural law thinkers.

[38] On the distinction between wants and reasons, see Joseph Raz, *The Morality of Freedom* (New York: Oxford University Press, 1986), 288–320.

of our well-being or flourishing. As *rational* animals, our fulfillment will include understanding, aesthetic experience, and having friendships. This is not the place to try to set out a full account of human well-being or flourishing. The point here is that human well-being is real fulfillment or perfection, which is constituted by various basic goods. Real fulfillment will *include* well-ordered pleasure, that is, pleasure taken in, or enjoyment of, appropriate activities or conditions – activities or conditions that are of themselves, or on the first level, really fulfilling. But our well-being does not *consist in* pleasure or in the satisfaction of desires.[39]

What then must be said about pleasure? As we saw earlier, the first two types of pleasure are either the conscious delight in or the consequence of some other condition or activity. It is clear that in these cases, pleasure is not what makes the condition or activity intrinsically good; rather, its being pleasurable, in these cases, is a *consequence* of its being intrinsically good. The enjoyment of playing tennis is a good because playing tennis is a genuine good. On the other hand, the enjoyment of a harmful activity is bad. If someone enjoys killing persons, the character or quality of this enjoyment, not being really separable from its object (that is, it is formally specified by its object), is in itself disordered.[40] Therefore, a type-one pleasure (conscious enjoyment of an activity) is truly good – we mean valuable here, not necessarily *morally* good – only if the activity of which it is the experiential aspect is good, that is, fulfilling or perfective, for the person. The same is true of type-two pleasures. That is, a pleasure consisting in the satisfaction of a desire is a good (a perfection of one's condition) only if the desire that is satisfied is for a genuine good, that is, for something truly perfective.

However, someone might object that type-three pleasures (pleasures as sensations) are a distinct case. These are often pursued as detached

---

[39] It is also important to see that human fulfillment is not just individualistic. The self in whose fulfillment one is naturally interested, the fulfillment of whom one's natural inclinations point to, is not an isolated individual. One has various unions with other people, and so one is interested in the fulfillment not only of oneself as an individual but also of all those with whom one is in communion – family, fellow citizens, neighbors, ultimately, all persons. So, the fulfillment of other people naturally interests one; it is an improvement of one's condition since one is not an isolated individual but has various forms and measures of unity with other people. Both egoism and altruism are mistaken; both presuppose a false dichotomy between one's own good and that of others. See John Finnis, *Natural Law and Natural Rights* (New York: Oxford University Press, 1980), 141–143.

[40] This is true even if one could have a sadistic pleasure without anyone actually being harmed, say, through well-placed electrodes.

from other activities. Moreover, one might argue that even what was said about the first two types of pleasure is only generally true. It is sometimes possible to have the experience of an activity without performing the real activity. In various instances people desire the pleasure or experience instead of, or even as detached from, any genuinely fulfilling activity. And, it might be argued, in these cases it seems that the pleasure is in itself good, independently of any associated activity.

Our reply is that the central reality of the good, what is worthwhile, is what is really perfective or fulfilling. So, first, if a pleasure or experience leads one away from a genuine good, then it is a disordered pleasure, and is not good and should not be pursued. But, second, pursuing an experience as isolated from genuine fulfillment (that is, isolated in the content of one's intention) always involves to a certain extent a retreat from reality into fantasy. Preferring mere experience to what is genuinely fulfilling is an escapism, a preference of appearance or fantasy over reality. It is, therefore, a disordered pleasure.[41]

By pursuing pleasure in this way, as detached from reality, one uses, and implicitly views, the body as a mere external means to one's end – a state existing in consciousness.[42] Thus, one treats one's body as a mere external tool. One is not regarding the experience or sensation as a bodily reality (which it, in fact, is), but one is after the sheer feel, or as it is sometimes put (in a different context), the quale of the experience,[43] regardless of how that feeling was obtained or how it is instantiated. Thus, one's bodily self is treated as a mere extrinsic means to what is viewed as alone of value (in this instance), the sheer feel or quale of an experience.

This point can be clarified by seeing that pleasurable sensations (type-three pleasures) can be related to real goods or harms in three different ways. First, one may experience a pleasant sensation in performing an activity, or undergoing an activity, which is itself really fulfilling. An example is the pleasure one experiences in eating. Here what one does and what one desires is the eating. One desires to eat, of course, on the bodily level

---

[41] Germain Grisez, *Way of the Lord Jesus, Vol. 1, Christian Moral Principles* (Chicago: Franciscan Herald Press, 1983), 208–210.

[42] On hedonism as a species of "mentalism," see Shelly Kagan, "The Limits of Well-Being," in *The Good Life and the Human Good*, ed. Ellen Frankel Paul, Fred D. Miller, Jr., and Jeffrey Paul. (Cambridge, UK: Cambridge University Press, 1992), 169–189.

[43] The term, of course, occurs most frequently in debates about the reducibility or nonreducibility of consciousness to the physical. See, for example, Ned Block, "Troubles with Functionalism," in *Readings in Philosophical Psychology*, vol. 1 (Cambridge, MA: Harvard University Press, 1980), 268–305.

without necessarily deciding to have such a desire. Usually, the object of this desire is not simply the pleasure one experiences in eating, but the total object: the pleasurable act of eating.[44] One desires, for example, to eat an apple, and this act is pleasant.

Second, the pleasant sensation may be attached to an activity that is harmful. Aquinas discussed the example of someone who found the taste of dirt pleasant. In this case, the pleasure is not a good because the activity it accompanies is bad (harmful). Similarly, if a man gets pleasure from molesting a child, this pleasure is not a good, although the harm it is attached to may not be (or even include) a physical harm, or at least not a purely physical one. Just as fear or anger should not lead us to perform acts that are actually harmful, so the desire for type-three pleasures should not lead us to do so. But, what is more, whether a pleasure is an intrinsic good or not depends on whether it is associated with a real perfection or a harmful condition. The pleasures of the sadist or child molester are *in themselves* bad; it is false to say that such pleasures are bad only because of the harm or pain involved in their total contexts. It is false to say, "It was bad for him to cause so much pain, but at least he enjoyed it." Pleasure is secondary, an aspect of a larger situation or condition (such as health, physical and emotional); what is central is what is really fulfilling.

Third, one might ask whether the pleasant sensation could, at least theoretically, be attached to an action that is neither harmful nor fulfilling, but is, as it were, neutral? Is that really possible? The answer is that where there is a choice – as opposed to something done indeliberately, that is, where the action comes up for deliberation – preferring the mere experience to another option cannot really leave those other goods unaffected. If the action is an object of deliberation, then there must be an alternative which in some way, however slight, contributes to a genuine good. And we ought not to prefer an option that realizes only a pleasant experience without contributing to a larger good to another option that realizes or contributes to a whole good.[45] One ought not to be deterred from contributing to a real (or whole) good by pursuit of a mere experience. Also, such a choice cannot leave unaffected the inner harmony of the emotional side of oneself (here, the desire for pleasure in general, though the emotional side, of course, includes more than that) with one's reasoned pursuit of intelligible goods. Such a choice subordinates reason to emotion, introducing disharmony in the self. In other words, pursuing

[44] Cf. Butchvarov, op. cit., 90–98.
[45] Cf. Finnis, op. cit., 37–42.

sheer pleasure apart from an intelligible good involves (a) a preference of mere experience to a real good and (b) a disharmony of the emotional part of oneself in relation to reason. It remains that pleasure is a second-order good, but only if connected to a first-order good.

This means that it is not always wrong to choose to do an act because it is pleasurable. Pleasure *is* a good when it is an aspect of the realization of a genuine good (the conscious delight in having the good or the satisfaction of the desire for a good). So, there is nothing wrong with eating breakfast because it tastes good. There is nothing wrong with being motivated by pleasure to have sexual intercourse with one's spouse (provided one desires union *with her* as opposed to using her for an experience of fantasy). In these cases, one desires and intends the pleasurable and fulfilling activity itself. The pleasure is not detached from the fulfilling activity; one's attention and concentration are rightly set on the real, fulfilling activity. Far from deterring one from realizing basic goods, in these cases the pleasure attracts one to them. But it *is* wrong to pursue a pleasurable experience, of whatever type, *as detached* from a genuinely fulfilling activity or condition because this involves a preference, on one level or another, of mere experience to what is really fulfilling – a subordination of reason to emotion (though whether the choice is a *serious* wrong or a slight one depends on other factors).

A hedonist might object, using an argument stated by W. D. Ross. In his book *The Right and the Good* Ross first argues that virtue is intrinsically good. He argues that if we compare two states of the universe with equal amounts of pleasure, but one with virtuous persons and the other with vicious ones, it is clear that we would judge the first state of the universe better.[46] He then presents a similar argument concerning pleasure:

> It seems at first sight equally clear that pleasure is good in itself. Some will perhaps be helped to realize this if they make the corresponding supposition to that we have just made; if they suppose two states of the universe including equal amounts of virtue but the one including also widespread and intense pleasure and the other widespread and intense pain.[47]

We should note, however, that Ross goes on significantly to qualify his conclusion. He later argues that pleasure is only prima facie a good and that neither vicious pleasures (such as those of a sadist) nor even undeserved pleasures are intrinsically good.[48]

---

[46] Cf. Aristotle, op. cit., Bk. VII, Chapter 8.
[47] W. D. Ross, *The Right and the Good* (London: Oxford University Press, 1930), 135.
[48] Ibid., 149–154.

We suspect that Ross's argument makes explicit the reason why many people do hold that pleasure is *simply* a good (whereas actually pleasure *is* a good, but only given other conditions). However, as Ross himself makes clear later in his book, this argument does not show that pleasure is a good *by itself*. For example, knowledge of science or philosophy is just by itself inferior to such knowledge joined with pleasure. In general, being fulfilled or perfected and enjoying such objects or activities is preferable to being fulfilled in them without enjoyment. Or, more precisely, enjoyment of fulfilling activities (in oneself or in others) is *part of* (i.e., is an aspect of) one's fulfillment (and this Ross's argument *did* show). But, while understanding just by itself is a good, and so too with health, friendship, marriage, and skillful performance, pleasure is not like these others. Pleasure is good only when it is an aspect or consequence of a genuinely fulfilling activity or condition – a fact not contradicted in the least by the previous point made by Ross. In this respect, pleasures may be compared to other physiological functions: coagulation of blood is, in the appropriate circumstances, good – a part of the healthy functioning of an animal. But in other circumstances (say, within the heart, caused by an arrhythmia), it is disordered and bad. Similarly, one cannot reasonably separate the pleasure from the activity it is attached to and count it as a good. One cannot reasonably say, for example, that what the sadist is doing is bad, but his enjoyment is good. No, to take pleasure in a harmful activity, whether the activity is harmful to oneself or to another person, is itself a defect. Sadistic pleasure has in itself a defect, a disorder.

In sum, pleasure is not a good like understanding or health, which are goods or perfections by themselves. That is, they are good in themselves even if in a context that is overall bad or if accompanied by many bads. By contrast, pleasure is good (desirable, worthwhile, perfective) if and only if attached to a fulfilling or perfective activity or condition. Pleasure is *like* other goods in that a fulfilling activity or condition is better with it than without it. But pleasure is *unlike* full-fledged goods in that it is not a genuine good apart from some other fulfilling activity or condition.

VI. Hedonistic Drug-Taking

This point has clear implications for the ethical questions concerning drug-taking. There are, of course a variety of drugs, taken for various purposes. In this context, we are interested in drugs that alter, in some way, one's feelings or consciousness, psychoactive substances. Sheridan Hough has helpfully distinguished four kinds of psychoactive drugs: (1) prescription drugs, such as codeine or Demerol; (2) over-the-counter medications, such as cough syrup and antihistamines; (3) legal nonmedical substances, such as alcohol and nicotine; and (4) illegal drugs, such as marijuana, cocaine, heroin, and LSD.[49] We abstract here from the question whether this or that drug ought to be legal. That is, we ask whether a use of psychoactive substances in a very specific way could be morally upright.

Usually, by "recreational drug use" is meant taking a drug simply for pleasure, rather than to enable or enhance other activities, or to remedy health problems: for example, for therapeutic purposes, to wake up, help one sleep, help one relax, enhance an athletic performance, or heighten one's attention for study. In many such cases, the drug's side effect may make use of the drug morally wrong (as with anabolic steroids). In some cases the purported benefit is illusory, and the argument given to oneself to justify its use is a rationalization. Many so-called mind-enhancing drugs actually do nothing of the sort. Still, some drugs do have the effect of helping one remain awake or alert (caffeine, for example). But our topic is recreational drug use, not every type of drug use or abuse.

We do not think all recreational drug use is wrong. A further distinction is necessary. Let us take alcohol as an example, and consider two very different types of social gatherings where alcoholic drinks are served.[50] In the first gathering, the participants attend in order to socialize; they drink alcoholic beverages to modify their feelings, to be sure, but they do this to enhance their socializing. That is, in this social gathering, the modification in feelings is subordinate to, or an aspect of, a genuine perfection, namely, friendship or social communion. In the other gathering, let us suppose, the participants come in order to get drunk, to get a "high," and the socializing is subordinate to that modification in their consciousnesses. In the first case, the intention is directed to the fulfilling activity as well as the pleasure, or the pleasurable fulfilling activity; in the second case, the intention is directed to the feeling, the fulfilling activity being viewed as a mere extrinsic means.[51] The use of drugs at both gatherings could

49 Sheridan Hough, "The Moral Mirror of Pleasure: Considerations about the Recreational Use of Drugs," in *Drugs, Morality and the Law*, ed. Steven Luper-Fay and Curtis Brower (New York: Garland, 1994), 133–134.

50 We owe this example to Germain Grisez, *The Way of the Lord Jesus*, Vol. 2, *Living a Christian Life* (Quincy, IL: Franciscan Press, 1993), 534–540.

51 Sheridan Hough also notes this difference when discussing recreational drug use. Discussing J. O. Urmson's explanation of Aristotle's position on pleasure, Hough says: "Urmson says that the intemperate person does not enjoy an activity that involves a particular sensation, but is instead focused on the feeling alone. [A reference to Urmson, *Aristotle's Ethics* (New York: Basil Blackwell, 1988), 107.] Certainly, drugs can be taken simply in

be described as "recreational," but only the latter qualifies as "purely hedonistic" drug-taking.[52]

Moreover – and this is the point important for our purposes here – there is a profoundly different attitude to one's body and to other people in this second type of drug-taking. In such an act, one's body is viewed as an extrinsic means to the sheer feeling. One's body and the whole real situation itself is viewed as extrinsic to the state of affairs one is seeking. In such a choice, one treats the body as a mere extrinsic means: one regards the body as outside the subject, and so as a mere object. Therefore, the content of such a choice includes a disintegrity, a reduction of one's bodily self to the level of an extrinsic instrument. A certain contempt for the body inheres in such choices. Therefore, the choice to take a drug simply for the feeling, rather than to enhance participation in real goods, is a choice whose object includes a disharmony between the conscious aspect of the self and the bodily aspect of the self.

Hedonism points people in the wrong direction, or, more precisely, it advises people to focus too narrowly. Hedonism narrows one's focus to an effect, or effects, in *consciousness*, ignoring, or reducing to the status of mere means, what is *really* the case, including especially what is the case with the bodily aspect of the self. The goal of the hedonistic drug-taker is the sheer feeling: how the feeling is obtained; what one does to one's body to attain that feeling is not part of the goal, but a mere means. Therefore, in the drug-taker's intention, one's body does not participate in the good sought after, but is treated as a mere extrinsic means. So, in hedonistic drug-taking, one alienates oneself from one's body, and the act violates the basic good of self-integration. The hedonistic drug-taker adopts a dualistic and contemptuous attitude toward one's body.

order to produce a certain sensation apart from a 'drug activity', and it is *this* sort of drug use, intemperately pursued, that strikes most people as 'base', not the temperate pursuits of the chef or oenophile, or, indeed, the usual taking of drink at weddings and parties" (Hough, op. cit., 170).

[52] Even here the adjective "purely" is needed. As we have indicated, there is nothing wrong with doing an act for the pleasure; it is morally problematic only to pursue the pleasure as detached from a fulfilling activity.

4

Abortion

What is killed in an abortion? It is obvious that some living entity is killed in an abortion. And no one doubts that the moral status of the entity killed is a central (though not the only) question in the abortion debate. Is what is killed in abortion a distinct, living human individual? Is what is killed in abortion a person? Is what is killed in abortion the same type of entity as you and I? Once more, the issue of what you and I are, of what makes us be entities with full moral worth, or subject of rights, is central to a controversial and fundamental moral issue.

It is often claimed that the abortion debate is a disagreement between those who follow the hard facts of science and recognize that what science uncovers is important, on the one hand, and religious persons who think abortion is wrong because they have a religious belief in the soul and have accepted on faith that the soul is present from conception onward. But the reality is actually very close to the opposite of that picture. First, as we will show in a moment, what science says, in particular, the science of embryology, favors the pro-life side, not those who defend abortion. Second, it is the defenders of abortion who often identify – usually only implicitly – the self with a subject or a series of conscious states other than the living body, rather than the human, physical organism. The issue is not whether we have a soul but whether we have a body, or more precisely, whether we are bodily beings. After all, one does not first examine to see whether the soul is present and from that observation conclude that there is or is not a human being present. Rather, one examines to see whether there are characteristics – physical characteristics – which indicate the presence of a human being, however small he or she is, and from that conclusion one further concludes (if one does hold that human souls exist) that the human soul must be present. So, it is defenders of abortion who distance themselves from the body, and it is the pro-life side that defends the point that we are essentially bodily beings, living bodies of a particular sort.

We shall approach the issue step by step, first, setting forth some (though not all) of the evidence that demonstrates that what is killed in abortion – a human embryo – is indeed a human being and then examining the ethical significance of that point.

I. The Biological Issue: Human Embryos and Fetuses Are Complete (Though Immature) Human Beings

It will be useful to begin by considering some of the facts of sexual reproduction. The standard embryology texts indicate that in the case of ordinary sexual reproduction, the life of an individual human being begins with the joining of sperm and ovum, which yields a genetically and functionally distinct organism, possessing the resources and active disposition for internally directed development toward human maturity.[1] In normal conception, a sex cell of the father, a spermatozoon (sperm), unites with a sex cell of the mother, an oocyte (ovum). Within the chromosomes of these sex cells are the DNA molecules (and other cytoplasmic factors) which constitute the information that guides the development of the new

---

[1] The standard texts in embryology and developmental biology clearly assert this. For example, "In this text, we begin our description of the developing human with the formation and differentiation of the male and female sex cells or gametes, which will unite at fertilization *to initiate the embryonic development of a new individual*" (emphasis added). William J. Larsen, *Human Embryology*, 3rd ed. (Philadelphia: Churchill Livingstone, 2001), 1. "Human development begins at fertilization when a male gamete or sperm (spermatozoon) unites with a female gamete or oocyte (ovum) to form a single cell – a zygote. This highly specialized, totipotent cell marked the beginning of each of us as a unique individual." Keith Moore and T. V. N. Persaud, *The Developing Human, Clinically Oriented Embryology*, 7th ed. (New York: W.B. Saunders, 2003), 16. "It needs to be emphasized that life is continuous, as is also human life, so that the question, 'When does (human) life begin?' is meaningless in terms of ontogeny. Although life is a continuous process, fertilization (which, incidentally, is not a 'moment') is a critical landmark because, under ordinary circumstances, *a new, genetically distinct human organism is formed* when the chromosomes of the male and female pronuclei blend in the oocyte" (emphasis added). Ronan O'Rahilly and Fabiola Mueller, *Human Embryology and Teratology*, 3rd ed. (New York: John Wiley & Sons, 2000), 8; in Scott Gilbert, *Developmental Biology*, 7th ed. (Sunderland, MA: Sinnauer Associates, 2003), Chapter 7 is entitled: "Fertilization: Beginning a New Organism." The first sentence of that chapter reads: "Fertilization is the process whereby two sex cells (gametes) fuse together *to create a new individual* with genetic potentials derived from both parents" (emphasis added; p. 183).

individual brought into being when the sperm and ovum fuse. When the sperm and ovum join, they cease to be and give rise to an entirely new and distinct organism, originally a single cell.[2] This organism, the human embryo, begins to grow by the normal process of cell division – it divides into two cells, then four, eight, sixteen, and so on (the divisions are not simultaneous, so there is a three-cell stage, and so on). This embryo gradually develops all of the organs and organ systems necessary for the full functioning of a mature human being. His or her development (sex is determined from the beginning) is very rapid in the first few weeks. For example, as early as eight or ten weeks of gestation, the fetus has a fully formed beating heart, a complete brain (though not all of its synaptic connections are complete – nor will they be until sometime *after* the child is born), a recognizably human form, feels pain, cries, and even sucks his or her thumb.

There are three important points we wish to make about this human embryo. First, the embryo is from the start *distinct* from any cell of the mother or of the father. This is clear because it is growing in its own distinct direction. Its growth is internally directed to its own survival and maturation, a distinct end from the survival and flourishing of the mother in whose body this distinct organism resides. Second, the embryo is *human*: it has the genetic makeup characteristic of human beings.

Third, and most important, this new human embryo is a *whole*, though obviously immature, human being. Clearly, the gametes whose union brings into existence the embryo are not whole or distinct organisms. They are not only genetically but also functionally identifiable as parts of the male or female potential parents. Each has only half the genetic material needed to guide the development of an immature human toward full maturity, and none of these cells will survive long. They clearly are destined either to combine with an ovum or sperm or to degenerate. Even when they succeed in causing fertilization, they do not survive; rather,

---

[2] This occurs when the sperm enters the ovum, for at that point the sperm ceases to be (breaking up in the process, so that only the genetic materials within its nucleus and minor components of the sperm cytoplasm persist and are active after penetration). The ovum also ceases to be, for after the entrance of the sperm the new entity that results repels penetration by any (more) sperm, the exact opposite of its previous developmental trajectory, namely, tending toward union with a sperm. Hence at this point the sperm and the ovum join, cease to be, and generate a new organism. This new organism has the developmental trajectory toward the mature stage of a human organism. It is a stable body that – provided only a suitable environment and nutrition, and barring accident or disease – will actively develop itself to the mature stage of a human being. This is the mark of the existence of a distinct, whole (though immature) human organism.

their genetic (and cytoplasmic) material enters into the composition of a distinct, new organism.

But none of this is true of the human embryo, from the zygote and blastula stages onward. The combining of the sperm and the ovum generates what the standard texts in human embryology identify as a new and distinct organism. The human embryo, from beginning of fertilization onward, is fully programmed actively to develop himself or herself to the mature stage of a human being. And unless deprived of a suitable environment or prevented by accident or disease, this embryo *will* actively develop itself in its own distinct direction, toward its own survival and maturity. The direction of its growth is not extrinsically determined, but is in accord with the genetic information and cytoplasmic factors within it. The human embryo is, then, a whole (though immature) and distinct human organism – a human being.[3]

If the embryo were not a complete organism, then what could it be? It has been shown that it is not a part of the mother or of the father, unlike the sperm cells and the ova. Nor is it a disordered growth such as a teratoma. These do not have the internal resources to actively develop themselves to the mature stage of a human. Perhaps someone will say that the early embryo is an intermediate form – something that regularly emerges into a whole (though immature) human organism but is not one yet. But what could cause the emergence of a new substantial entity, and cause it with regularity? It is clear that after conception, that is, from the zygote stage on, the major development of this organism is controlled and directed from within, that is, by the multicellular organism itself. None of the changes that occur to the embryonic human being during normal gestation generate a new direction of growth.[4] Rather, all of the changes (for example, those involving nutrition and environment) either facilitate

---

[3] Conjoined twins are distinct organisms and are *internally oriented toward* completion or wholeness, but because of a defect in their development (either in the separation generating the second embryo or in a partial fusion of two embryos) they fail to achieve organic completeness and so share many organs. They are both organically (and personally) one in many respects but also distinct organisms (and distinct persons) at the same time. Despite their organic incompleteness, however, they are quite unlike somatic cells or organs, which are *fully* oriented to being *only* parts of a larger organism. See Chapter 1, Section VII.

[4] This point is also argued, in a different context, where it is shown that applying Aquinas's philosophical principles to the embryological data known today (and unknown in Aquinas's days) leads to the conclusion that the human being comes to be at fertilization, in: John Haldane and Patrick Lee, "St. Thomas Aquinas on Human Ensoulment," *Philosophy* 78 (2003), 255–278. Cf. Robert Pasnau's reply to this article: "Souls and the Beginning of Life," *Philosophy* 78 (2003), 515–531, and Haldane and Lee's reply, "Rational Souls and the Beginning of Life," *Philosophy* 78 (2003), 532–540.

or retard the internally directed growth of this individual. These facts are sufficient to show that the human embryo is a whole, though immature, human being, an individual member of the species *homo sapiens*.[5]

In sum, the immediate product of the successful union of the sperm and the ovum has a developmental trajectory entirely different from the sperm or the ovum (which will degenerate or cease to be in the union with each other); it is toward the mature stage of a human being. If this new organism is provided a suitable environment, and sufficient nutrition, then, barring accident or disease, it *will* actively develop itself to the mature stage of a member of the human species. Hence the joining of the sperm and the ovum generates a new human organism; it produces a distinct organism with the active disposition, or ability from within (as opposed to an ability acquired by an extrinsic change), to develop itself in accord with its own internal (genetic and cytoplasmic) information to the next more mature stage of a human being. In monozygotic twinning, a second human embryo is generated with the division at some stage of a hitherto unitary and single human organism.[6] And, should humans ever be cloned, cloning would produce the same result by combining what is normally combined and activated in fertilization, that is, the full genetic code plus the ovular cytoplasm. (So, just as fertilization produces a new and complete, though immature, human organism, the same would be true of cloning.)

Perhaps because the political debate has of late centered on the use of human embryos for stem cell research, there has been a renewed focus in

---

[5] The question we are examining in this section is a *factual* one: whether the human embryo is a whole member of the species *homo sapiens*. As long as the question is made clear and is not confused with the *evaluative* question whether this individual is a subject of rights, there is general agreement among embryologists and developmental biologists (see note 1) that the human embryo is a distinct, whole human individual. See the report, Subcommittee on Separation of Powers to Senate Judiciary Committee S-158, 97 Congress, 1st Session, 1981. It says in part: "We must consider not only whether unborn children are human beings but also whether to accord their lives intrinsic worth and value equal to those of other human beings. The two questions are separate and distinct. It is a scientific question whether an unborn child is a human being, in the sense of a living member of the human species. It is a value question whether the life of an unborn child has intrinsic worth and equal value with other human beings. Those witnesses who testified that science cannot say whether unborn children are human beings were speaking in every instance to the value question rather than the scientific question. No witness raised any evidence to refute the biological fact that from the moment of human conception there exists a distinct individual being who is alive and is of the human species. No witness challenged the scientific consensus that unborn children are 'human beings,' insofar as the term is used to mean living beings of the human species" (p. 11).

[6] See pp. 123–125.

the last few years on the specifically biological or embryological question of when a distinct human individual comes to be. And so some have raised objections to the standard position.

One argument is that monozygotic twinning shows that the embryo in the first several days of its gestation is not a human individual. It seems that both twins can be traced back to a single zygote at his or her origin and so the zygote (and the embryo before twinning becomes impossible) is not yet a determinate individual – not yet this human being rather than that one. And so (the argument goes) what exists up to about day 14, after which twinning does not seem possible, is a merely a group of cells from which one or more human beings will develop, but is not yet an individual organism, and hence not yet a human being.[7]

First, as a conceptual matter, the possibility of twinning, of splitting into two individuals, provides no evidence at all against the present existence of an individual prior to the splitting taking place. From the fact that *A* can split into *B* and *C*, it simply does not follow, nor does the fact at all suggest that *A* was not an individual before the division. Logically speaking, there are three possibilities. *A* might have been an amalgam or aggregate of *A* and *B*. But also *A* might have ceased to exist and *B* and *C* have come to be from the constituents that once went into *A* (though we do not think this is the most plausible account of what happens in human monozygotic twinning). Or, finally, it is possible that *A* was an individual and is identical with *B* or *C*, that is, that a new individual is generated by the splitting off from the whole of which it once was a part (which we think is the most likely account of what goes on in most cases of human monozygotic twinning). So, the mere fact of the division does nothing to show that prior to the division, *A* could not have been a determinate, single individual (though itself composed of parts).

In nature, determinate individuals split and generate new entities all the time: an individual somatic cell reproduces by splitting into two "daughter cells," – here a determinate individual cell *A* ceases to be and gives rise to two new individual cells, *B* and *C*. A flatworm is divided into two halves, and the result is two flatworms.[8] Here *A* produces *B* and *C* but is identical with either *B* or *C*. A plant is divided (a cutting is taken from it) and the result is two plants, *B* and *C*, with one being identical with the

[7] For example, Lee Silver, *Re-Making Eden, How Genetic Engineering and Cloning Will Transform the Family* (New York: Avon Books, 1998), Chapter 3.
[8] Indeed, for several asexual species of flatworms, splitting is their *only* form of reproduction. For a brief overview of flatworm biology, see A. Sanchez Alvarado, "Planarians," *Current Biology* 14 (18) (September 21, 2004), R737.

original, rooted plant A from which the cutting was taken and the other developing into a new individual plant of the same species. These events, of course, do nothing to show that prior to those divisions there was not an individual cell, an individual worm, or an individual plant.

Second, as an empirical matter, there is abundant evidence to show that prior to monozygotic twinning, there is a single, developing organism. There is extensive internally coordinated development from day 1 until day 14 (when twinning becomes impossible) that is *only* compatible with the existence of an individual, developing organism. So it is reasonable to conclude that during twinning, a new organism is generated with separation of the some of the cells[9] of a developing individual from physical and functional unity with the other cells.[10] The position that individuality is not attained until twinning becomes impossible (after day 14) makes inexplicable the internally directed development from day 1 until day 14. Suppose twinning occurs on day 6: prior to day 6 there must have been a single multicellular organism, for all of the cells of this system functioned together as a unit, oriented toward the development and maintenance of the system as a whole.

A cutting can be obtained from a plant, and a flatworm can be divided into two flatworms. In each case, it is obvious that a new individual is generated by the division of parts from a single whole (parts that can regenerate the missing cells and structures so as to become whole individuals in their own right, once they are divided from the rest of the original organism). The evidence indicates that this same type of event occurs with most monozygotic twinning in human beings. That is, in most monozygotic twinning, a single embryonic human being exists until the splitting of some cells from this first embryo, and this division generates a second embryo.[11]

---

[9] In most monozygotic twins the cells are from the inner cell mass after the fifth day. (See Moore and Persaud, op. cit., 147–150; Bruce M. Carlson, *Human Embryology and Developmental Biology* (Ann Arbor, MI: Mosby, 2004), 55–58.)

[10] In most cases, one or more of the developing organs are shared – the chorion, and sometimes also the amnion. If division occurs after day 9, there is likely to be sharing of permanent organs and so conjoined twins result. See the works cited in note 1.

[11] It is possible that with monozygotic twinning the original organism dies and gives rise to two new organisms. However, we think that this is not what occurs, at least in most cases, since in many instances there is an obvious unity of plan of development between the zygote, on the one hand, and one (but not both) of the twins, on the other hand. An example occurs with some twins in whom only one suffers from trisomy 21: evidently, one of the twins is generated by the splitting and exhibits a unique plan of development that differs from the other twin. See J. G. Rogers, S. M. Voullaire, and H. Gold, "Monozygotic Twins Discordant for Trisomy 21," *American Journal of Human Genetics* 11 (1982),

The clearest evidence that the embryo in the first two weeks is not a mere aggregate of cells but is a unitary organism is this: if the individual cells within the embryo before twinning were each independent of the others, there would be no reason why each would not regularly develop on its own. Instead, these allegedly independent, noncommunicating cells regularly function together to develop into a single, more mature member of the human species.[12] This shows that interaction is taking place between the cells from the very beginning (even within the zona pellucida, before implantation), restraining them from individually developing as whole organisms and directing each of them to function as a part of a single, whole organism continuous with the zygote. Thus, prior to an extrinsic division of the cells of the embryo, these cells together do constitute a single organism.[13]

Another related argument for the denial that human embryos are whole human beings is based on the totipotency of the cells in the first several days, up to day 14 or 16. Because of this some have contended that prior to day 14 (or according to some, day 16), there really isn't a unitary organism at all, but only diverse cells waiting to (somehow) become one.[14] Speaking

143–146; T. Hassold, "Mosaic Trisomies in Human Spontaneous Abortions," *Human Genetics*, 11 (1982), 31–35; Angelo Serra and Roberto Columbo, "The Identity and Status of the Human Embryo: The Contribution of Biology," in *The Identity and Status of the Human Embryo, Proceedings of the Third Assembly of the Pontifical Academy for Life*, ed. Juan de Dios Vial Correa and Elio Sgreccia (Vatican City: Libreria Editrice. Vaticana, 1999), 169ff.

Monozygotic twinning is of course comparatively rare. Most monozygotic twinning (about two-thirds) occurs between the fifth and ninth days after fertilization, and the twins share a common amnion. About one-third of the cases of monozygotic twinning occur before the fifth day and so each twin has its own chorion (and amnion). (See Moore and Persaud, op. cit., 147; Carlson, op. cit., 55. Perhaps some cases of twinning occur in the first cleavage, where a one-celled embryo (a zygote) divides into two one-celled embryos. It is more likely in this type of case than in others that the first human embryo ceases to exist and gives rise to two others.

[12] Benedict Ashley and Albert Moraczewski, "Cloning, Aquinas, and the Embryonic Person," *The National Catholic Bioethics Quarterly* 1 (2001), 189–201.

[13] It is also possible in the first several days for two embryos to fuse and become one. This, however, does not show that prior to that fusion there were not two embryos, two human beings. The evidence that there were is, again, the internally coordinated activities on the part of two distinct embryos. Biologically the process seems similar to grafting or transplanting an organ; only here, it is all of the organs of a distinct embryo that are transplanted. It is possible that both embryos die and give rise to a new embryo, but it seems more likely that one survives and receives the cells of the other one that dies, though it may be difficult or impossible to tell which one survived and which one died.

[14] For example, Bailey, loc. cit.; Barry Smith and Berit Brogaard, "Sixteen Days," *Journal of Medicine and Philosophy* 28 (2003), 45–78. This argument was made by Joseph Donceel in 1970, S. J. Joseph Donceel, "Immediate Animation and Delayed Hominization,"

of the embryo in the first few days, and noting that its cells are totipotent, Smith and Brogaard write:

The cells form a mere mass, being kept together spatially by the thin membrane (the *zona pellucida*), which is inherited from the egg-cell before fertilization, but there is no causal interaction between the cells. They are separate bodies, which adhere to each other through their sticky surfaces and which have at this point only the bare capacity for dividing (they neither grow nor communicate).[15]

Smith and Brogaard conclude that the embryo is only an aggregate of cells and that a multicellular organism does not come to be until about day 16, that is, at gastrulation – the process by which cells migrate in determinate directions to form three layers in the embryo, the ectoderm, mesoderm, and endoderm, the germ layers that form the rudiments of the basic body plan of the different organ systems.

This argument, however, ignores an abundance of evidence indicating that the cells within the embryo from day one onward function as parts of the whole embryo rather than as independent units. Smith and Brogaard dismiss the zona pellucida as a film incidentally related to the blastomeres inside, and the unity among the blastomeres is interpreted as merely spatial and arising incidentally rather than from any internal unitary direction. But in fact the zona pellucida shows a resiliency amidst extrinsic pressures exerted on it as the embryo travels down the uterine tube and into the uterus. And it has this resiliency for the whole time, and only that time, in which it is needed.

And, what is more significant, the blastomeres are not mere passive passengers falling down the uterine tube and then becoming stuck onto the uterus. Rather, within the embryo in the first few days, before implantation, there is complex and coordinated activity. On day 3 or 4 *compaction* occurs, which is the process in which the cells change their shapes and align themselves closely together. And compaction is the first step toward *cavitation*, that is, the process (at day 4) in which an inner cavity is formed within the embryo and the embryo differentiates itself into the inner cell mass (which will later develop into the parts of the embryo not discarded at birth) and the trophoblast (which will later develop into the placenta, an organ of the embryo, though temporary, as are, for example, baby

Theological Studies 31 (1970), 76–105, and was presented again by Norman Ford in 1988, Norman Ford, *When Did I Begin?* (New York: Cambridge, 1988), 115ff.; it was recently revived by various authors, for example, Smith and Brogaard, op. cit., 45–78. Patrick Lee replied to Donceel and Ford's version of this argument in *Abortion and Unborn Human Life* (Washington, DC: Catholic University of America Press, 1996), 79–104.

[15] Smith and Brogaard, op. cit., 53.

teeth).[16] On day 5 or 6, as the embryo enters the uterus, it "hatches" from the zona pellucida, preparing to begin implantation. At the same time, the trophoblast cells secrete an enzyme that erodes the epithelial lining of the uterus and creates an implantation site for the embryo.

Moreover, the trophoblast itself becomes differentiated (about day 5 or 6) into various levels (cytotrophoblast and syncytiotrophoblast) in preparation for developing the vital contacts with the mother's blood system (the embryo will circulate its own blood but will exchange oxygen and wastes with the mother's blood, first through connecting microvilli and eventually through the umbilical cord, developed from the trophoblast). Around the same time, the trophoblast produces immunosuppressive factors signaling the mother's system to accept the embryo rather than attack it as a foreign substance. In order for the embryo as a whole to survive, this complex series of activities must occur and they must occur in a timely, ordered sequence; and this complex sequence of activities occurs with predictable regularity. Clearly, these activities, compaction, cavitation, and implantation itself, are organized processes performed by the embryo as a whole.[17]

The test of whether a group of cells constitutes a single organism is whether they form a stable body and function as parts of a whole, self-developing, adaptive unit. But compaction, cavitation, the changes occurring earlier to facilitate these activities, and implantation – all of these activities are clear cases of the cells acting in coordinated manner for the sake of a self-developing and adaptive whole.[18] In other words, such

---

[16] Even at the two-cell stage, already the embryo is producing the glycoprotein that will later guide that compaction process.

[17] At several points, Miller and Brogaard claim that the early embryo before day 16 lacks its own integrated mechanism for restoring stability upon encountering environmental difficulties (Miller and Brogaard, "Sixteen Days," op. cit., 69, 71). However, first, the claim that an entity must have such homeostatic mechanisms in order to be an organism is not argued for at all (we think, on the contrary, that internally coordinated, self-perfective activity, such as internally coordinated development toward maturity – which certainly *is* present in the early embryo – is sufficient indication that there is an organism). Second, the zona pellucida, even though it is inherited in some way from the ovum, clearly fits the definition of such a protective mechanism, as does the product of the glycoprotein, produced at the two-cell stage and then distributed throughout the cells' surfaces (but more concentrated at their top ends, so that each cell has a polarity), which helps restrain the cells from separation and independent development from day 2 onward.

[18] It was once thought that the first few cleavages in the embryo were governed by the "maternal" mRNA, and on that basis Philip Peters, for example, argued that the embryo is not a distinct human being until the six- or eight-cell stage – about day 4. (See Philip G. Peters, "The Ambiguous Meaning of Human Conception," *University of California, Davis Law Review*, 40 (2006), 199ff. However, in the last two decades, numerous studies have shown that the expression of key genes in the embryonic DNA begins to occur as

activities are evidently ordered to the survival and maturing of the whole embryo. This shows that the unity of the blastomeres (the cells of the early embryo) to each other is substantial (that is, together they make up one organism) rather than incidental (where the unity accrues to many whole organisms). This is compelling evidence that what exists from day 1 to day 16 is not a mere aggregate of cells but a multicellular organism.

The immediate product of the successful union of the sperm and the ovum *already has within itself* the full program that will, if all goes well, specify the timing and sequence of its first cleavages, and guide its development up to and through compaction, differentiation into embryoblast and trophoblast, hatching, implantation, gastrulation, differentiation of the rudiments of the nervous system, and so on. In other words, the whole cascade of changes from before the first cleavage on up to gastrulation and beyond is already programmed within the zygote and clearly constitutes a single overall developmental trajectory. The sequence of changes in the embryo from day 1 up to, say, day 14, is necessary and preparatory for what occurs afterward, and is a unitary trajectory of development. It is unlike, for example, the separate sequences of events undergone by the sperm and the ovum before fertilization. Fusion of the gametes does produce – as we have seen – a fundamentally different developmental trajectory. By contrast, the human embryo's cells (from day one onward) form a stable body and work together to produce a single direction of

early as the one-cell stage. It is true that many maternal mRNAs are translated in the first few days of development (which does *not* mean, however, that these maternally *derived* mRNAs and proteins are extrinsic or distinct agents – instead, at this point they are parts of the new embryonic organism). However, the transition to control of development by the unique genome of the embryo begins even at the one-cell stage. (See E. Memili and N. L. First, "Zygotic and Embryonic Gene Expression in Cow: A Review of Timing and Mechanisms of Early Gene Expression as Compared with Other Species," *Zygote* 8 (1) (February 2000), 87–93; E. M. Thompson, E. Legouy, and J. P. Renard, "Mouse Embryos Do Not Wait for the MBT: Chromatin and RNA Polymerase Remodeling in Genome Activation at the Onset of Development," *Development* 124 (22) (1998) 4615–4625.) Moreover, this transition is gradual and its sequence is internally determined: there is as it were a zygotic "clock" scheduling when different embryonic genes will begin to be transcribed. M. Zuccotti, M. Boiani, R. Ponce, S. Guizzardi, R. Scadroglio, S. Garagna, and C. A. Redi, "Mouse Xist Expression Begins at Zygotic Genome Activation and Is Time by a Zygotic Clock," *Molecular Reproduction and Development* 3 (2002), 14–20; L. Martin-McCaffrey, F. S. Willard, A. J. Oliveira-dos-Santos, D. R. Natale, B. E. Snow, R. J. Kimple, A. Pajak, A. J. Watson, L. Dagnino, J. M. Penninger, D. P. Siderovski, and S. J. D'Souza, "RGS14 Is a Mitotic Spindle Protein Essential from the First Division of the Mammalian Zygote," *Developmental Cell* 7 (2004), 763. For more on this topic, see Maureen L. Condic, Robert P. George, and Patrick Lee, "Do Human Beings Begin at Conception?" forthcoming.

growth, which is toward the mature stage of a human organism. Hence the immediate product of the union of the sperm and the ovum is not an intermediary entity between the gametes and embryo; it *is* the embryo, the human organism at the earliest stages of his or her development.

Again, not only does the position that the embryo is only a mass of cells before day 16 provide no explanation for the complex, ordered, regular sequence of events from day 1 to day 16; but it also provides no explanation for the sudden unification of these now hundreds of cells (at day 16) into a unit. These events occur with predictable regularity, and so an explanation *is* needed. By contrast, the view proposed by the standard embryology texts does provide intelligible explanations of the relevant events. Fertilization occurs because both the sperm and the oocyte are internally oriented to such an event. The successful union of the sperm and the ovum produces a new and distinct organism, and the sequence of events after that occurs because they are internally coordinated by the increasingly complex and differentiated new organism itself.

Another attempt to deny that the early human embryo is a whole human being is based on a comparison between the human embryo and a somatic cell, that is, any cell of our body besides a sex cell. Proponents of this argument claim that each of our own somatic cells has as much potential for development as any human embryo. Here is their argument: cloning has shown that each of our cells has the genetic information necessary for producing an entire human embryo, when joined to an enucleated (nucleus removed) oocyte and placed in the right environment. Each cell has the entire DNA code; it has become specialized (as muscle, skin, etc.) by most of that code being turned off. In cloning, those portions of the code previously deactivated are reactivated. And so (the argument goes), the potentiality of the human embryo is no different than that of any of our somatic cells – a skin cell, for example – and therefore the human embryo has no more value or worth than a skin cell, hundreds of which we shed every day.[19]

But this argument is fallacious. Of course, in *one* respect a somatic cell and a human embryo *are* similar: namely, each contains within it the entire genetic code (the genetic material). However, in the human embryo, even

---

[19] Silver, op. cit., 54–56; Ronald Bailey, *Liberation Biology: The Scientific and Moral Case for the Biotech Revolution* (Amherst, NY: Prometheus Books, 2005), Chapter 5. We have replied to earlier presentations of this argument by Bailey *National Review Online*, reprinted at http://reason.com/rb/rbo80601.shtml (2001); William J. Fitzpatrick, "Totipotency and the Moral Status of Embryos," *Journal of Social Philosophy* 35 (2004), 108–122.

at the one-cell stage, the program is totally active; in the somatic cell most of this information is "switched off." The argument simply ignores the profound and decisive differences between the two. No somatic cell has the active disposition to become a mature human being. No somatic cell will actively develop itself to a mature stage of a human being, requiring only a suitable environment for its natural development. Cloning generates a new organism, rather than merely placing a cell in an environment suitable for its growth.[20] Somatic cells, in the context of cloning, are analogous, then, not to embryos, but to gametes (spermatozoon and oocyte). Just as a human being who is generated as a result of the union of gametes was never a spermatozoon or an oocyte, a human being who is generated by a process of cloning (should this occur in the future) was never a somatic cell. But you and I truly were once embryos, just as we were once fetuses, infants, and adolescents. These are merely stages in the development of the enduring organism – the human being – we are. Moreover, the argument comparing human embryos to somatic cells ignores the most obvious difference between any of our cells and a living human embryo. Each of our cells is a mere part of a larger organism; but the embryo himself or herself is a complete, though immature, human organism (human being). Somatic cells are not, and embryonic human beings are, distinct, self-integrating living beings actively disposed to direct their own maturation as members of the human species. Thus, if a skin cell dies, the human being does not; the human being lives on. If a human embryo dies, the entire human organism is dead, and cannot be replaced.

II. No-Person Arguments: The Dualist Version

Defenders of abortion may adopt different strategies to respond to these points. Most will grant that human embryos or fetuses are human beings.

---

[20] William Fitzpatrick describes the enucleated egg into which a somatic cell is placed in the cloning process, as a "merely a suitable environment" (see Fitzpatrick, op. cit., 113). That is a mistake. Rather, what he refers to as "ooplasmic environment," together with an electrical stimulus to effect fusion, in fact radically changes the *internal* developmental trajectory of the cell, evidently, therefore, producing a substantial change. That is, it generates a *whole* organism, whereas before, the somatic cell was only a *part* of an organism. There is a radical difference – a difference between a part and a whole – between a cell that has all of the *information* for the production of a mature organism but most of which is latent (as is the case with every somatic cell) and a unicellular or multicellular organism that has the *active disposition to develop oneself* in accord with that information (which is the case with the zygote and early embryo, whether he or she is produced by fertilization or by cloning).

However, they then distinguish "human being" from "person" and claim that embryonic human beings are not (yet) persons. They hold that while it is wrong to kill persons, it is not always wrong to kill human beings who are not persons.

Sometimes it is argued that human beings in the embryonic stage are not persons because embryonic human beings do not exercise higher mental capacities or functions. Certain defenders of abortion (and infanticide) have argued that in order to be a person, an entity must be self-aware.[21] They then claim that, because human embryos and fetuses (and infants) have not yet developed self-awareness, they are not persons. Others have advanced the same claim on the ground that (they argue) in order for one entity to be the same person as an entity at a later stage, there must be a psychological continuity between them and thus each must possess self-awareness.[22]

These defenders of abortion raise the question: where does one draw the line between those who are subjects of rights and those that are not? A long tradition says that the line should be drawn at *persons*. But what is a person, if not an entity that has self-awareness, rationality, and so on?

However, this argument is based on a false premise. It implicitly identifies the human person with a consciousness which inhabits (or is somehow associated with) and uses a body; the truth, however (as we argued in Chapter 1), is that we human persons are particular kinds of physical organisms. The argument here under review grants that the human organism comes to be at conception, but claims nevertheless that you or I, the human person, comes to be only much later, say, when self-awareness develops. But if this human organism came to be at one time, but *I* came to be at a later time, it follows that I am one thing and this human organism with which *I* am associated is another thing.[23]

[21] Mary Ann Warren, "On the Moral and Legal Status of Abortion," in *The Problem of Abortion*, 2nd ed., ed. Joel Feinberg (Belmont, CA: Wadsworth, 1984), 102–109; Michael Tooley, *Abortion and Infanticide* (New York: Oxford University Press, 1983); Peter Singer, *Practical Ethics*, 3rd ed. (New York: Cambridge University Press, 1993).

[22] For example, Peter McInerney, "Does the Fetus Have a Future-Like-Ours?" *Journal of Philosophy* 87 (1990), 264–268; Jeff McMahan, *The Ethics of Killing: Problems at the Margins of Life* (New York: Oxford University Press, 2002); for the persistence of the person, McMahan also requires sameness of that part of the brain in which conscious states are realized – so he allows late abortions (after twenty weeks) but not early ones.

[23] Recall that body–self dualists may identify the self with a subject of experiences (e.g., Tooley, *Abortion and Infanticide*, loc. cit.) or with a series of experiences (proponents of the psychological continuity criterion of personal identity, e.g., Sydney Shoemaker, "Survival and the Importance of Identity," in Daniel Kolak and Raymond Martin, *Self and Identity: Contemporary Philosophical Issues* (New York: Macmillan, 1991), 267–273;

But this is false. We are not consciousnesses that *possess or inhabit* bodies nor are we merely embodied minds. Rather, we *are* living bodily entities. Recall (as we argued in more detail in Chapter 1) that we understand what an entity is by examining the kinds of actions it performs. If a living thing performs bodily actions, then it is a physical organism. Now, those who wish to deny that we are physical organisms think of *themselves*, what each of them refers to as *I*, as the subject of self-conscious acts of conceptual thought and willing (what many philosophers, ourselves included, would say are nonphysical acts). But this "I" is identical with the subject of physical, bodily actions, and so is a living, bodily being (an organism). Sensation is a bodily action, and it is an action performed by the organism as a whole (and not just its brain). The act of seeing, for example, is an act that an animal performs with the eyeballs and the optic nerve, just as the act of walking is an act that one performs with the legs. But it is clear in the case of human individuals that it must be the same entity, the same single subject of actions, that performs the act of sensing and that performs the act of understanding. When I know, for example, that *This is a book*, it is by my understanding, or a self-conscious intellectual act, that I apprehend what is meant by "book," apprehending what it is (at least in a general way). But the subject of that proposition, what I refer to by the word "This," is apprehended by sensation or perception. Clearly, it must be the same thing – the same I – which apprehends the predicate and the subject of a unitary judgment (again, for more details, see Chapter 1).

So, it is the same substantial entity, the same agent, which understands and which senses or perceives. And so what all agree is referred to by the word "I" (namely, the subject of conscious, intellectual acts) is identical with the physical organism which is the subject of bodily actions such as sensing or perceiving. Hence the entity that I am and the entity that you are – what you and I refer to by the personal pronouns "you" and "I" – is in each case a human, physical organism (but also with nonphysical capacities). Therefore, since you and I are *essentially* physical organisms, *we* came to be when these physical organisms came to be. But there are no scientific or philosophical grounds for doubt that the human organism comes to be at conception. Thus you and I came to be at conception; *we* once were embryos, then fetuses, then infants, just as we were once toddlers, preadolescent children, adolescents, and young adults.

Jennifer Whiting, "Personal Identity: The Non-Branching Form of 'What Matters'," in *The Blackwell Guide to Metaphysics*, ed. Richard Gale (Malden, MA: Blackwell Publishers, 2002), 190ff.), or with an embodied mind (that is, conscious experiences as realized in a part of the brain, e.g., McMahan, loc. cit.).

So, how should we use the word "person"? Are human embryos persons or not? People may stipulate different meanings for the word "person," but we think it is clear that what we normally mean by the word "person" is that substantial entity that is referred to by personal pronouns – "I," "you," "she," and so on. It follows, we submit, that a person is a distinct subject with the natural capacity to reason and make free choices. That subject, in the case of human beings, is identical with the human organism, and therefore that subject comes to be when the human organism comes to be, even though it will take him or her at least several months to actualize the natural capacities to reason and make free choices, natural capacities which are already present (albeit in radical, i.e., root, form) from the beginning. So it makes no sense to say that the human organism came to be at one point but the person – you or I – came to be at some later point. To have destroyed the human organism that you are or I am even at an early stage of our lives would have been to have killed you or me.

III. No-Person Arguments: The Evaluative Version

Let us now consider a different argument by which some defenders of abortion seek to deny that human beings in the embryonic and fetal stages are "persons" and, as such, ought not to be killed. Unlike the argument criticized in the previous section, this argument grants that the being who is you or I came to be at conception, but contends that you and I became valuable and bearers of rights only much later, when, for example, we developed the proximate, or immediately exercisable, capacity for self-consciousness. Inasmuch as those who advance this argument concede that you and I once were human embryos, they do not identify the self or the person with a nonphysical phenomenon, such as consciousness.

They claim, however, that being a person is an accidental attribute. It is an accidental attribute in the way that someone's being a musician or basketball player is an accidental attribute. Just as you come to be at one time, but become a musician or basketball player only much later, so, they say, you and I came to be when the physical organisms we are came to be, but we became persons (beings with a certain type of special value and bearers of basic rights) only at some time later.[24] Those defenders of abortion whose view we discussed in the previous section disagree with the pro-life position on an ontological issue, that is, on what kind of

---

[24] Judith Thomson, "Abortion," *Boston Review*, 1995, at bostonreview.mit.edu/BR20.3/thomson.html; Ronald Dworkin, *Life's Dominion: An Argument about Abortion, Euthanasia, and Individual Freedom* (New York: Knopf, 1993).

entity the human embryo or fetus is. Those who advance the argument now under review, by contrast, disagree with the pro-life position on an evaluative question. To clarify this point, let us summarize the basic pro-life argument. It can be set out in five steps:

1. You and I are intrinsically valuable (in the sense that makes us subjects of rights).
2. We are intrinsically valuable in virtue of what we are (what we are essentially), instead of in virtue of accidental characteristics.
3. What we are is each a human, physical organism. (We are human, physical organisms essentially.)
4. Human, physical organisms come to be at conception. (Shown in Section I.)
5. Therefore, what is intrinsically valuable (as a subject of rights) comes to be at conception.

In the last section (and in Chapter 1) we examined attempts to deny step #3. In this section we defend step #2.

In an article written in 1995, Judith Thomson argued for this position by comparing the right to life with the right to vote. Thomson argued that, "[i]f children are allowed to develop normally they will have a right to vote; that does not show that they now have a right to vote."[25] So, according to this position, it is true that we once were embryos and fetuses, but in the embryonic and fetal stages of our lives we were not yet valuable in the special way that would qualify us as having a right to life. We acquired that special kind of value and the right to life that comes with it at some point after we came into existence.

We can begin to see that this view is mistaken by considering Thomson's comparison of the right to life with the right to vote. Thomson fails to advert to the fact that some rights vary with respect to place, circumstances, talents, and other factors, while other rights do not. We recognize that one's right to life does not vary with place, as does one's right to vote. One may have the right to vote in Switzerland, but not in Mexico. Moreover, some rights and entitlements accrue to individuals only at certain times, or in certain places or situations, and others do not. But to have the right to life is to have *moral status at all*; to have the right to life, in other words, is to be the sort of entity that can have rights or entitlements to begin with. And so it is to be expected that *this* right

25 Thomson, "Abortion," loc. cit.

would differ in some fundamental ways from other rights, such as a right to vote.

In particular, it is reasonable to suppose (and we will give reasons for this in a moment) that having moral status at all, as opposed to having a right to perform a specific action in a specific situation, follows from an entity's being the *type of thing* (or substantial entity) it is. And so, just as one's right to life does not come and go with one's location or situation, so it does not accrue to someone in virtue of an acquired (i.e., accidental) property, capacity, skill, or disposition. Rather, this right belongs to a person, a substantial entity, at all times that he or she exists, not just during certain stages of his or her existence, or in certain circumstances, or in virtue of additional, accidental attributes.

The pro-life position is that human beings are valuable as subjects of rights in virtue of *what* we are, not in virtue of some attribute that we acquire some time after we have come to be. Obviously, defenders of abortion cannot maintain that the accidental attribute required to be a person, or valuable as a subject of rights (additional to being a human individual), is an *actual* behavior. They of course do not wish to exclude from personhood people who are, say, in reversible comas. So, the additional attribute will have to be a capacity or potentiality of some sort. Thus, they will have to concede that reversibly comatose human beings will be persons because they have the potentiality or capacity for higher mental functions.

But there is a sense in which human embryos and fetuses also have a capacity for higher mental functions. Human embryos and fetuses cannot, of course, immediately perform such acts. Still, they are related to such acts differently than, say, a canine or feline embryo is. They are members of a natural kind – a biological species – whose members, if not prevented by some extrinsic cause, in due course develop the immediately exercisable capacity for such mental functions. The fact that they do shows that members of this species come to be with whatever it takes to *develop* that immediately exercisable capacity, given a suitable environment and nutrition, and that only the adverse effects on them of other causes will prevent it.[26]

Discussing an acquired ability, we recognize that one can have a certain ability (or capacity) and yet require intermediate steps to actualize it. If asked, "Does Jane have the capacity to run a marathon?" it is perfectly

---

[26] This morally significant feature is true of *every* whole member of the human species, not just of its paradigm instances, contrary to Jeff McMahan's interpretation of the "nature-of-a-kind argument" in "Fellow Creatures," *Journal of Ethics* 9 (2005), 353–380.

accurate to reply, "Yes, after some training she will succeed." But a similar point is true of basic, natural capacities, that is, capacities one possesses simply because of the kind of thing one is. The human embryo has within itself – or herself, since sex is determined from the beginning – all of the positive reality needed to actively develop herself to the point where she will perform higher mental functions, given only a suitable environment and nutrition, and so she now has the natural capacity for such mental functions. One could also call this capacity an "ultimate capacity,"[27] or a "second-order capacity," since it is the capacity to acquire a more proximate, or first-order, capacity.[28]

So, we must distinguish two sorts of capacity or potentiality for higher mental functions (conceptual thought and free choice) that a substantial entity might possess: first, an immediately (or nearly immediately) exercisable capacity to engage in higher mental functions; second, a basic, natural capacity to develop oneself to the point where one does perform such actions. But on what basis can one require the first sort of potentiality – as do proponents of the position we are now considering – which is an accidental attribute, and not just the second? There are three decisive reasons *against* supposing that the first sort of potentiality is required to qualify an entity as a bearer of the right to life.

First, the developing human being does not reach a level of maturity at which he or she performs a type of mental act that other animals do not perform – even animals such as dogs and cats – until at least several months after birth. A six-week-old baby lacks the *immediately (or nearly immediately) exercisable* capacity to perform characteristically human mental functions.[29] So, if full moral respect were due only to those who possess a nearly immediately exercisable capacity for characteristically human mental functions, it would follow that six-week-old infants do not deserve full moral respect. If abortion were morally acceptable on the grounds that the human embryo or fetus lacks such a capacity for characteristically human mental functions, then one would be logically committed to the view that, subject to parental approval, human infants could be disposed of as well.

[27] J. P. Moreland and B. Rae Scott, *Body and Soul: Human Nature and the Crisis of Ethics* (Downers Grove, IL: InterVarsity Press, 2000), 203–204.

[28] Eric T. Olson, *The Human Animal: Personal Identity without Psychology* (New York: Oxford University Press, 1997), 86.

[29] Stuart Derbyshire, "Locating the Beginnings of Pain," *Bioethics* 13 (1999), 21ff.; R. Joseph, "Fetal Brain and Cognitive Development," *Developmental Review* 20 (1999), 97–98.

Second, the difference between these two types of capacity is merely a difference between stages along a continuum. The *proximate* capacity for mental functions is only the development of an underlying potentiality that the human being possesses simply by virtue of the kind of entity it is. The capacities for reasoning, deliberating, and making free choices are gradually developed, or brought toward maturation, through gestation, childhood, adolescence, and so on. But the difference between a being that deserves full moral respect and a being that does not (and can therefore legitimately be disposed of as a means of benefiting others) cannot consist only in the fact that, while both have some feature, one has more of it than the other. A mere *quantitative* difference (having more or less of the same feature, such as *the development* of a basic natural capacity) cannot by itself be a justificatory basis for treating different entities in *radically* different ways. Between the ovum and the approaching thousands of sperms, on the one hand, and the embryonic human being, on the other hand, there *is* a clear difference in kind. But between the embryonic human being and that same human being at any later stage of its maturation, there is only a difference in degree.

One might object to this that sometimes one *must* draw a line at some arbitrary point: if there are no more than quantitative differences among infants, fetuses, embryos, and sperm and ova, then one simply must pick a dividing line somewhere along that continuum.[30] However, there *is* a fundamental difference (as shown earlier) between the gametes (the sperm and the ovum) on the one hand, and the human embryo and fetus, on the other. When a human being comes to be, then a substantial entity that is identical with the entity that will later reason, make free choices, and so on, begins to exist. So, those who propose an accidental characteristic as qualifying an entity as a bearer of the right to life (or as a "person" or being with "moral worth") are *ignoring* a radical difference among groups of beings (a difference in kind, not a mere difference in degree), and instead fastening onto a mere quantitative difference as the basis for treating different groups in radically different ways. In other words, there are beings a, b, c, d, e, and so forth. And between a's and b's, on the one hand, and c's, d's, and e's, on the other hand, there is a *fundamental difference*, a difference in kind not just in degree. But proponents of the position that being a person is an accidental characteristic ignore that difference and pick out a mere difference in degree between, say, d's and e's, and make that the basis for radically different types of treatment.

[30] Thanks to Don Marquis for bringing this objection to our attention.

That violates the most basic canon of justice: similars should be treated similarly.

Third, being a distinct human being (whether immature or not) is an either/or matter – a thing either is or is not a distinct human being.[31] But the acquired qualities that could be proposed as criteria for personhood come in varying and continuous degrees: there is an infinite number of degrees of the *development of* the basic natural capacities for self-consciousness, intelligence, or rationality. So, if human beings were worthy of full moral respect (as subjects of rights) only because of such qualities, and not in virtue of the kind of being they are, then, since such qualities come in varying degrees, no account could be given of why basic rights are not possessed by human beings in varying degrees. The proposition that all human beings are created equal would be relegated to the status of a superstition. For example, if developed self-consciousness bestowed rights, then, since some people are more self-conscious than others (that is, have developed that capacity to a greater extent than others), some people would be greater in dignity than others, and the rights of the superiors would trump those of the inferiors where the interests of the superiors could be advanced at the cost of the inferiors. This conclusion would follow, no matter which of the acquired qualities generally proposed as qualifying some human beings (or human beings at some stages) for full respect were selected. Clearly, developed self-consciousness, or desires, or so on, are arbitrarily selected degrees of development of capacities that all human beings possess in (at least) radical form from the coming into existence of the human being until his or her death. So, it cannot be the case that *some* human beings *and not others* possess the special kind of value that qualifies an entity as having a basic right to life, by virtue of a certain degree of development. Rather, human beings are valuable as subjects of rights, *in virtue of what (i.e., the kind of being) they are*; and *all* human beings – not just some, and certainly not just those who have advanced sufficiently along the developmental path as to be able immediately (or almost immediately) to exercise their capacities for characteristically human mental functions – possess that kind of value and that right.[32]

---

[31] For defense of this proposition, see Chapter 1, Section VII.

[32] In arguing against Lee's article "The Pro-Life Argument from Substantial Identity: A Defense," *Bioethics* 18 (2004), 249–263, Dean Stretton claims that the basic natural capacity of rationality also comes in degrees and that therefore the argument we are presenting against the position that moral worth is based on having some accidental characteristic would apply to our position also (Dean Stretton, "Essential Properties and the Right to Life: A Response to Lee" *Bioethics* 18 (2004), 264–282).

Since human beings are valuable in the way that qualifies them as having a right to life in virtue of what they are, it follows that they have that right, whatever it entails, from the point at which they come into being – and that (as shown earlier) is at conception.[33]

However, Stretton misconstrued the argument and the criterion Lee (along with many others) has proposed for the right to life. Lee argued that defenders of abortion have no good reason to base the right to life on developed capacities for conceptual thought and free choice rather than on basic, natural capacities for such acts – capacities which are possessed by unborn, as well as more mature, human beings. However, the conclusion of Lee's argument was not that the criterion for the right to life is natural capacities, but that it is *being a certain type of substance*. He then proposed that the genuine criterion for having a right to life is *being a person*, that is, a distinct substance of a rational nature (the classic Boethian or Thomistic definition of "person.")

Stretton treated the natural capacity for higher mental functions as just another acci-dental attribute – as a property inhering in the thing (substance), as opposed to an expres-sion of what the thing is. So it is not surprising that "the natural capacities view" seemed to raise the same problems as do other accidental characteristics proposed as conferring a right to life. However, in Lee's article in *Bioethics*, 2004, he stressed that the criterion for the right to life is not a capacity that inheres in an entity, but "being a certain kind of thing, that is, having a specific type of substantial nature" (p. 254). A *rational animal* (Lee said) is "a type of substance, and . . . being rational (having the natural capacity for conceptual thought and free choice) is a specific difference, a feature expressing (in part) what the substance is instead of an accidental characteristic" (p. 256).

Moreover, Stretton's arguments presuppose that there is only a difference in degree, or a mere quantitative difference, between human beings and their natural capacities, on the one hand, and other animals and their natural capacities, on the other hand. But we hold that human beings (and some of their natural capacities, such as those for concep-tual thought and free choice) *do* differ in kind, and not just in degree, from other animals (and their natural capacities – see Chapter 2). For more on these issues, see Patrick Lee, "Substantial Identity and the Right to Life: A Rejoinder to Dean Stretton," *Bioethics* 21 (2007), 93–97.

[33] Don Marquis's position that fetuses deserve full moral respect because they "have a future like ours" also seems to identify the ground of personhood or full moral worth in an accidental attribute (Don Marquis, "Why Abortion Is Wrong," *Journal of Philosophy* 86 (1989), 182–202). However, a being A can have a future like ours only if it is true that, absent some accident or violence, *A itself* would persist into infancy, childhood, etc. In other words, Marquis's position rests on reference to a strong ground of persistence – one that admits counterfactuals being true of the persisting, and thus enduring, entity. And if that is true, then it seems that A *itself* (given the arguments earlier), from the moment it (he or she) comes to be, would merit full moral respect. But if A merits full moral respect, then deliberately depriving A of *any* basic good, including life itself, will be unjust, not only depriving him or her of a rich future like ours – unless one wants to say that only consciously experienced realities can be basic goods (goods valuable as ends, rather than just as means, for someone). In other words, it seems that the difference between the position we are defending and Marquis's position concerns what is good *for* an individual, not directly with the question which are the individuals we should care about, or who are subjects of rights. For a defense of the proposition that life itself is a basic good, where Marquis's position does seem to diverge from ours, see Chapter 5, Section IV.

For, if the right to life is based on being a certain type of substance, having a certain substantial nature, then just having such a substantial nature will qualify one as having full moral worth and a right to life. To be sure, persons (substances with a rational nature) are not all equal – some are more intelligent or morally better than others. But since having a right to life follows upon just *being a person*, then being a person is sufficient to give one *full* moral worth, and so in that sense *equal* dignity – just as, by analogy, if a property simply follows upon being an animal, then it is fully possessed by every animal, even though not all animals are equal. (For example, it follows upon the *nature* of an animal that it has parts that move other parts, and so it is a property *fully* possessed by all animals.)

In sum, human beings are valuable (as subjects of rights) in virtue of what they are. But what they are are human, physical organisms. Human, physical organisms come to be at conception. Therefore, what is intrinsically valuable (as a subject of rights) comes to be at conception.

IV. The Argument that Abortion Is Justified as Nonintentional Killing

Some "pro-choice" philosophers have attempted to justify abortion by denying that all abortions are intentional killing. They have granted (at least for the sake of argument) that an unborn human being has a right to life but have then argued that this right does not entail that the child in utero is morally entitled to the use of the mother's body for life support. In effect, their argument is that, at least in many cases, abortion is not a case of intentionally killing the child, but a choice not to provide the child with assistance, that is, a choice to expel (or "evict") the child from the womb, despite the likelihood or certainty that expulsion (or "eviction") will result in his or her death.[34]

Various analogies have been presented by people making this argument. Famously, Judith Thomson compared the mother's gestating a child to allowing someone the use of one's kidneys, and others have compared gestation to donating an organ. We are not *required* (morally or as a matter of law) to allow someone to use our kidneys, or to donate organs to others, even when they would die without this assistance (and we could

---

[34] Judith Jarvis Thomson, "A Defense of Abortion," *Philosophy and Public Affairs* 1 (1971), 47–66; reprinted, among other places, in *The Problem of Abortion*; Eileen McDonagh, *Breaking the Abortion Deadlock: From Choice to Consent* (New York: Oxford University Press, 1996); Margaret Olivia Little, "Abortion, Intimacy, and the Duty to Gestate," *Ethical Theory and Moral Practice* 2 (1999), 295–312.

survive in good health despite rendering it). Analogously, the argument continues, a woman is not morally required to allow the embryo or fetus the use of her body. Let us call this "the bodily rights argument."[35]

It may be objected that a woman has a special responsibility to the child she is carrying, whereas in the cases of withholding assistance to which abortion is compared, there is no such special responsibility. Proponents of the bodily rights argument have replied, however, that the mother has not voluntarily assumed responsibility for the child, or a personal relationship with the child, and we have strong responsibilities to others only if we have voluntarily assumed such responsibilities[36] or have consented to a personal relationship which generates such responsibilities.[37] True – say proponents of this argument – the mother may have voluntarily performed an act which she knew may result in a child's conception, but that is distinct from consenting to gestate the child if a child is conceived. And so (according to this position) it is not until the woman consents to pregnancy, or perhaps not until the parents consent to care for the child by taking the baby home from the hospital or birthing center, that the full duties of parenthood accrue to the mother (and perhaps the father).

In reply to this argument we wish to make several points. It seems true that in some cases abortion is not intentional killing, but a choice to expel the child, the child's death being an unintended, albeit foreseen and (rightly or wrongly) accepted, side effect. However, these constitute a small minority of abortions. In the vast majority of cases, the death of the child in the womb is precisely the object of the abortion. In most cases the end sought is to avoid being a parent; but abortion brings that about only by bringing about the death of the child. Indeed, the attempted abortion would be considered by the woman requesting it and the abortionist performing it to have been unsuccessful if the child survived. In most cases abortion is intentional killing. Thus, even if the bodily rights argument succeeded, it would justify only a small percentage of abortions.

Still, in some few cases abortion is chosen as a means precisely toward ending the condition of pregnancy, and the means to bring that about is the removal of the child. A pregnant woman may have less or more

[35] Cf. Francis J. Beckwith, "Arguments from Bodily Rights: A Critical Analysis," in *The Abortion Controversy: 25 Years after Roe v. Wade*, 2nd ed., ed. Louis Pojman and Francis J. Beckwith (Belmont, CA: Wadsworth, 1998), 132–150.

[36] Thomson, "A Defense of Abortion," loc. cit.

[37] Little, loc. cit. Id., "The Permissibility of Abortion," in *Contemporary Debates in Applied Ethics*, ed. Andrew I. Cohen and Christopher Wellman (New York: Blackwell Publishers, 2005), 27–40.

serious reasons for seeking the termination of this condition, but if that is her objective, then the child's death resulting from his or her expulsion will be a side effect rather than the means chosen. For example, an actress may wish not to be pregnant because the pregnancy will change her figure during a time when she is filming scenes in which having a slender appearance is important; or a woman may dread the discomforts, pains, and difficulties involved in pregnancy. (Of course, in many abortions, there may be mixed motives: the parties making the choice may intend both ending the condition of pregnancy and the death of the child.)

Nevertheless, while it is true that in some cases abortion is not intentional killing, it is misleading to describe it simply as choosing not to provide bodily life support. Rather, it is actively expelling the human embryo or fetus from the womb. There is a significant moral difference between *not doing* something that would assist someone, and *doing* something that causes someone harm, even if that harm is an unintended (but foreseen) side effect. It is more difficult morally to justify the latter than it is the former. Abortion is the *act* of extracting the unborn human being from the womb – an extraction that usually rips him or her to pieces or does him or her violence in some other way.

It is true that in some cases, causing death as a side effect is morally permissible. For example, in some cases it is morally right to use force to stop a potentially lethal attack on one's family or country, even if one foresees that the force used will also result in the assailant's death. Similarly, there are instances in which it is permissible to perform an act that one knows or believes will, as a side effect, cause the death of a child in the womb. For example, if a pregnant woman is discovered to have a cancerous uterus, and this is a proximate danger to the mother's life, it can be morally right to remove the cancerous uterus with the baby in it, even if the child will die as a result. A similar situation can occur in ectopic pregnancies. But in such cases, not only is the child's death a side effect, but the mother's life is in proximate danger. It is worth noting also that in these cases *what is done* (the means) is the correction of a pathology (such as a cancerous uterus or a ruptured uterine tube). Thus, in such cases, not only the child's death, but also the ending of the pregnancy are side effects. So, such acts are what traditional casuistry referred to as *indirect* or *nonintentional*, abortions.

But it also is clear that not every case of causing death as a side effect is morally right. For example, if a man's daughter has a serious respiratory disease and the father is told that his continued smoking in her presence will cause her death, it would obviously be immoral for him to continue the smoking. Similarly, if a man works for a steel company in a city with significant levels of air pollution, and his child has a serious respiratory problem, making the air pollution a danger to her life, certainly he should not continue living (with his family) in that city. He should move, we would say, even if that meant he had to resign a prestigious position or make a significant career change.

In both examples (a) the parent has a special responsibility to his child, but (b) the act that would cause the child's death would avoid a harm to the parent but cause a significantly worse harm to his child. And so, although the harm done would be a side effect, in both cases the act that caused the death would be an unjust act and morally wrongful as such. The special responsibility of parents to their children requires that they at least refrain from performing acts that cause terrible harms to their children in order to avoid significantly lesser harms to themselves.

But (a) and (b) also obtain in intentional abortions (that is, those in which the removal of the child is directly sought, rather than the correction of a life-threatening pathology) even though they are not, strictly speaking, intentional killing.[38] First, the mother has a special responsibility to her child, in virtue of being her biological mother (as does the father in virtue of his paternal relationship). The parental relationship itself – not just the voluntary acceptance of that relationship – gives rise to a special responsibility to a child.

Proponents of the bodily rights argument deny this point. Many claim that one has full parental responsibilities only if one has voluntarily assumed them. And so the child, on this view, has a right to care from his or her mother (including gestation) only if the mother has accepted her pregnancy, or perhaps only if the mother (and/or the father?) has in some way voluntarily begun a deep personal relationship with the child.[39]

One argument to support the proposition that parents have special obligations to their children, even unborn ones, has been that by voluntarily having sexual intercourse they tacitly consent to care for the child,

---

[38] Notice that we define direct or intentional abortion in a way that includes *both* expelling the child with the intent to kill *and* expelling the child foreseeing the child's death, with the intent to end the pregnancy. Where the correction of a pathological condition is intended and the ending of the pregnancy and the child's death are side effects, the act is an indirect or nonintentional (but foreseen) abortion (and this may or may not be justified, depending on other morally relevant factors). We contend that although not every intentional abortion is intentional killing, every intentional abortion is objectively morally wrong.

[39] Little, loc. cit.

since they voluntarily perform an action (sexual intercourse) which they know could result in a child. David Boonin has replied to this argument, however, that we do not give tacit consent to all of the results of what we voluntarily bring about, but only to what is directly included in the states of affairs we voluntarily create. This reply of Boonin seems correct to us. The basis for the special responsibilities we have to our children from their beginning is not tacit consent.

A second argument to show that parents have special responsibilities to their children from conception on has been that their voluntary action has caused the child to be in an especially imperiled condition.[40] The point is that one is, in general, responsible for the foreseen consequences of one's actions, even if one has also tried to prevent them. Boonin calls this the negligence version of the "responsibility objection" (because it is often illustrated by comparisons with harms caused by drunk driving).

Boonin replies, however, that we must distinguish between being responsible for someone's neediness and being responsible for the fact that they exist, with the result that they are in need. In the first case, he says, we do have a special responsibility to give assistance, but not, he says, in the second case. More precisely: if we are responsible for the fact that, given that someone exists, he stands in need of our assistance, then we do have a special responsibility to provide him assistance. But if we are responsible for the fact that someone exists, with the result that he stands in need of our assistance, then, says Boonin, this fact does not ground any special duty to provide assistance to this person. He then argues that abortion is an instance of the second type, not the first.

For example, suppose a physician gives a patient a life-saving drug, but the drug has a side effect of causing the kidney ailment in which he will die unless he is given the use of someone else's kidneys (by being hooked up to him or her), and the physician happens to have the right blood type to provide such assistance. Since the physician is not responsible for the patient's dependency condition, Boonin argues, but only for his continued existence, his causing him to exist at this time does not ground any special responsibility to that patient. Boonin argues that unborn babies are analogous to this patient: by conceiving them, we do not precisely cause their dependency condition, but we cause them to exist, with the result that they are in a dependency condition.

But it is not clear that the reason why the physician lacks special responsibilities to this patient involves factors that are analogous to a pregnancy.

[40] Beckwith, loc. cit.; Lee, *Abortion and Unborn Human Life*, loc. cit.

The physician did not bring this patient into being, but in a generous act extended his life. The fact that he thus extended the life of this patient, but with the *result* that he *later* develops this urgent need is quite distinct from conceiving a child. In the conception of a child the parents cause a child to come to be and *at the same time* cause him or her to come to be in an imperiled, or radically dependent, condition. The parents' action directly places the child in an imperiled condition, for the coming to be of an immature human being and his or her coming to be in an imperiled (or dependent) condition are identical. Suppose I am in a motorboat in a lake and speeding past the pier I knock three or four children into the lake. We suppose Boonin would agree that certainly here I *am* responsible for their being in a dependency condition and that I owe it to them to go back and try to help them out of the water, lest they drown. However, following Boonin's principles, we might also claim that I was only responsible for their being in the water, not for their being in an imperiled condition. It is not my fault, I might argue, that they do not know how to swim, and so their dependency condition is a consequence of what I do, but it is not something I am responsible for. But clearly, it is at least dubious to distinguish between my causing them to be in the water (for which I am responsible) and their being in a dependency condition due to their inability to swim (for which, the claim would be, I am not responsible). But, likewise, it is at least dubious to distinguish between a child's existing (for which I am responsible) and his existing in an imperiled condition (for which, the claim is, I am not responsible).

Still, Boonin's book raises an important question: what is the source of our special responsibilities to our children, provided that we do have such responsibilities, and when do those responsibilities commence? In particular, do those special responsibilities come to be only when we have voluntarily assumed them? Or do they come to be with the coming to be of the child himself or herself?

First, we think it is clear *that* parents do have special responsibilities to their children, anterior to their having voluntarily assumed them. Suppose a mother takes her baby home after giving birth, but the only reason she did not get an abortion was that she could not afford one. Or suppose she lives in a society where abortion is not available (perhaps very few physicians are willing to do the grisly deed). She and her husband take the child home only because they had no alternative. Moreover, suppose that in their society, people are not waiting in line to adopt a newborn baby. And so the baby is several days old before anything can be done. If they abandon the baby and the baby is found, she will simply be returned to them. In such a case the parents have not voluntarily assumed responsibility, nor have they consented to a personal relationship with the child. But it would surely be wrong for these parents to abandon their baby in the woods (perhaps the only feasible way of ensuring she is not returned), even though the baby's death would be only a side effect. Clearly, whatever the precise explanation of *why* it is so, parents do have a responsibility to make sacrifices for their children, even if they have not voluntary assumed such responsibilities, or given their consent to the personal relationship with the child.

What is the source of this special responsibility? The first step in answering this question, we think, is to reject the idea – implicitly supposed by the bodily rights argument – that we have a primordial right to construct a life simply as we please, and that others have claims on us only very minimally or through our consent (either directly or indirectly through our consent to a relationship).[41] On the contrary, we are by nature members of communities. Our moral goodness or character consists to a large extent (though not solely) in contributing to the communities of which we are members. We ought to act for our genuine good or flourishing (we take that as a basic ethical principle), but our flourishing involves being in communion with others. And communion with others of itself – even if we find ourselves united with others because of a physical or social relationship which precedes our consent – entails duties or responsibilities. Moreover, the contribution we are morally required to make to others will likely bring each of us some discomfort and pain. This is not to say that we should simply ignore our own good for the sake of others. Rather, since what I am, who I am, is in part constituted by various relationships with others, not all of which are initiated by my will, my genuine good includes the contributions I make to the relationships in which I participate. Thus,

---

[41] Boonin argues (*A Defense of Abortion*, 176–177) that the child is not made worse off by being conceived and then aborted. He does not put this forward as a sufficient condition for the morality of abortion (since he recognizes that he must also show – though, we think, he fails in this – that there are no other grounds for special responsibility owed to the child). However, he does present it as providing some support for his claim that the mother has no special responsibility to provide bodily life support. That is, *if* the child were left worse off before any of one's interactions with him or her than before, *then* one would have an obligation to continue bodily life support, and his answer is that the child is not left worse off. In effect, his claim is that by conceiving the child and then aborting him or her, one has not harmed the child (also see F. M. Kamm, *Creation and Abortion* (New York: Oxford University Press, 1992), 8off.). However, to see if one has harmed someone, one must compare the condition the person is in before *the contemplated action* versus after that action. Otherwise, one could claim that one did not harm one's six-week-old son or daughter by killing him or her, which is clearly wrong.

the life we constitute by our free choices should be in large part a life of mutual reciprocity with others.

For example, I may wish to cultivate my talent to write and so I may want to spend hours each day reading and writing. Or I may wish to develop my athletic abilities and so I may want to spend hours every day on the baseball field. But if I am a father of minor children, and have an adequate paying job working (say) in a coal mine, then my clear duty is to keep that job. Similarly, if one's girlfriend finds she is pregnant and one is the father, then one might also be morally required to continue one's work in the coal mine (or steel mill, factory, warehouse, etc.).

In other words, I have a duty to do something with my life that contributes to the good of the human community, but that general duty becomes specified by my particular situation. It becomes specified by the connection or closeness to me of those who are in need. We acquire special responsibilities toward people, not only by *consenting* to contracts or relationships with them, but also by having various types of unions with them. So, we have special responsibilities to those people with whom we are closely united. For example, we have special responsibilities to our parents, and brothers and sisters, even though we did not choose them.

The physical unity or continuity of children to their parents is unique. The child is brought into being out of the bodily unity and bodies of the mother and the father. The mother and the father are in a certain sense prolonged or continued in their offspring. So, there is a natural unity of the mother with her child, and a natural unity of the father with his child. Since we have special responsibilities to those with whom we are closely united, it follows that we in fact do have a special responsibility to our children anterior to our having voluntarily assumed such responsibility or consented to the relationship.[42]

---

[42] David Boonin claims, in reply to this argument (in an earlier and less developed form, presented in Lee's *Abortion and Unborn Human Life*, 122), that it is not clear that it is impermissible for a woman to destroy what is a part of, or a continuation of, herself. He then says that to the extent the unborn human being is united to her in that way, "it would if anything seem that her act is *easier* to justify than if this claim were not true." (Boonin, *A Defense of Abortion*, 230.) But Boonin fails to grasp the point of the argument (perhaps, understandably, since it was not expressed very clearly in the earlier work he is discussing). One has a duty to care for oneself (and persons united with one) in a way that one does not have with respect to others. And the unity of the child to the mother is the basis for this child being related to the woman much differently than other children. We ought to pursue our own good *and the good of others with whom we are united in various ways*. If that is so, then the closer someone is united to us, the deeper and more extensive our responsibility to the person will be.

An additional point is one brought out well by Alasdair MacIntyre (though not applied by him to the abortion issue). Namely, we have received benefits from our parents and society and therefore have a duty to help others who are in need in similar ways that we have been. As Mac-Intyre explains, we become mature practical reasoners and thus are able to participate fully in human flourishing only in, "a set of relationships to certain particular others who are able to give us what we need."[43] But once we reach that stage, we then find ourselves in a network of relationships of giving and receiving. And we owe to this community a kind of giving that cannot be calculated or restricted in advance. We *ought* to enter this network of relationships, this pool of giving and receiving, but to enter it is to assume an obligation to give to individuals from whom we have not received, and to be ready to give without restrictions or conditions:

> We receive from parents and other family elders, from teachers and those to whom we are apprenticed, and from those who care for us when we are sick, injured, weakened by aging, or otherwise incapacitated, and others in gross and urgent need have to rely on us to give. Sometimes those others who rely on us are the same individuals from whom we ourselves received. But often enough it is from one set of individuals that we receive and to and by another that we are called on to give.[44]

MacIntyre speaks of being *called on* to be a parent: as part of this network of giving and receiving we are called on, that is, we are morally *required*, to step up and do our part. Moreover, our part is a role or a service that may require giving more than we have received and giving to those from whom we have received little or nothing.

> For to participate in this network of relationships of giving and receiving as the virtues require, I have to understand that what I am called upon to give may be quite disproportionate to what I have received and that those to whom I am called upon to give may well be those from whom I shall receive nothing. And I also have to understand that the care that I give to others has to be in an important way unconditional, since the measure of what is required of me is determined in key part, even if not only, by their needs.[45]

In sum, we are beneficiaries of being members of a network of giving and receiving, and this network of giving and receiving involves duties toward those from whom we have received nothing, and with whom we

---

[43] Alasdair MacIntyre, *Dependent Rational Animals: Why Human Beings Need the Virtues* (Chicago: Open Court, 1991), 98ff.

[44] Ibid., 98.

[45] Ibid., 108.

have not entered any voluntary association. Thus, I *ought* to help my child, and so I have special responsibilities to my child, because to help him or her is a duty I incur as part of entering that network of giving and receiving, which is constitutive of flourishing as a virtuous person. To ignore or downplay these bodily connections that generate specific responsibilities – claiming that all duties arise from acts of consent – is another manifestation of a general disregard for the significance of the bodily nature of human persons.

The second point (in the overall argument that intentional abortion, even when it is not intentional killing, is unjust) is this: in the types of cases we are considering, the harm caused (death) is much worse than the harms avoided (the difficulties in pregnancy). Pregnancy can involve severe impositions, but it is not nearly as bad as death – which is total and irreversible. One need not make light of the burdens of pregnancy to acknowledge that the harm that is death is in a different category altogether.

The burdens of pregnancy include physical difficulties and the pain of labor, and can include significant financial costs, psychological burdens, and interference with autonomy and the pursuit of other important goals.[46] These costs are not inconsiderable. Partly for that reason we owe our mothers gratitude for carrying and giving birth to us. However, where pregnancy does not place a woman's life in jeopardy or threaten grave and lasting damage to her physical health, the harm done to other goods is not total. Moreover, most of the harms involved in pregnancy are not irreversible: pregnancy is a nine-month task – if the woman and man are not in a good position to raise the child, adoption is a possibility. So the difficulties of pregnancy, considered together, are in a different and lesser category than death. Death is not just worse in degree than the difficulties involved in pregnancy; it is worse in kind.

Some have recently argued, however, that pregnancy can involve a unique type of burden. They have argued that the *intimacy* involved in pregnancy is such that if the woman must remain pregnant without her consent, then there is inflicted on her a unique and serious harm. Just as sex with consent can be a desired experience but sex without consent is a violation of bodily integrity, so (the argument continues) pregnancy involves such a close physical intertwinement with the fetus that not to allow abortion is analogous to rape – it involves an enforced intimacy.[47]

---

[46] McDonagh, op. cit., Chapter 5.
[47] David Boonin, *A Defense of Abortion*, 2003 84; Little, op. cit., 300–303.

However, this argument is based on a false analogy. Where the pregnancy is unwanted, the baby's "occupying" the mother's womb may involve a harm; but the child is committing no injustice against her. The baby is not forcing himself or herself on the woman, but is simply growing and developing in a way quite natural to him or her. The baby is not performing any action that could in any way be construed as aimed at violating the mother.[48] So the comparison with sex without consent is a false analogy.

It is true that the fulfillment of the duty of a mother to her child (during gestation) is unique and in many cases does involve a great sacrifice. The argument we have presented, however, is that being a mother *does* generate a special responsibility and that the sacrifice morally required of the mother is less burdensome than the harm that would be done to the child by expelling the child, causing his or her death, to escape that responsibility. The argument we have presented equally entails responsibilities for the father of the child. His duty does not involve as direct a bodily relationship with the child as the mother's, but it may be equally or even more burdensome. In certain circumstances, his obligation to care for the child (and the child's mother), and especially his obligation to provide financial support, may severely limit his freedom and even require months or, indeed, years of extremely burdensome physical labor. Historically many men have rightly seen that their basic responsibility to their family (and country) has entailed risking, and in many cases, losing, their lives. Different people in different circumstances, with different talents, will have different responsibilities. It is no argument against any of these responsibilities to point out their distinctness.

So, the burden of carrying the baby, for all its distinctness, is significantly less than the harm the baby would suffer by being killed; the mother and father have a special responsibility to the child; it follows that intentional abortion (even in the few cases where the baby's death is an unintended but foreseen side effect) is unjust and therefore objectively immoral.

---

[48] In some sense, being bodily "occupied" when one does not wish to be *is* a harm; however, the child does not (as explained in the text), neither does the state, inflict this harm on the woman, in circumstances in which the state prohibits abortion. By prohibiting abortion, the state would only prevent the woman from performing an act (forcibly detaching the child from her) which would unjustly kill this developing child, who is an innocent party.

5

Euthanasia

Thought and debate about euthanasia obviously involve different conceptions of what a human person is. Suppose Grandfather has a stroke, his son and daughter call the ambulance, and he is brought to the hospital. As a result of the stroke he loses significant memory and becomes demented. Suppose he no longer recognizes his family and can no longer carry on a conversation. Members of his family come to visit him. They spontaneously react: "That's just not Grandfather anymore. Grandfather – the lovable, affable person we have known for years – is just not there any more!" Understandable reaction. But some proponents of euthanasia articulate this reaction into an argument. It is wrong to kill persons (they argue), but the person who was living at his family's home exists no longer. True, it would be wrong to kill Grandfather, but *that* (meaning the human organism now hooked up to various tubes in the hospital) is not Grandfather. So, a week later the doctors in charge propose that this isn't really Grandfather any more either and that therefore we should withdraw nutrition and hydration (though his system is still metabolizing the nutrition). Keeping this organism alive who, or which, is not Grandfather, and is not a person, is futile. Proponents of euthanasia add that the doctors should be allowed to hasten the demise of this organism by more active methods. In short: it is not a person, so it is not murder to kill it.

If the entity that was lying in his bed and talking to you two weeks ago (Grandfather) is not the same entity as the one these doctors proposed to kill, but plainly it *is* the same human organism, this can only be because Grandfather is not a human organism.[1] What then is Grandfather; that is,

---

[1] The debate about euthanasia in many ways mirrors the debate about abortion.

what is he when he is alive and conscious before his trip to the hospital? Proponents of euthanasia are usually not so clear about the answer to this question. But if Grandfather is not a human organism, then he must be either a spiritual subject somehow associated with a human organism, or a series of experiences – a nonsubstantial consciousness sustained or embodied somehow in this organism during certain stages of its existence. In other words, this popular argument for euthanasia relies on an implicit denial that we are essentially bodily beings. The body and bodily life are treated as interesting tools or instruments – good just insofar as, and for as long as, they enable *us* to have and enjoy various experiences.

For example, speaking of human beings in so-called persistent vegetative state, Peter Singer argues as follows:

> In most respects, these human beings do not differ importantly from disabled infants. They are not self-conscious, rational, or autonomous, and so considerations of a right to life or of respecting autonomy do not apply. If they have no experiences at all, and can never have any again, their lives have no intrinsic value. Their life's journey has come to an end. They are biologically alive, but not biographically.[2]

Thus, it is often assumed that only conscious experiences are intrinsically valuable (that is, valuable for their own sake), and so the conclusion is drawn that when one's life becomes devoid of them or the pleasant experiences become outweighed by the unpleasant ones, one's life lacks net value. Like the other issues we have examined, the idea of *what a human person is* is central to the euthanasia debate.

I. Human Life and Personhood Near the End of Life

We argued in Chapter 1 that human persons are not spiritual subjects who *have* bodies; they are not just series of experiences, mere consciousnesses, or conscious information related to their bodies as software to the hardware in a computer. Human persons are living, organic animals – free and rational animals, but essentially animals nonetheless. What *I* am, the thing the word "I" refers to (or "he," "him," and so on) is a human, physical organism. So, the time that this human organism comes to be is the time that I come to be. Moreover, I do not cease to be until this physical organism ceases to be. The accidental characteristics or properties I

---

[2] Peter Singer, *Practical Ethics*, 2nd ed. (New York: Cambridge University Press, 1993), 395. This can be found reprinted on the Internet at http://icarus.uic.edu/~strian1/pechapter7.htm.

have are distinct from the thing that I am. Such accidental properties as my height, my shape, my color can come to be or cease to be at a different time than the time that I come to be or cease to be. However, since *human, physical organism* expresses what I am, rather than a property I have, I cannot come to be or cease to be at a different time than the time that this human organism comes to be or ceases to be. It is the same with all human beings, of course. Thus, it makes no sense to say that the same physical organism that Grandfather was is lying on the hospital bed, but Grandfather has ceased to be. Since Grandfather is essentially a human, physical organism, he cannot cease to be until the physical organism that he is ceases to be.

It is also important to note again (as shown in Chapters 1–3) that every human being is an animal with the basic natural capacity to reason and make free choices, even though something may prevent the actualization of that natural capacity. When thinking of "capacities" or potentialities, one often thinks of such capacities as the ability to play a musical instrument, to work mathematical problems, or to speak a language. Such abilities, however, are quite different from the more basic potentialities such as the abilities to move, to grow, to see, and to reason. In the Aristotelian tradition the former were called *habitus* and the latter were classified as natural powers.

The distinction is important. The ability to play the piano and the ability to speak a language are refinements, or specifications, of more basic potentialities – basic capacities to move and to think. The specific abilities to play the piano or to speak a language are acquired by repeated acts, which in some manner dispose the agent so that a more basic potentiality becomes more specific or perfected. That is, the specific abilities are in fact dispositions to exercise an already existing potentiality in a particular way. However, it is clear that not all abilities can be of this sort. Acquired dispositions presuppose more basic capacities, and ultimately there must be capacities which a thing has in virtue of the kind of being it is, that is, in virtue of its nature. And so each thing must have some basic potentialities not acquired by repeated action, but possessed as part of its nature. And these basic potentialities may require time to be actualized. Even so, since they are basic, natural capacities, the substantial entity will have them from the time it comes to be and will continue to have them for as long as it exists. This is true of unborn human beings and of infants, but it also is true of a human being with severe dementia, or in coma, or in so-called persistent vegetative state. They possess the basic capacities to reason and make free choices, but a defect in their brains – perhaps quite temporary – prevents the actualization of those capacities. Finally, this is true of severely retarded children and anencephalic infants.[3] Thus, unborn human beings, infants, comatose human beings, human beings with severe dementia, and other disabled human beings are all human persons.

II. The Human Individual Remains a Person during His or Her Whole Duration

One might grant that an unconscious or severely demented human being *is* the same individual who was intrinsically valuable a few weeks ago, but argue that this individual is no longer intrinsically valuable. One might express this thought by saying, "This is no longer a person." Notice that this argument is distinct from the last argument, even though either of these might sometimes be expressed by claiming that the individual "is (no longer) a person." However, one might mean that either the individual who was a person has ceased to be (the argument replied to in the last section) or the same individual has ceased to be intrinsically valuable, and, in that sense, has ceased to be a person. This second position will be examined in this section. Speaking of an advanced Alzheimer's victim, Ronald Dworkin says that,

... he is no longer capable of the acts or attachments that can give [life] value. Value cannot be poured into a life from the outside; it must be generated by the person whose life it is, and this is no longer possible for him.[4]

Could it be reasonable to say that *you* exist throughout a time, but that you have moral status and rights during only a certain portion of that time? A first difficulty can be expressed as follows. If a thing itself could continue to be but cease to be valuable as a subject of rights, then there would be no reason why a being could not have the property that qualifies him or her for personhood or moral worth (e.g., self-consciousness, in the sense of immediately exercisable self-consciousness), then lack that property, then have it again, and so on. Suppose human beings hibernated for one-month period every year. Would it not still be wrong to kill a human being during his or her hibernating periods? Clearly it would be. But severely demented human beings or human beings in a so-called

---

[3] On this point also see John Finnis, "The Philosophical Case against Euthanasia," in *Euthanasia Examined: Ethical, Legal and Clinical Perspectives*, ed. John Keown (New York: Cambridge University Press, 1995), 68–70.

[4] Ronald Dworkin, *Life's Dominion: An Argument about Abortion, Euthanasia, and Individual Freedom* (New York: Vintage Books, 1992), 230.

persistent vegetative state are in situations not significantly morally different from such human beings. They still are identical to the beings that at some point clearly do have intrinsic value.

As we argued in Chapter 4, Section III, human beings are intrinsically valuable as subjects of rights in virtue of what they are. Just as they cannot come to be and then acquire intrinsic value at a later time in their life, so they cannot continue to be but lose their intrinsic value as a subject of rights. To base the intrinsic value of a being on an accidental attribute – such as consciousness or the immediately exercisable capacity for consciousness – is to base a radical moral difference on a mere quantitative ontological difference. We treat beings who are subjects of rights radically differently from the way we treat other beings. The basis for that radical difference in treatment must be some radical difference in the different types of beings treated differently. Between any human being and a corpse or an aggregate of tissues and organs there *is* a radical difference. But the difference between a healthy, self-conscious human being and a human being incapacitated, even severely incapacitated, is only a difference in degree. It is unjust, then, to pick out such an accidental attribute as self-consciousness or the immediately exercisable capacity for self-consciousness and make that the criterion for whether someone should be treated as a subject of rights or not. Thus, a human being is valuable as a subject of rights in virtue of what he or she is (a person, a subject with the basic nature capacity for conceptual thought and free choice even if he or she cannot right now actualize that basic capacity). And so a human being remains a subject of rights, someone who has a right not to be intentionally killed, for as long as he or she exists.[5]

III. Why Suicide and Euthanasia Are Morally Wrong

There are various arguments against suicide and euthanasia. For example, one might argue that such acts violate God's dominion. Here, however, we will argue that the reason why suicide and euthanasia are wrong is that they are choices contrary to the intrinsic good of a human person. Such acts are contrary to the openness to the fulfillment of oneself and others, which is the standard (we maintain – see Chapter 2, Section III) for morality.[6]

---

[5] See further arguments for this point in Chapter 4.

[6] Some sources for this position: Robert P. George, *In Defense of Natural Law* (New York: Oxford University Press, 1999); Germain Grisez, Joseph Boyle, and John Finnis, "Practical Principles, Moral Truth and Ultimate Ends," *American Journal of Jurisprudence* 33 (1988),

As we argued in Chapter 2, the ultimate reasons for choice are not just arbitrary desires. Rather, the ultimate reasons for action, the objects desired for their own sake, are genuine fulfillments or objective perfections of both oneself and other persons. To apprehend a condition or activity as *really fulfilling* or *perfective* (of me and/or of others like me) is to recognize it as a fitting object of pursuit, that is, an object worth pursuing. The basic moral norm, we contend, is that we should choose fully in accord with the truth about what is really perfective or fulfilling for ourselves and other persons. To choose in a way that respects all of these human perfections, both in ourselves and in others, is to respect human persons and to choose morally well. To choose to act against a fundamental human good is to act against some intrinsic good of a human person. For, to make such a choice is to substitute one's own subjective preference for the objective standard provided by what is objectively fulfilling.

Human life itself is a fundamental human good (we defend this later, Section V). Thus, we ought to respect this good. But the choice to destroy a human life is contrary to respecting human life. And so we ought never to choose precisely to destroy a human life, whether of another person or our own. To do so is implicitly (and sometimes explicitly as well) to adopt the attitude that this human life is not objectively good, but is good only if I desire it. To choose to destroy one instance of a basic good for the sake of other instances of goods is to adopt the attitude that human goods, including human lives, are only conditionally good. It is to exclude from one's benevolence or appreciation an instance of intrinsic human good. It is, in effect, to adopt the attitude that it is not an intrinsic good.[7]

Thus, the choice to kill an innocent human life, whether one's own or another's, even for the sake of avoiding terrible suffering, is intrinsically immoral. Euthanasia and suicide are contrary to the intrinsic dignity of human persons.

99–151; John Finnis, Joseph M. Boyle, Jr., Germain Grisez, *Nuclear Deterrence, Morality and Realism* (Oxford and New York: Oxford University Press, 1987), Chapters 9–11; John Finnis, *Fundamentals of Ethics* (Washington, DC: Georgetown University Press, 1983); John Finnis, *Aquinas: Moral, Political, and Legal Theory* (New York: Oxford University Press, 1998); William E. May, *An Introduction to Moral Theology* (Huntington, IN: Our Sunday Visitor, 1994); T. D. J. Chappell, *Understanding Human Goods: A Theory of Ethics* (Edinburgh: Edinburgh University Press, 1998); Mark C. Murphy, *Natural Law and Practical Rationality* (New York: Cambridge University Press, 2001).

7 For arguments against the utilitarian or consequentialist attempt to justify direct killing, see Finnis, Boyle, and Grisez, op. cit., Chapter 9 and Patrick Lee, *Abortion and Unborn Human Life* (Washington, DC: Catholic University of America Press, 1996), Chapter 5.

IV. Intentional Killing versus Causing Death as a Side Effect

This does not mean, however, that we must always take all measures possible to preserve someone's life, our own included. While it is always morally wrong intentionally to kill a human person, it is sometimes morally right to choose not to use certain means to preserve someone's life, because of the burden of those means. For example, someone with cancer may choose not take a course of chemotherapy if doing so offers little or no chance of bringing complete recovery – it is quite expensive, and it would block spending time with one's family. Such a choice is not disrespectful of the basic good of life. Rather, it is a choice not to use certain means of extending life on the grounds that these means involve a diminishing of one or more basic goods, or on the grounds that adopting these means is incompatible with pursuing other goods (one's other responsibilities).

Such diminishing of basic goods is a side effect of what one does; it is not the same as choosing against a basic good, and it does not necessarily involve a lack of appreciation or commitment to those goods that are diminished (or destroyed) as a side effect. Indeed, some diminishing or destruction of basic goods as a side effect is strictly unavoidable. Every choice we make is a choice to pursue and enhance some goods and not others. Thus every choice we make involves a diminishing or at least a nonenhancing of some basic goods as a side effect of what we directly (intentionally) do.

On the other hand, a choice to kill a human life *is* incompatible with a love for that life: such a choice involves – as proponents of euthanasia themselves often openly testify – the judgment or attitude that some lives are not worth living, that some lives are mere means to some other condition, a denial of the intrinsic dignity of the person killed.

If one chooses to kill in order to end suffering, one sees (at least initially) that continuing to live does instantiate a human good, but that escaping pain would also instantiate a good.[8] To act *against* the first reason (as opposed simply to not acting on it), one must judge that the second reason (escaping pain) is preferable to it. But one can make such a judgment only on the supposition that the good offered by the second alternative (escape from pain) is of a higher order than the good offered by the first alternative

---

[8] Thus, Frances Kamm is correct when she argues that it is not incoherent to view such killing as bringing about a good, namely, the cessation of pain. (Cf. Frances Kamm, "A Right to Choose Death?" *Boston Review* (1998), reproduced on the Internet at http://bostonreview.mit.edu/BR22.3/Kamm.html.) However, it *is* unreasonable and immoral to choose the destruction of a basic good as a *means* toward realizing that good.

(human life). But it could be of a higher order only if human life were not a basic and intrinsic good. Thus, the choice to kill as a means toward escaping pain involves, at least implicitly, the attitude that human life is not a basic and intrinsic good.

One might object: life is a basic, intrinsic good, but it can be outweighed by the prospect of a greater good, such as relief from excruciating pain. However, how can one objectively measure that the worth of a human life is less than the relief from pain? Human life is an irreducible, basic human good (a point we defend in Section V). It is not a mere means to an ulterior or ends, and so death is the total and, from the natural standpoint, irreversible loss of an intrinsic and irreducible basic human good. Pain that cannot be relieved is a bad, but it is not the irreversible and total destruction of an intrinsic, basic good. It is only one's emotional reaction to the pain that moves one to judge, erroneously, that it is objectively worse than death. So, the judgment that one's life can be destroyed for the sake of some other good or to avoid such an evil is tacitly a judgment that this life does not have basic, intrinsic worth, and so it is a denigration of the basic good of life.

It has sometimes been objected that there is no morally significant difference between actively killing a dying person and letting him die.[9] Therefore (the argument continues), since everyone admits that it is sometimes morally right to let someone die (that is, choose not to use a lifesaving treatment), then it also is morally right in some cases to choose to kill a dying person. However, this argument is mistaken. If killing were the same as withholding or withdrawing lifesaving treatment, then *everything* we did other than lifesaving attempts would be cases of killing. For in every choice we make to pursue some good other than the saving of someone's life, we are doing something which has the side effect of not saving someone's life. If this objection were correct, then, as John Finnis points out, the choice to take one's children for a walk – thus passing up the opportunity to take a plane to Kolkata to save street children – would be as murderous as deliberately blanketing those same children with machine gun bullets.[10] We cannot actively pursue every aspect of every person's fulfillment all of the time, but we are morally required at least not to choose precisely to act *against* (that is, to destroy, damage, or impede) one instance of a basic

---

[9] For example, James Rachels, "Active and Passive Euthanasia," reprinted in several places, for example: *Social Ethics, Morality and Social Policy*, 5th ed., ed. Thomas A. Mappes and Jane S. Zembaty (New York: McGraw-Hill, 1997), 61–66.

[10] John Finnis, "Understanding the Case against Euthanasia," in *Euthanasia Examined*, 64–65.

good for the sake of others. The basic moral requirement is of a respect and appreciation for all the basic goods, both in ourselves and in others. Such respect and appreciation is incompatible with a choice to destroy one instance of a basic, intrinsic good for the sake of others.

It is important to see that the difference between intentionally killing and causing death as a side effect is not primarily a difference in physical behavior. The same physical behavior – for example, injecting a patient with morphine – might in one case be carrying out a choice to relieve pain with the side effect of hastening death, and in another case carry out a choice to kill in order to relieve pain. Although the external results are the same, there is a tremendous moral difference between the two choices.

Moreover, not-doing something – an omission – can in some cases be a way of intentionally killing someone. Clearly, if someone withholds needed insulin from his wife in order to end her life, he intends her death just as much as if he had deliberately dropped arsenic in her orange juice. Similarly, if a relatively nonburdensome lifesaving treatment is withheld or withdrawn, then the reason probably is that one wants the death – in this case the omission is the means chosen for the sake of the death.[11]

Of course, really causing death as a side effect is not always morally right either. How does one decide when it is? Frances Kamm has argued that everyone already admits that we may let someone die, *if doing so would be for the patient's overall benefit.* In other words, we sometimes make the judgment (according to Kamm) that, "in this particular case, the greater good for the patient is relief of pain, and the lesser evil is loss of life...."[12] But if that is so, she argues, it should also be morally right to kill the patient in order to bring about this greater good. I believe Kamm is right that *if* that were the basis for not adopting those means, then it would be inconsistent to say that letting die can be permissible but not the killing. However, contrary to what Kamm assumes, people often make such judgments (that they should withhold lifesaving treatment) on the basis of something other than the denial of the patient's intrinsic dignity (which is what the judgment that a patient would be better off dead amounts to). Think of a concrete case. The patient who foregoes chemotherapy does not usually say to himself, "The total consequences of living two months without chemo-therapy will be objectively better, overall, than all of the consequences of living six months with

[11] Unfortunately, this kind of thing seems to be done frequently to Down syndrome babies.
[12] Kamm, op. cit., 2.

chemo-therapy." No, there usually is no futile attempt to calculate what all of the consequences will be in the two different scenarios and measure them against one another. Rather, people usually make such a judgment on the basis of the belief that their responsibilities to family and others could best be carried out in one way rather than the other. The criterion for whether one should do something that causes bad side effects is not whether doing so will produce the greatest net good, since that is a judgment that cannot be objectively assessed, but whether doing so is just and consistent with all of one's responsibilities.[13]

V. Human Life Is an Intrinsic Good

Apart from such untenable dualism and unacceptable ethical presuppositions, it might still be asked: must one really maintain that biological life is an intrinsic good? One might grant that we are bodily beings, rational animal organisms, and that we remain persons until biological death. Still, might one not argue that biological life, at least just by itself, is not an intrinsic good deserving of respect? In other words: biological life (it might be argued) is good only if connected with other conditions and experiences such as consciousness. So, when biological life ceases to bring about, or to be accompanied by, these other conditions, then it ceases to be valuable. Need one really be a body–self dualist in order to hold that the biological life of a human being in a persistent vegetative state, for example, with no hope whatsoever of regaining consciousness, is not in itself valuable?

To reply, we must recall what makes a condition or activity intrinsically valuable. As we explained earlier, the basic reasons for action are the various forms of personal perfection or fulfillment (see Chapter 3, Section V). That is, what makes a condition or activity intrinsically valuable, worth pursuing for its own sake, is that it is *fulfilling*. But it makes no sense to

---

[13] Cf. Finnis, "The Philosophical Case against Euthanasia," in *Euthanasia Examined*, 23–34. Note also that the examples Kamm gives of cases where all of us seem to condone doing evil to achieve a good are *not* cases of choosing to destroy, damage, or impede a basic human good. When one amputates a limb for the sake of the individual life, the limb is not a basic human good. The parts of one's body are good just to the extent to which they, as parts, contribute to the good of the whole. If through some pathology they cease to be able to contribute to the survival or flourishing of the whole, then they are not good but instead are harmful. This, of course, is the traditional principle of totality. It says, not that one may do a small evil for the sake of avoiding a greater, but that the goodness of the part consists in its contribution to the whole. But a whole person is not a part.

hold that the fulfillment of an entity is intrinsically valuable, and yet the entity itself is not. The entity itself cannot be viewed as a mere instrumental good or as a mere condition for the fulfillment or perfection of that entity. Thus, my genuine good includes my *being* as well as my *full-being*.

Moreover, while it is true that an intrinsic *part* of myself can be viewed as in some way instrumentally valuable – my bodily parts are called "organs," which is from the Greek word for instrument – it is impossible actually to view my whole self as merely instrumental to another good or as only conditionally good. One must value, at least implicitly, one's own being or preservation as in itself good. So, to view one's whole biological life as merely instrumentally or merely conditionally valuable is indeed, though perhaps only implicitly, to identify oneself with something other than that living bodily entity. Thus, to deny that one's biological life is intrinsically good is, at least implicitly, to adopt a body–self dualism. But what I am is a living bodily entity and the thing which I am is intrinsically valuable, so it follows that this bodily entity itself is intrinsically valuable. To deny that is to denigrate one's bodily life, to demean one's bodily person. Suicide and euthanasia necessarily involve a denigration of the very thing which you and I are, our bodily lives. The choice of suicide or euthanasia unavoidably involves a denial of the intrinsic dignity of the human person.

Still, it might be objected that my individual biological life is intrinsically good *while I have a capacity for consciousness*, but that it ceases to be good if I lose that capacity. Indeed, it might be objected that in some cases it is actually an evil. Suppose my continuing to live involves such suffering that I judge that this kind of life is not good. According to Gary Seay, for example, killing someone who is suffering, immediately produces a good because: "... it is not difficult to imagine the case of a dying patient whose entire conscious experience is wholly consumed by physical suffering so excruciating that his life has *nothing at all good about it*" (emphasis in original) (such cases are, in fact, all too common).[14] However, if the badness of the experience is the reason why one views one's life as bad, then one is not actually viewing one's life as bad in itself or per se bad. If life really were viewed as per se bad, then it would be viewed as bad at all times. Rather, the thought expressed earlier is actually that the life is bad when it brings about bad experience. But this means that life is viewed

[14] Gary Seay, "Do Physicians Have an Inviolable Duty Not to Kill?" *The Journal of Medicine and Philosophy* 26 (2001), 78.

as in itself neutral, and good or bad according to whether it brings about good experience or bad experience.

Yet, what is valuable cannot be mere experience, but must be the reality of which one may, or may not, have an experience.[15] To make experience the criterion for the value or goodness of a thing is to put things backward. Rather, we should judge the quality of our experience on the basis of the goodness or badness of that of which it is an experience. Thus, for example, I may take pleasure in the downfall of my enemy, but such pleasure is not a good. The character of my pleasure derives from the character of its object, not vice versa (see Chapter 3).

Moreover, although suffering is not in itself good, focusing only on experience rather than the realities involved in a situation can make us blind to the real value that our living with suffering can have. Although we are not writing a theological work here, it is worth noting that Christians believe that suffering is not meaningless and that, indeed, all of us are called to join our suffering to the sufferings of Christ. This does not mean that, according to Christian belief, we should always actively seek suffering or that we should not try to remove it or avoid it when possible. But it does mean that one may view suffering as not the ultimate evil and one may have a developed view as to why *living with* suffering is not in itself evil. One of the worst effects of the euthanasia mentality is to suggest, and subtly to convince many people, that what is valuable is only the quality of one's experience, and therefore if one's experience is negative, one's existence itself is negative. On the contrary, a person's being and real fulfillment are genuine goods, and are not just mere means to pleasant experience.[16]

---

[15] On this point much of our culture is, indeed – and not just on the euthanasia issue – profoundly confused. Much of our culture is hedonistic.

[16] Kevin O'Rourke believes that prolonging the life of a person in a persistent vegetative state, say, by providing nutrition and hydration through a feeding tube, does not benefit him since the treatment does not enable him "to pursue the spiritual purpose of life." O'Rourke has advanced this argument in several places. See, for example, his "Should Nutrition and Hydration Be Provided to Permanently Unconscious and Other Mentally Disabled Persons?" *Issues in Law and Medicine* 5 (1989), 181–196 and, with Benedict Ashley, *Health Care Ethics*, 4th ed. (Washington, DC: Georgetown University Press, 1997), 421–426. On his view, since permanently unconscious patients are not enabled to pursue life's spiritual purpose, its ultimate end, providing them with artificial nutrition and hydration is futile; no intrinsic good is promoted by this action. This position, however, is implicitly based on a body–self dualism, an identification of the self with something purely spiritual. For it conceives the goal of human life as something purely spiritual. However, if an entity is a living bodily being – as we have shown earlier – then his bodily life must be an important constituent of his fulfillment. A human being is a body–soul

VI. The Definition of Death

One might object that, while it is wrong intentionally to cause the death of a person, the standard criterion of death is wrong and that, as a consequence, what is often described as euthanasia is actually not killing a person at all. The standard criterion of death today is total and irreversible cessation of the functioning of the entire brain (or, as an indication that total brain death has occurred, irreversible cessation of circulatory and respiratory functions). This criterion grew out of the report, in 1981, of the President's Commission for the Study of Ethical Problems in Medicine and Biomedical and Behavioral Research[17] and the Uniform Determination of Death Act, formulated by the National Conference of Commissioners on Uniform State Laws, which served as the model for numerous state laws. The key statement of that Act was as follows: "An individual who has sustained either (1) irreversible cessation of circulatory and respiratory functions, or (2) irreversible cessation of all functions of the entire brain, including the brain stem, is dead."

Given this criterion, several individuals who apparently will never have consciousness, or regain it – anencephalic infants, irreversibly comatose individuals, and individuals in "persistent vegetative state" – are classified as living persons and therefore cannot, morally or legally, be killed. If, instead, the correct criterion of death were permanent cessation of *higher brain* functions, then it would follow that often what appear to be human persons actually are not, and so what often appears to be euthanasia is not killing a person.

Some neurologists and bioethicists reject total brain death as the criterion of death and argue for a *higher* brain criterion of death. The lower brain (approximately, those parts of the brain other than the neocortex) is generally involved in the integrative function of the brain (integrating or modulating the systems of the organism) and the higher brain (approximately, the neocortex) is generally involved in the capacities for consciousness, thought, and feeling. According to the higher brain criterion, the irreversible cessation of functioning of the higher brain causes irreversible loss of the capacity for consciousness, feeling, and conceptual thought. And, it is argued, since one must have these characteristics to be

composite, not just a soul, and so his bodily life and health is a constituent *part* of the achievement of his purpose and so is intrinsically good, not just a means toward other goods.

[17] This is reprinted in John D. Arras and Bonnie Steinbock, eds., *Ethical Issues in Modern Medicine*, 4th ed. (Mountain View, CA: Mayfield, 1995), 144–153.

a person, the irreversible cessation of function of the higher brain means that the *person* has died, even if perhaps the human *organism* continues to live.[18]

Let us first note that this move would change not just the *criterion* of death, but its *definition*. It is customary to distinguish between a definition of death, a criterion of death, and clinical tests. A *definition* of death is an expression of what it is – for example, as cessation of the integration of the organism or as the irreversible loss of personal characteristics, such as consciousness. A *criterion* of death is a detectable state of affairs that indicates that death – the ceasing to be of the human being or person – has occurred. A clinical *test* is some clinical or medical procedure to determine that the criterion of death has occurred. For example, clinical tests might include an EEG, tests to determine whether there is pupillary response, whether eye movements are elicited by vestibule-ocular reflex or by irrigating ears with cold water, whether there are corneal and gag reflexes, tests to check facial or tongue movement, and apnea tests (this is not a complete list).

Some neurologists and bioethicists argue that a human organism may suffer total (and irreversible) brain death but still survive, still live as a bodily, human being and a human person. Such thinkers agree on the definition of death – they agree that human beings are organisms, and that death is the irreversible cessation of integrative function of the body – but disagree on the empirical question of what biological criteria indicate that such loss of integration has occurred. However, the proposal to move to a higher brain death criterion involves a different definition of death as well as a disagreement about what a human person is.

But this proposal (to adopt a higher brain death criterion of death) mistakenly identifies the person with something other than the human organism. Proponents of this criterion concede that a human organism can continue to live after the higher brain (basically, the cerebral cortex) has irreversibly ceased to function. Yet they claim that the *person* has died. But we have shown that the human person is identical with the human organism that comes to be at conception; by the same token, the human person does not die until the human organism that he or she *is* dies. A human being in a coma is a disabled human person. The same is true for the human being who is in a so-called persistent vegetative state or a human being with anencephaly. It is clear that the numerically singular life

---

[18] See, for example, Karen Grandstrand Gervais, "Advancing the Definition of Death," in *Ethical Issues in Modern Medicine*, 155.

of the human organism continues uninterrupted, albeit severely disabled, before, during, and after he or she suffers severe brain damage resulting in coma or a "vegetative state." Thus, this argument for the higher brain criterion rests on the mistaken assumption – refuted earlier in Chapter 1 – that the human person is a consciousness or spirit which *has* or *inhabits* an organism.

However, one might object that, while the human person is a human organism, an entity is a human organism only if it (he or she) has a cerebral cortex capable of functioning and thus capable of being the substrate of thought. Severe brain damage causing permanent cessation of higher brain function (the objection continues) would cause a substantial change, that is, the ceasing to be of the human substance, and its replacement by a material substance of a different and lower kind.[19] However, when a material organism ceases to be, then the components that were *virtually* present in it – as parts of a whole rather than as actual, whole entities – become actual, whole entities. For example, the dying of a tree results in the actual existence of a multitude of lower level entities (perhaps cells), which were formerly only parts of the actual substantial whole. The death of an organism (or the ceasing to be of any substantial entity) is a breakdown or loss of unity. Hence, unless it is consumed or absorbed by a distinct substance, the death of an organism results in a *multitude* of lower level substantial entities. If a human being dies, then what it changes into (the corpse) is a multitude of substantial entities whereas before death cells and tissues were only parts of the whole. Thus, when a human being loses his immediate capacity for consciousness (and conceptual thought and free choice) such a loss is not his demise; rather the human being, the living substantial entity that is numerically identical with the living substantial entity which before had consciousness, reasoning, and free choice, continues to be, but suffers severe damage and acquires a severe disability.[20]

VII. The Criterion of Death

Several objections have been advanced against total brain death as the criterion for death. One objection is that the standard clinical tests often fail

---

[19] This seems to be the proposal of Julius Korein and Calixto Machado, "Brain Death: Updating a Valid Concept for 2004," in *Brain Death and Disorders of Consciousness*, ed. Calixto Machado and D. Alan Shewmon (Kluwer Academic/Plenum Publishers, 2004), 1–14.

[20] On this point also see: Jason Eberl, "A Thomistic Understanding of Human Death, *Bioethics* 19 (2005), 29–48.

to detect present brain functioning (even that above the level of activities of pockets of cells). More than a decade ago it was reported that some patients who passed standard clinical tests nevertheless later showed evidence of neurohormonal functioning (posterior pituitary function), and even cortical functioning.[21]

The most serious case against the criterion of total brain death has been presented by D. Alan Shewmon in the last decade. Shewmon has argued that many individuals who have suffered total and irreversible brain death have nevertheless survived, as shown by the fact that after total brain death they nevertheless performed actions which can only be attributed to the organism as a whole, and so total brain death does not necessarily result in the death of the whole human organism. Shewmon asserts that brain-dead patients have performed not only the organic actions of respiration and nutrition, but a long list of actions that they can perform must be attributed to the organism as a whole.[22]

Indeed, Shewmon and others have presented evidence to show that a brain-dead individual, "T. K.," continued to live, performing various integrative functions (including maturation to adulthood) for over twenty years – though ventilator-dependent and assisted by a feeding tube. The evidence that this individual has indeed suffered total brain death seems decisive. In 1998, while T. K. was still alive Shewmon reported that:

Cerebral edema was so extreme that the cranial sutures split. Multiple EEGs have been isoelectric, and no spontaneous respirations or brainstem reflexes have been observed over the past 14½ years. Multimodality evoke potential revealed

---

[21] Amir Halevy and Baruch Brody, "Brain Death: Reconciling Definitions, Criteria, and Tests," *Annals of Internal Medicine* 119 (1993), 519–525. Also see Robert M. Veatch, "Brain Death and Slippery Slopes," *Journal of Clinical Ethics* 3 (1992); Stewart J. Youngner, "Defining Death: A Superficial and Fragile Consensus," *Archives of Neurology* 49 (1992) 570–572.

[22] The actions included in Shewmon's list are homeostasis of a variety of mutually interacting chemicals, macromolecules, and physiological parameters (through the functions especially of liver, kidneys, cardiovascular and endocrine systems, but also of other organs and tissues), elimination, detoxification, and recycling of cellular wastes throughout the body, energy balance (involving interactions among liver, endocrine system, muscle, and fat), maintenance of body temperature (albeit at a lower than normal level), wound healing, fighting of infections and foreign bodies (through interactions among the immune system, lymphatics, bone marrow, and microvasculature), development of febrile responses to infection, successful gestation of a fetus in a brain-dead woman, and in one case, sexual maturation of a brain-dead child (and others). See D. Alan Shewmon, "The Brain and Somatic Integration: Insights into the Standard Biological Rationale for Equating 'Brain Death' with Death," *The Journal of Medicine and Philosophy* 26 (2001), 457–478, at 467–468.

no intracranial peaks, magnetic resonance angiography disclosed no intracranial blood flow, and neuroimaging showed the entire cranial cavity to be filled with disorganized membranes, proteinaceous fluids, and ghost-like outlines of the former brain.[23]

In 2006, T. K. died and a brain autopsy was performed. The pathologists and physicians who performed the autopsy and analyzed its results reported that the autopsy confirmed that the brain (including the brain stem) had indeed been completely destroyed. They concluded that:

Our pathologic findings at autopsy confirmed that his brain had been destroyed by the events associated with the episode of H influenzae type b meningitis, whereas his body remained alive (brain dead with living body) for an additional two decades, a duration of survival following brain death that far exceeds that of any other reports.[24]

Thus, Shewmon argues that counterexamples show that brain death does not necessarily constitute the death of the human individual.

Moreover, according to Shewmon, the brain is not, as was previously thought, the actual *integrator* of the various systems of the body, but is the modulator of a somatic integrative unity that is *already* present.[25] The unity of the human organism is "an inherently nonlocalizable, holistic feature involving the mutual interaction among all the parts,"[26] rather than the result of a single organ, such as the brain.

A neurologist might reply that in these cases of what appear to be the survival of human individuals – whole organisms that have survived brain death – what actually has occurred is that various groups of tissues and organs have been kept alive artificially. Perhaps it is not clear what aspects of bodily coordination or integration are sufficient to indicate that a whole human organism has survived. Thus, some neurologists question whether the actions observed in these cases can only be attributed to the organism as a whole rather than to cells or smaller sets of cells and tissues.

So, there is dispute among neurologists about the brain death criterion. We believe Shewmon has presented a strong case. Nevertheless, since

---

[23] D. Alan Shewmon, "Brainstem Death', 'Brain Death' and Death: A Critical Re-Evaluation of the Purported Equivalence," *Issues in Law and Medicine* 14 (1998), 125–145; D. Alan Shewmon, "Chronic 'Brain Death': Meta-Analysis and Conceptual Consequences," *Neurology* 51 (1998), 1538–1545.

[24] Susan Repertinger, William P. Fitzgibbons, Mathew F. Omojola, and Roger A. Brumback, "Long Survival Following Bacterial Meningitis-Associated Brain Destruction," *Journal of Child Neurology* 21 (July 2006), 591–595, at 595.

[25] Ibid., at 460ff.

[26] Ibid., 457.

(it seems) the majority of neurologists are still not convinced that an individual can actually survive (or actually has survived) brain death, we ourselves are not certain which side is correct. What is of central concern to the thesis of this book is this: even if the whole brain death *criterion* did turn out to be mistaken, the *definition* of death – an important part of the rationale behind that criterion – is certainly correct. The rationale for the criterion of whole brain death was that the human individual is a specific type of organism, and therefore he or she is alive for as long as the organism that he or she is continues to exist. Whole brain death is still thought by most neurologists to indicate that the human being has died because it is thought that the brain is the primary and necessary organizer of the tissues and organs into a single organism, and so, absent the function of the brain, there no longer is a single organism, but only an aggregate of organs and tissues. The empirical point (that a primary material organizer is needed, and at this stage of life it is the brain) is open to question. But the proposition that the person dies only with the cessation of the integrated functioning of the organism as a whole is on firm ground. As the President's 1981 Commission on Brain Death indicated, to move to a higher brain death criterion for the death of the person would substitute a new, and incorrect, *definition* of death for the traditional and sound one.[27] Thus, if one rejects the whole brain death criterion, this in

---

[27] Another serious problem for the higher brain death criterion is that it rests on the assumption that destruction of the neocortex necessarily means the permanent cessation of consciousness. But there also seem to be counterexamples to this assumption. D. Alan Shewmon reports several cases where children without neocortical functioning nevertheless are obviously conscious. "For some decades the assumption has prevailed that cortical function is absolutely necessary for consciousness, in terms both of adaptive interaction with the environment . . . and inner awareness of self and environment. . . . But this is more a dogma of neurological faith than a scientifically established fact." D. Alan Shewmon, "The ABC's of PVS: Problems of Definition," in *Brain Death and Disorders of Consciousness*, 217. Shewmon cites cases in which children without cortical function (as established by standard tests) clearly indicate signs of consciousness. For example: "The first was a girl with hydranencephaly, examined at age 13 years. The diagnosis [of neo-cortical death or apallia] was reliably established by the combination of classical findings on computed tomography (CT), and isoelectric electroencephalogram (EEG), and even a 'brain' biopsy revealing only meninges and a thin layer of gliotic tissue devoid of neurons. A more dramatic case of 'apallia' would be hard to imagine. Nevertheless, she manifested discriminative awareness of the environment, for example, consistently distinguishing close family members from others. . . . She had favorite pieces and types of music, to which she would consistently smile and vocalize, in contrast to other music, to which she consistently remained indifferent. On 'good days' she manifested visual tracking" (Ibid., 217).

no way implies the need for a new definition of death. The standard *definition* of death – the irreversible cessation of the integrated functioning of the organism as a whole – remains valid. If the brain death criterion is incorrect, then Shewmon's circulatory–respiratory criterion[28] appears to be the only valid alternative, but that would leave intact the definition of death as the irreversible loss of integrative function of the organism as a whole.

It is important to note, however, that even if Shewmon and others are right, and brain death is not (always) an indication that death has occurred, this would not preclude organ transplantation (as Shewmon himself indicates). A variant of the Pittsburgh non-heart-beating donor protocol is ethically sound. Suppose someone has signed a DNR (a "Do Not Rescuscitate" order – and independently of the decision to donate a heart) and he suffers asystole. After a short period (two or three minutes, provided other circumstances) one can be sure that his heart would not restart on its own. One would be able to restart it, perhaps, but the patient has signed a DNR and so members of the hospital staff are not going to do so. In such a situation, even if the patient is still alive, extracting his organs (perhaps including his heart, if it is viable) will not hasten his death. Here death is not intended, either as an end or as a means. Not only that, one does not even cause or hasten the patient's death as a side effect; one does not cause or hasten his death at all (whether the correct criterion of death is total brain death or irreversible cardiopulmonary cessation).[29]

VIII. Human Life and Dignity

Perhaps the most popular argument on behalf of euthanasia or suicide is that there are various conditions that make continuing to live a severe

[28] The circulatory–respiratory criterion should not be confused with the older cardiopulmonary criterion. The cardiopulmonary criterion referred only to the operations of the heart and lungs. The circulatory–respiratory criterion is based on the idea that, as Shewmon puts it, "What is of the essence of integrative unity is neither localized nor replaceable – namely the anti-entropic mutual interaction of all the cells and tissues of the body, *mediated in mammals by circulating oxygenated blood*" (emphasis added; Shewmon, "The Brain and Somatic Integration,", 476).

[29] This is basically the Pittsburgh protocol, but on that protocol the patient is declared dead – though tests have not been performed to determine brain death (these would require a longer period than the two minutes, presently waited on the Pittsburgh protocol). We believe this procedure is ethically correct. The important point is that the extraction of the organs does not hasten death.

*in*dignity, and therefore in choosing to kill, one is not choosing to destroy what retains intrinsic value. "Granted," the argument could be made, "one ought not to kill any person whose life retains dignity or intrinsic worth. Still, to live as a vegetable, or as severely demented, or as completely dependent on others and burdensome to them – to continue to have biological life but without *meaningful life* – is a fate worse than death. To kill oneself in such a situation is not to choose to destroy something that preserves intrinsic value or dignity since one's dignity has already been lost." Indeed in certain cases, it is argued, life is the evil and death the good. Dworkin claims: "Just as Justice Rehnquist was wrong to assume that there is no harm in a patient's living on as a vegetable, so it would be wrong to assume that there is no harm in living on demented."[30]

A variant of this argument – usually not clearly stated – is that there are two types of death: death *with* dignity and death *without* dignity. The proponent of this argument may or may not grant that death itself is bad, but the argument is that death without dignity is *much worse* than death with dignity, and it is morally upright to pursue the latter and avoid the former.

To understand where these arguments go wrong, we must uncover what is meant by "dignity." As a beginning, we can agree on examples of dignity and indignities. We all would agree, for example, that being in a hospital with little privacy, almost completely dependent on others, without control over one's bowels or feeding, is, in some sense, to suffer *in*dignities, or in some way to lose dignity. On the other hand, we are apt to refer to an elderly person who maintains a healthy routine and calmly visits her relatives as "dignified," or as exhibiting "dignity."[31]

Dignity, however, is not a distinct property, a quality one might know by intuition. Though there are different types of dignity, in each case the word refers to a property or properties – different ones in different circumstances – that cause one to *excel* and thus elicit or merit respect from others. There are four types of real dignity, plus a *sense of*, or *awareness of*, dignity, that must be distinguished. First, in aristocratic countries (and even to a certain extent in our own) those of a higher class have a certain dignity not possessed by persons in lower classes. Thus, the loss of a job or the loss of financial status can harm one's dignity in this sense.

---

[30] Dworkin, op. cit., 232.
[31] See Germain Grisez and Joseph Boyle, *Life and Death with Liberty and Justice: A Contribution to the Euthanasia Debate* (Notre Dame, IN: University of Notre Dame Press, 1979), 179–182.

Second, and of greatest interest to us here, there is the dignity of a person or personal dignity. The dignity of a person, whatever that consists in, is that whereby a person excels other beings, especially other animals, and merits respect or consideration from other persons. As we argued in Chapter 2, what distinguishes us from other animals, what makes us persons rather than things, is our capacity to shape our own lives, our capacity for rationality and free choice. And, as we also explained in Chapter 2, the capacities to reason and make free choices are basic, natural capacities, possessed by every human being, even those who cannot immediately exercise these capacities. Dignity in this sense derives from the kind of substantial entity one is, a human being – and this is dignity in the most important sense. Because it is based on the kind of being one is, one cannot lose this dignity as long as one exists.

A third type of dignity is dignity *in action or choice* (though this may overlap with the manifestation of dignity, it is at least conceptually distinct). Thus, one can distinguish between *having* dignity and *acting with* dignity.[32] Acting with dignity is an action or choice that manifests an underlying dignity; the action itself also is dignified, in the sense that it excels other types of action and being acted upon. Of course, one speaks of dignified action usually in the moral sense of excellence. Thus, one can make choices and live one's life in a dignified manner in relation to severe suffering and indignities (of other types).[33] Christians look to the passion and death of Jesus as ways in which a man bore sufferings and indignities in a courageous manner, and thus showed great dignity in action amidst suffering indignities.

Fourth, there is a type of dignity that varies in degrees, which is the *manifestation* or *actualization* of those capacities that distinguish us from other animals. Thus, slipping on a banana peel (being reduced for a moment to a passive object) and losing one's independence and privacy

---

[32] On this distinction, see Michael J. Meyer, "Dignity, Death and Modern Virtue," *American Philosophical Quarterly* 32 (1995), 45–56.

[33] It is worth noting that dignity as independence and control is only relative. All people are dependent on others for the attainment of their ends. Moreover, as Jyl Gentzler points out: "For the majority, though, who are very young, elderly, unhealthy, or disabled, the fact of their dependency and neediness is more obvious [than that of most of us in affluent countries], since they need additional help in order to have their needs met in a world designed to assist others. But this fact about the design of our social world has no *direct* bearing on the value of the lives of different sorts of human beings" (Jyl Gentzler, "What is a Death with Dignity?" *The Journal of Medicine and Philosophy* 28 (2003), 461–487, at 468).

(especially as regards our baser functions) are events that detract from our dignity in this sense. However, note that while this dignity seems to be harmed by various situations, it never seems to be completely removed. Moreover, this dignity, which varies in degrees, is distinct from the more basic dignity that derives from the kind of substantial entity one is.

In addition to the different types of real dignity, it is important to distinguish one's sense of dignity. Something may harm one's *sense of* dignity without removing one's real dignity. Everyone who becomes dependent on others *feels* a certain loss of dignity. Yet their dignity, in either of the first three of the four senses of dignity distinguished, may not have been harmed at all. Often one's sense of dignity can be at variance with one's real dignity (in all of the first three senses). Those who are sick and who bear their suffering in a courageous or holy manner, often inspire others even though they themselves may feel a loss of dignity. In other words, not only must basic personal dignity be distinguished from secondary or manifested dignity, but dignity in both these senses must be distinguished from felt or sensed dignity.

So, replying to the argument based on the concept of dignity, we must remember the distinction between different types of dignity and the distinction between these and a *sense* or *feeling* of dignity. In truth, every human being has a basic real dignity based simply on being a person – that whereby he excels other animals and has in him what makes him deserving of respect and consideration from all other persons. It is precisely this truth that is at stake in the debate about suicide and euthanasia.

There are conditions that harm our dignity in the fourth sense discussed earlier (the manifestation of our more basic dignity) – conditions such as being dependent on others, loss of privacy, preoccupation with pain. These conditions are certainly bad. None of us desires to be in these conditions, and we should work to remove or alleviate such conditions in sick and elderly people as much as possible. But that does not mean that it would be right to kill someone (or oneself) to prevent those indignities. First, death itself is bad, the destruction of an intrinsic good. So, to choose death to avoid indignities (in the sense of loss of independence, which is the *manifestation* of an underlying dignity) is to act against what has basic, intrinsic dignity for the sake of an ulterior end. But the end does not justify the means. Second, the very act of killing a person with the supposed justification that the one killed has lost his dignity, or is about to lose his dignity, denies the *intrinsic personal* dignity of the one killed. And so it is contrary to dignity in action.[34]

No one wants to die without dignity. But we do not really want to die now *with* dignity either.[35] Death itself is never a dignity – it is, in a way, the supreme indignity. We may bear suffering and death well, and whether we do so depends, in part, on whether we continue to treat ourselves as well as others as persons with intrinsic dignity; that is, persons who have dignity simply because they are persons. Thus, the argument that death without dignity is much worse than death with dignity and therefore it is permissible to seek the latter to avoid the former, confuses the process of dying (which may or may not be accompanied by some of the indignities in the senses we have described) with death itself, which is an indignity (not a moral indignity, but a destruction, a loss).

Finally, another way of construing death as in some cases actually in itself good and life evil has been proposed. Ronald Dworkin has argued that one may view life as a work of art or drama that one composes, and death as its boundary. The boundaries of a work of art help make it what it is, that is, contribute to its beauty and unique statement. Analogously, Dworkin argues that in some cases death is good because it is the way one chooses to end one's life:

We should distinguish between two different ways in which it [i.e., death] might matter: because death is the far boundary of life, and every part of our life, including the very last, is important; and because death is special, a peculiarly significant event in the narrative of our lives, like the final scene of a play, with everything about it intensified, under a special spotlight.[36]

It is worth noting that if this argument worked, it would justify suicide and not, we think, any other kind of euthanasia. Moreover, it would also justify suicide for many reasons other than to escape suffering or pain.

To reply to this remarkable claim, several things must be noted. The analogy or metaphor of life as a work of art should not be left at the vague level. The analogy is helpful in many ways. It helps to emphasize

---

[34] It is worth remembering here that there is a distinction between death and the process of dying. The process of dying may in many ways assault our dignity, in the sense of its manifestation, but it is not a loss of one's basic dignity as a person and it need not involve a loss of dignity in action. It must be conceded that death itself, since it is one's ceasing to be or destruction, is a loss of dignity. But that argues *against* hastening death, not for it.

[35] Grisez and Boyle op. cit., 179.

[36] Ibid., 209.

how one should see one's life as in part constituted by one's choices, and it helps to emphasize the importance of trying to organize one's life and of viewing it in its unity. Still, the respects in which the analogy fails, that is, the respects in which life is *not* like a work of art, should also be noticed. Most importantly: in a work of art the entire composition (though not the natures of all of the components) is within the artist's control; every aspect of the work of art is there only because of the will of the artist. Not so in human life: there are aspects of human life that inevitably have their structure and constitution prior to devising by human will. We do constitute our characters by our choices, but we do not constitute other aspects of our being by our choice. Specifically, our biological and intellectual components have the structures they have, to a very great extent, independently of our will, and so they cannot be compared very well to works of art. (Even the aspect of us which we do constitute by our choices, our moral character, is not exactly like art – in that art is an external product produced by external actions, while our character is internal and constituted by interior acts of will.) Thus, the goodness or badness of the biological and intellectual dimensions of ourselves is not constituted by our designing or shaping them. Human life (including health) and knowledge of truth are in themselves good prior to their being pursued by choice, and their structures are not directly subject to free or artistic design. Failure to understand these points perhaps explains in part the initial appeal of arguments like Dworkin's.

However, the most important point is that, the death itself is simply not an artistic product. There may be various desirable effects of the death; for example, its timing may be more or less apt for various reasons. But the death itself is the destruction of a life.

One's own death itself is plainly not an act that one performs. That is, although one can perform the act of choosing to kill, and one can do something that causes one's death, one's actual death is something that, whether one wishes it or not, occurs to a human being rather than an action one performs. This is because it is a *ceasing to be*, not the actualization of any potentiality that one possesses. Therefore, death as such is the privation of the life of an organism, and so the death itself is in no way a good. There could be aesthetic *effects* of one's dying or there could be a certain appropriateness about when one dies, but these are in reality distinct from the death itself. One might as well face it: death itself *is* an indignity.[37] It is an indignity because it is the destruction of that

---

[37] Cf. Grisez and Boyle, op. cit., 179–182.

which has intrinsic dignity, the dignity of a person. In some ways it is the supreme indignity – the point at which lower forces finally submerge the life of a person.[38] That being so, the object of choice in a suicide adopted as a means toward making one's "life as a whole" more apt in some way (though how it does so is obscure, to say the least) remains the destruction of one's life. Hence such a choice is morally wrong.

[38] The human *soul* continues to exist after death, and as Christians we believe there will be a resurrection of the body. However, the human soul is not the whole person, and so death itself is the destruction of a person. These points can be denied only by denying that a human person is essentially a body–soul composite, a rational animal.

6

Sex and the Body

No one doubts that dualism has often influenced views of sexual morality. Platonists, for example, have sometimes viewed sexual activity as inherently bad, since in their view it lowered the spirit, which is the true self, to a preoccupation for the merely bodily. On the other hand, dualism has often led to a somewhat opposite view, namely, sexual libertinism. For, if the self is a spirit, or a consciousness, and the body is outside the self, then bodily sexual activities may be viewed as rather unimportant – useful perhaps to obtain pleasure (viewed as an effect in one's consciousness), to relieve tension, or so on. If one's body, or one's animality, is viewed as extrinsic to what one really is, then one might also conclude that what happens within the realm of the bodily or animal is of itself quite irrelevant to what occurs to one's real self. Perhaps the sexual may *receive* some important significance or meaning, but – if the self is a pure consciousness – it does not have within its nature, or inherently, any significance or value.

We believe that such views are more commonplace than one might first expect. Indeed, in our judgment, keeping firmly in mind that the human person is bodily, and not just a consciousness possessing or inhabiting a body, is a key to understanding the basic issues in sexual ethics. We will distinguish between contemporary forms of sexual libertinism and contemporary forms of sexual liberalism, but we will show that each, in its own way, implicitly views the self as a pure consciousness and the body, or the animality of the human person, as a mere extrinsic tool. We will then show that the traditional view of sexual activity – that sexual activity is morally right only within marriage, and as open to new life and embodying marital commitment – is the only view consistent with the bodily nature of the human person. Understanding this will enable one to see why nonmarital sexual acts (including homosexual acts) are intrinsically incapable of actualizing or promoting a genuine human good. Indeed, we shall argue that such nonmarital sexual acts are always and in principle contrary to intrinsic personal goods (self-integration and marriage) and as such harm the character of those freely choosing to engage in them.

It is often assumed in treatments of sexual ethics that the central argument from natural law theory against nonmarital sexual acts is simply that such acts are unnatural, that is, contrary to the direction inscribed in the reproductive or procreative power. This argument, which used to be described as "the perverted faculty argument," is easily disposed of.[1] It is then assumed that only prejudice motivates the conviction that the acts mentioned earlier are morally wrong.[2]

Some contemporary natural law theorists, however, have articulated much more powerful arguments in sexual ethics. In this chapter we present a natural law argument for the proposition that sexual acts are morally right only within marriage – an argument first developed in detail by Germain Grisez[3] and subsequently presented by others influenced by his thought[4] – and we show that nonmarital sexual acts, and academic defenses of them, inevitably involve, at least implicitly, a dualistic view of the self.

---

[1] It is not clear, for example, that acting against the orientation of a biological power (including the sexual power) is necessarily wrong, nor is it clear that all of the acts mentioned earlier are really *contrary* to that direction (instead of being outside it.) It is worth noting that among the recent natural law theorists who have developed new arguments in sexual ethics, one would have to include Pope John Paul II. Cf. *Familiaris Consortio*, Pt. III. At *Veritatis Splendor* (*The Splendor of Truth*), #48, the pope specifically rejects the sort of argument just mentioned. On the pope's position here: Patrick Lee, "The Human Body and Sexuality in the Teaching of Pope John Paul II," in *John Paul II's Contribution to Catholic Bioethics*, ed. Christopher Tollfsen (The Netherlands: Kluwer Academic Publishers, 2004), 107–120.

[2] See, for example, Andrew Sullivan, *Virtually Normal: An Argument about Homosexuality* (New York: Alfred Knopf, 1995), 19–55; id., *The Conservative Soul* (New York: Harper, 2006), 76–99.

[3] Germain G. Grisez, *The Way of the Lord Jesus, Volume 2: Living a Christian Life* (Quincy, IL: Franciscan Press, 1993), 633–656.

[4] For example, John Finnis, "Law, Morality, and 'Sexual Orientation'," *Notre Dame Journal of Law, Ethics and Public Policy* 9 (1995): 11–39; id., "The Good of Marriage and the Morality of Sexual Relations: Some Philosophical and Historical Observations," *American Journal of Jurisprudence* 42 (1997), 97–134; Robert P. George and Gerard V. Bradley, "Marriage and the Liberal Imagination," *Georgetown Law Review* 84 (1995), 301–320. Much of the present chapter appeared in the following article (though we develop the argument here and reply to recent objections): Patrick Lee and Robert P. George, "What Sex Can Be: Self-Alienation, Illusion, or One-Flesh Union," *American Journal of Jurisprudence* 42 (1997), 135–157.

The argument we propose centers on the choice to engage in a non-marital sexual act and the relationship between this choice and what is genuinely fulfilling for the persons involved in that act. We argue that in order for a choice to engage in sex to be respectful of the basic, intrinsic goods of persons, this choice must (1) respect the integration of sexuality of the person with the person as a whole, and thus respect the basic good of marriage, and (2) constitute a choice to participate in the real and basic good of marital union, rather than to induce in oneself and one's partner(s) a merely illusory experience of interpersonal unity. We shall argue that chaste marital intercourse[5] is really and literally lovemaking and that it really consummates or renews the marriage, that is, the two-in-one-flesh unity of a man and a woman. And we shall argue that if sexual acts do not consummate or renew marriage, they either involve self-alienation (and so violate the first requirement) or constitute the pursuit of a merely illusory experience (and so violate the second requirement). Either way, they involve a diminishing of respect for the good of marriage. So, if our view is right, sex offers a unique and profound human possibility, a possibility denied, incidentally, by liberationists who claim to have a more enlightened and appreciative view of sex. At the same time, the abuse of sex is a degradation of persons and a denigration of the bodily or animal aspect of the self.

The central question in sexual ethics is, under what conditions is a sexual act morally right? There are, basically, three positions contending for dominance in the contemporary debate. First, some hold the "liberationist" position that as long as no other, more general moral norms are violated, such as those prohibiting lying, deception, and exploitation, sexual acts are morally good (or, at least, innocent), since they are pleasurable. Second, others adopt the "liberal" view that sexual acts between people are morally right as long as they in some way express genuine love or affection; the relationship such acts symbolize or express, on this view, need not be marital. Third, the position we shall argue for is the "traditional" view, that to be morally right, sexual acts must embody or actualize marital union. In Section I, we set out the traditional view of marriage and explain how in marriage sexual acts initiate or renew marital communion. In Section II, we criticize the liberationist position. In Section III, we criticize the liberal position. In Section IV we reply to objections. And in Section V, we argue that only the traditional position

---

[5] By "chaste" marital intercourse is meant marital intercourse that is done with mutual respect and the right intentions.

can give a plausible account of why incest, pedophilia, bestiality, sex with multiple partners, and so on, are morally wrong.

I. Sex and Marriage

In our judgment, the key to understanding the relationship between sexual ethics and the body is first to see how sexual acts realize a basic value within marriage. But to consider that question we must first examine (in a general way) what marriage is.

There are three main views of marriage. First, some thinkers have held that marriage is an institution which is defined by its instrumental relation to procreation.[6] On this view, marriage is essentially a contractual union, and its extrinsic purpose is the conceiving and rearing of children. Proponents of this view usually hold that marriage should also, ideally, involve a friendship between the husband and wife. Marital union involves an agreement concerning acts of sexual intercourse, and sexual intercourse within marriage is conceived not only as serving procreation, but also, secondarily, as symbolizing the marital friendship. Still, the relationship between husband and wife is conceived as *in itself* nonbodily, and sexual intercourse is viewed as extrinsic (an extrinsic means) to procreation (or, failing that, to marital friendship).

A second view, certainly more popular these days, is that marriage is essentially a friendship, procreation is an extrinsic addition to that relationship, and sexual acts are extrinsic symbols or expressions of love or of the couple's personal communion. On this view there is no *intrinsic* or *essential* relationship between marriage and procreation. A couple may wish to have children, and having children may even be viewed as contributing to their marital relationship. But procreation is not viewed as intrinsically linked with marriage. As a consequence, on this view there is no reason why "marriage" should refer only to man–woman relationships, or, to express the same point differently, why (if this view is consistently worked out, which is not always the case) there is any morally significant difference between homosexual and heterosexual relationships.

The third view of marriage, the traditional view, is the one we propose. On this view, marriage is the community formed by a man and a woman who publicly consent to share their whole lives, in a type of relationship

---

[6] In *De Bono Coniugali* St. Augustine held explicitly that marriage is an instrumental good. He added, however, that ideally there should be a friendship between husband and wife, and that this friendship is intrinsically good: St. Augustine, *De Bono Coniugali*, 9.9.

oriented toward begetting, nurturing, and educating of children together. This community is naturally oriented to procreation, and is naturally fulfilled by it, though it also is good in itself and not a mere means to procreation.

Every society has some way or regulations for determining the ways and the contexts in which children come to be and are raised. This is a necessity. For, it is both desirable and inevitable that children will come to be. The question for society and for people who engage in acts (sexual acts) by which children might come to be is the following. What should society and those who engage in such acts do to provide a suitable environment in which children might come to be and flourish? That is, what must society and those in society who engage in sexual acts do in order to be fair to the children who will come to be through sexual acts?

The answer is that those couples who perform sexual acts should first form a community that will be dedicated to the raising and educating of children who might come to be. State-run organizations, business enterprises, even communes (groups composed of sexual partners) are not the groups most suitable for the raising and educating of children.[7] In virtually every society it is recognized that the best arrangement for bearing and raising children is to ensure that the parents themselves in some way form a society oriented to bearing and raising children (this is true of polygamous societies as well, though we hold that polygamous marriages violate the equality of man and woman in marriage and are not, in the end, most suitable for raising children). Thus, marriage is the community formed by a man and a woman who publicly consent to share their lives, in a type of relationship oriented toward begetting, nurturing, and educating of children together. Even though this or that particular marriage may not result in children, marriage is the *sort* of relationship *that would be fulfilled by* bearing and raising children together. This openness to procreation, as the community's natural fulfillment, distinguishes this community from other types of community.

Moreover, sexual acts have a tendency, in most people at least, to create a strong feeling of bonding and an expectation of a deeper, noninstrumental relationship. And the desire to have children is often, and naturally, an outgrowth of a romantic love between and a man and a woman. When a

---

[7] Of course, in some cases, as with the death of one or more of the biological parents, such arrangements are the best that can be had, but they are not optimal. See Linda J. Waite and Maggie Gallagher, *The Case for Marriage* (New York: Broadway Books, 2000), Chapter 9.

man and a woman love each other, they naturally tend to desire to form a life together, and (often) to have children together.[8] Thus, marriage is the society whose distinctive purpose is the provision of a stable and protective environment not only for bearing and raising children but also for romantic love, a love that is itself intrinsically linked to bearing and raising children. Rightly understood, marriage has a twofold end – one end with two aspects, the marital communion itself and procreation.[9]

The next question is, how should this society – marriage – be related to this end or goal of bearing and raising children? Reflecting on this question, one can see that marriage – the community specifically dedicated, in a quite distinctive way, to the bearing and raising of children – is a unique and complex society. The relation of marriage to the goal of bearing and raising children cannot (or should not) be one of simple means to an end. Marriage is not a mere contractual union like that of a roof-repair company, or even a tutoring group, where the activity of the group is instrumental to an end or goal extrinsic to the relationship itself, with the result, also, that once the end is achieved the reason for the unity of the group has also ended. To view the marriage as merely instrumental is to denigrate the union of the man and the woman; it would reduce their union to that of a mere means.

On the other hand, the bearing and raising of children should not be understood as a mere means to personal communion: this would reduce the children to objects or instruments in relation to the good of their parents.[10] Thus, marriage must be seen both as a personal communion between a man and a woman that is in itself good, and not a mere means toward bearing and raising children, but at the same time as the type of community which must be formed so that *if* children come to be, then they come to be in an environment suitable for their flourishing. Marriage is oriented to bearing and raising children in a somewhat indirect way: the marital communion of the spouses is intrinsically good and by itself a worthy motive for choosing to marry, *but*, this community must be such that it can provide a suitable environment for bearing and raising children, and is naturally *fulfilled* by bearing and raising children. Because of its orientation both to procreation and to the personal communion of the

---

[8] Grisez, , op. cit., 574–576.

[9] This point is explained quite clearly by John Finnis in "Law, Morality, and 'Sexual Orientation'," 11–39; id., "The Good of Marriage and the Morality of Sexual Relations," 97–134.

[10] This point is often relevant in discussions about reproductive technology.

spouses, the good of marriage requires a sharing of whole lives (that is, an open-ended, all-inclusive unity), stability, and exclusivity.[11]

Thus, on the third view of marriage, marriage is good in itself, and not merely an instrumental good in relation to procreation. At the same time, marriage is naturally fulfilled or unfolds in bearing and raising children; children are not related to marriage merely as an extrinsic addition or afterthought. Thus, if a married couple do not have children for some reason, their marriage is fully a marriage and remains good in itself (which is difficult to maintain on the first view), but also lacks its natural fulfillment (which is denied on the second view).[12]

In this type of community, sexual intercourse is not merely an extrinsic symbol or a pursuit of pleasure. In sexual intercourse between a man and a woman (whether married or not), a *real* organic union is established. This is a literal, biological point. Human beings are organisms, albeit of a particular type.[13] An organic action is one in which several bodily parts – tissues, cells, molecules, atoms, and so on – participate. Digestion, for example, involves several smaller, chemical actions of individual cells. But the several components of digestion form a unitary, single action. The subject of this action is the organism. So, the organism is a composite, made up of billions of parts. Its unity is manifested and understood in its actions. For most actions, such as sensation, digestion, and walking, individual male or female organisms are complete units. The male or female animal organism uses various materials as energy or instruments to perform its actions, but there is no internal orientation of its bodily parts to any larger whole of which it is a part, with respect to those actions. (This is precisely why we recognize individual male and female organisms as distinct, complete organisms, in most contexts.) However, with respect to one function the male and the female are *not* complete, and that function is reproduction. In reproductive activity the bodily parts of the male and the bodily parts of the female participate in a single action, coitus, which is oriented to reproduction (though not every act of coitus actually reproduces), so that the subject of the action is the male and the female as a biological unit.[14] Coitus is a unitary action in which the male

---

[11] Grisez, op. cit., 555–584.

[12] For this reason the couple may wish to adopt a child or join together in some other parental-like activity.

[13] See Chapter 1.

[14] Note also that the teleology of sexual acts belongs to them as groups primarily. That is, one cannot say that each and every spermatozoon is designed to join with an oocyte, and so if this particular one does not, it has failed. If so, it would be hard to explain

and the female become really biologically one.[15] In marital intercourse, this bodily unity is an aspect of, the biological matrix of, the couple's more comprehensive, marital communion.[16]

teleologically why there are millions of spermatazoa ejaculated in intercourse. Rather, the design of the bodies is that *some sperm or other at some time or other* joins with an oocyte. The same is true with individual instances of sexual intercourse. That is, the functional orientation belongs to acts of sexual intercourse as a group, primarily, and only indirectly to the individual acts. That is, the individual act of intercourse is oriented to reproduction, as a member of a set, some of which will reproduce.

[15] Of course, not every instance of two entities sharing in an action are instances of two entities becoming biologically one. In this case, however, the potentiality for a specific type of act, reproduction, can be actualized only in cooperation with the opposite sex of the species. The reproductive bodily parts are internally oriented toward actuation together with the bodily parts of the opposite sex. So, although the bodily parts of the male and the female are not interdependent for their continued life (as the bodily parts are to each other in a male organism or the bodily parts to each other in a female organism), there is a real biological unity. Note also that, strictly speaking, men and women engaging in sexual acts do not choose to reproduce; what they can choose and do is to perform reproductive-type acts, some of which may (they may or may not hope) reproduce.

[16] Gareth Moore denies that sexual intercourse establishes a real biological unity: "Principally, this approach [he is speaking of Germain Grisez's clear explanation of this idea in his *Living a Christian Life*, op. cit., 553–681, at 570] confuses two very different things: the automatic *functioning* of glands, organs and other parts of an animal, and the *voluntary activity* of an animal.... Animal reproduction is not a function of an animal or of a pair of animals, but the result of the successful functioning, in combination, of the products of their organs.... We might in a pinch speak of male and female reproductive organs as incomplete, if by that is meant that one cannot achieve reproduction without the other, but the male and female animals are in no sense incomplete. So neither is a mating pair a single complete organism; it is simply two organisms cooperating in a joint activity of mating" (Gareth Moore, O. P., "Natural Sex: Germain Grisez, Sex, and Natural Law," in *Revival of Natural Law*, ed. Nigel Bigger and Rufus Black (Burlington, VT: Ashgate, 2001), 225).

This objection reveals a selective reductionism: why not go further (as John Finnis observed regarding a similar objection raised earlier by Andrew Koppelman) and say it is not the organs that reproduce, nor the sperm and the ovum, but the pronuclei of the sperm and the ovum, and so on. Cf. Finnis, "The Good of Marriage and the Morality of Sexual Relations," 128. Finnis is replying to Koppelman's "Is Marriage Inherently Heterosexual?" *American Journal of Jurisprudence* 42 (1997), 67, n. 77.

Moore is correct to point to somewhat of a gap between the sexual act suited for reproduction and the success of that act, but it is a gap only in terms of distance on the part of the male and in terms of what the male and the female have direct control over. This gap does not affect the question what or who is the subject of this action: the subject of this action is the male and female organisms themselves, acting as a unit. It is a mistake to try to deny, on account of this gap, that what the male and female do together, sexual intercourse, is a reproductive act, reproductive in the sense that it is teleologically oriented to reproduction, an act that *fully succeeds*, at least from the biological point of view, only if reproduction occurs. Likewise, it is mistaken to say that the male and female are only "mating" and not jointly performing an act that neither of whom is capable of performing by himself or herself, that is, a reproductive-type act. Hence it is also a mistake to attribute reproduction only to the products of the animals' organs rather than to

When a couple chooses to form the kind of community distinguished by its openness and orientation to procreation, then the organic unity effected in sexual intercourse has a continuity with their community. In sexual intercourse they unite (become one) precisely in that respect in which their community is defined and naturally fulfilled. So (in marriage) this bodily unity is not extrinsic to their emotional and spiritual unity. The bodily, emotional, and spiritual are the different levels of a unitary, multileveled, personal, marital communion. Therefore, in such a community, sexual intercourse actualizes the multileveled personal communion. The sexual intercourse of spouses is not an extrinsic symbol of their love, or a mere means in relation to procreation. Rather, their sexual intercourse embodies, or actualizes, their marital communion. In that way the chaste sexual intercourse of husband and wife instantiates a basic human good: the good of marital union.

In sexual intercourse the husband and the wife become biologically one, but they do so precisely as man and woman, precisely as potential father and mother. So, in this act they share their procreative power (even if some condition distinct from their sexual act makes procreation impossible).[17] The full exercise or fulfillment of this potential would include conception, gestation, and bearing and raising the child, that is, bringing the child, the concrete prolongation and fruit of their love, to maturity – physically, emotionally, intellectually, and morally. Thus in their sexuality, in the procreative potential which they share with each other, there is a dynamism toward fatherhood and motherhood, and so, a dynamism which extends the present unity of the spouses indefinitely into the future. This *reality* is the basis for the profound significance that most people rightly sense is attached to sexual intercourse.

the animals themselves. We do not in the least deny that the male and the female remain two distinct complete organisms in many respects. However, it is also true that since the nature and unity of a substance is known through its actions and since the male and the female *do* regularly, and by internal tendency, jointly actuate themselves, with respect to reproduction, as a single unit, they are also biologically *in*complete with respect to those actions, and so become organically or biologically one when jointly performing those types of actions.

Moore's (and Koppelman's) objection is like saying that a woman does not breast-feed her child, but her milk does, or that you or I are not breathing, our lungs (and diaphragm) are. Living bodily actions must be attributed to whole organisms, and the sex cells are manifestly operating as instrumental causes of the whole animal organisms of which they are parts (even when at a distance as in the case of the male). Otherwise, the basic principle of explanation, that the cause must be proportionate to the effect (in this case, a new animal) would be violated.

17 See Section IV.

It is certainly true that there *are* unions or arrangements in the first two understandings of the word "marriage" as set out in the preceding – contractual unions in the first case and friendships in the second case. In some societies, men have viewed their wives only as mothers of their children, and have sought romantic relationships elsewhere (as on the first view). Also, many couples today regularly perform sexual acts together, but view their relationships as having nothing inherently connected to procreation (as on the second view). Both these types of relationships have at times been called "marriage." But these societies or arrangements are fundamentally distinct from the intrinsic good of marriage.

In the first two types of relationship, sexual acts are *extrinsic* to the personal communion of the couple.[18] Only in the third type, only in marriage as a one-flesh union of spouses, is the sexual intercourse part of, or constitutive of, the personal bodily communion itself.

II. Sex and Pleasure

Now we turn to the question whether sexual acts outside marriage are objectively morally right. One view of sexual acts which is perhaps not the most popular, but is currently gaining ground, is the view that while some sexual acts may have a tremendous emotional (or other) significance or depth, there is no valid reason why all such acts must have such significance. In fact, on this view, as long as concerns about health, honesty, and liberty are met, there is nothing wrong with even the most promiscuous forms of sexual behavior. Frederick Elliston presents an argument for this position:

For at least some of the people some of the time sex is fun. Whatever else may be true of it, at the barest level sex remains an intensely pleasing physical activity.... Granted the two earlier provisos [no coercion, no deception], sex is good for this reason, if for no other.[19]

Later he sums up this view: "Insofar as promiscuity maximizes the pleasures that can be derived from sex, it is good; and insofar as the prohibition against promiscuity is a limitation on the pleasures to be derived from sex, it is unwarranted – in a word, 'bad'."[20] He adds that one can also argue,

---

[18] Or more, if more than two are engaging in the sexual act.
[19] Frederick Elliston, "In Defense of Promiscuity," in *Philosophical Perspectives on Sex and Love*, ed. Robert M. Stewart (New York: Oxford University Press, 1995), 152.
[20] Ibid.

in the spirit of John Stuart Mill, that "the freedom to be promiscuous can contribute to the full growth of the human personality."[21]

Among the implications of this view, it would seem to follow that there is nothing wrong, at least in principle, with prostitution. For, if it is pleasant for one party, why may it not be merely profitable for the other party? Proponents of the morality of prostitution grant that there is often coercion, exploitation, and other bad effects associated with prostitution. But, they argue, these are not necessary or inevitable features of commercial sex. On this basis, Lars Ericsson argues that prostitution should be viewed as morally upright: "If two adults voluntarily consent to an economic arrangement concerning sexual activity and this activity takes place in private, it seems plainly absurd to maintain that there is something intrinsically wrong with it."[22]

However, we argue that it is wrong to treat one's sexuality, or another's, as a mere extrinsic instrument, and that this is done in sexual acts chosen for the sole immediate purpose of pleasure (even when there is an ulterior end, such as commercial gain or relaxation). Sexual acts done for the sole immediate purpose of pleasure, and not intended as embodying, expressing, or symbolizing personal communion, constitute mere masturbation, either solitary or mutual. And we shall argue that masturbatory sex is objectively morally wrong.

As we indicated in Chapter 3, there are three types of pleasure: first, the enjoyment of, or an appetitive reaction to, some fulfilling activity or condition, such as the pleasure in playing tennis (not a specific sensation, but the enjoyment or satisfaction of the game as a whole). Second, "pleasure" may refer to a specific type of sensation, such as the taste of an apple or the euphoric sensation produced by a drug. And, third, we obtain pleasure from the satisfaction of a desire, for example, the pleasure we obtain from completing any job or from solving a crossword puzzle. Here we are interested in the second sense of "pleasure," that is, as a specific type of sensation. The position we are examining claims that sex just for pleasure (as a type of sensation or effect in one's consciousness) is morally right, provided there is no deception, coercion, or violence.

In Chapter 3 we proposed two points about pleasure as a type of sensation. First, pleasure (in this sense) is not just by itself a genuine good. It is, or it should be, icing on the cake. It is good only if it is attached to an activity or condition that is already good, good in the sense of fulfilling or

---

[21] Ibid. Mill himself, it should be noted, did not advocate promiscuity.

[22] Lars O. Ericsson, "Charges against Prostitution: An Attempt at Philosophical Assessment," *Ethics* 90 (1980), 338–339.

perfective. Consider, for example, sadistic pleasures. One does not wish to say that Smith's sadism was bad but at least he got pleasure from it. Rather, when one takes pleasure in an inappropriate object, the pleasure itself is bad. So, bodily pleasure is not *of itself* a good.

The second point we wish to recall about pleasure is that when it *is* attached to an activity or condition that is already fulfilling, then it adds to its goodness or fulfillment. We can see this point when we consider that it is better, for example, to have learning with pleasure than without it. So, pleasure is not a good just by itself, it must be connected to an *appropriate* object in order to be a good; but it does positively add to the overall condition. The question is, what must the object of a pleasure be like in order to be appropriate? Pleasure that is a good cannot be sadistic, or derived simply from destruction. Also, it is clear that a good pleasure must not be an *illusory* one – for example, the pleasure one might obtain from believing that so-and-so admired one is illusory if so-and-so does not really admire one. Illusory pleasures take us away from reality, and from what is genuinely good.

These examples, though, suggest (as we argued in more detail in Chapter 3) that there is a basic criterion for distinguishing between good pleasures and bad ones. In general, what does make an object or activity really good and worthy of pursuit? When we act for a reason, that is, when we guide our actions by reason or understanding, then the *point* of our acting is something that we understand to be really *fulfilling* or *perfective* of us and of others we care about. What makes an object or activity good and worth pursuing is that it is really *fulfilling* or *perfective*. Pleasure is not by itself, or is not always, really fulfilling – as is clear from the examples of sadism and illusory pleasures. So, pleasure is good only if it is an experience of, or an aspect of, a condition or activity that is already genuinely fulfilling. The condition or activity must first be really fulfilling, and *then* pleasure taken in it is an additional fulfillment.

Now to pursue pleasure as a type of sensation when it is not connected to a genuine good is morally wrong, even though it may or may not be *seriously* morally wrong. For, to pursue pleasure as unconnected to a genuinely fulfilling activity or condition is, at least to some degree, a retreat from reality. If the pleasure is chosen *instead of* pursuing a real good, then the choice is morally wrong (though not necessarily seriously wrong).[23] Our choices ought to be in accord with a respect and love for

---

[23] As we shall see, choices which alienate the bodily self from the intentional self in the *sexual* domain *are* serious, since they also involve a denigration of the good of marriage and an attitude to the person-as-sexual (oneself or another) as a mere impersonal thing for use.

real human goods, precisely because such goods are intrinsic aspects of the well-being and fulfillment of human persons – ourselves and others. So, just as we should not be deterred by contrary emotions from choosing a genuine good, so we should not be deterred from choosing a real good by a mere desire for pleasure.[24]

Moreover, a choice to pursue sexual pleasure apart from the genuine good of personal communion (the only good that can be immediately realized in a sexual act) involves a denigration of one's (and others') sexuality. Masturbatory sex is a choice to use one's sexuality (and perhaps that of others) as a mere means toward pleasure and thus involves treating one's sexuality (and perhaps others' sexuality) as a mere object for use and as *subpersonal*.[25]

An analogy will clarify the point. Suppose a husband begins to regard his wife as a mere servant or as a mere means toward his own ends. To regard her in this way *in itself* diminishes the personal harmony between them. He has ceased to regard her as an end in herself, as a subject, and regards her as merely a means, an object. His relation to her, then, is lacking in what it should have. This is true even before he performs any external act to manifest this defect in his relation to her. Something similar happens with the masturbator and his body (or his sexuality) – only here the disharmony involves different aspects of the same person, rather than two distinct persons. The masturbator treats his sexuality (and perhaps that of others) as a mere *extrinsic* means, and thus an impersonal (or

---

[24] Sometimes simulating an activity is not a pursuit of sheer pleasure or an experience bereft of real fulfillment, but a form of play: for example, simulating the flying of an airplane, or the coaching of a football team, as in computer games. Why couldn't having sex with Susan, one might object, be justified as "playing house," that is, playing husband and wife? Note, first, that if this were so, it would justify adultery as well as premarital sexual relations. Note also that no one would think it wrong for John and Susan to pretend to be husband and wife in a play or movie, provided they did not engage in acts intended to be sexually arousing. The difference is that when people engage in sex, their sexual desire and their physical activity are aimed at something quite real – the sexual arousal and bodily contact or union with the other – making sexual acts quite different from saying lines in a play or movie, or other types of simulation. It is clear, then, that the fundamental act is not play (although there may, of course, be some playfulness during their sexual act).

[25] It is in this way, for example, that one might take heroin. A drug addict takes heroin simply for the feeling; how he gets that feeling and what reality that feeling is attached to (in this case, certain neurons firing in his brain) is completely irrelevant to his immediate aim. Thus, he is using his body to get that feeling. His end is the conscious feeling, as a content. His means is a chemical change produced in his body. But he treats his body as a mere extrinsic means, as a mere object, not as an intrinsic aspect of the subject, which in reality it is. Such a choice inherently involves contempt for the body.

depersonalized) object, in relation to the goal of a certain type of feeling. Therefore, the choice to have masturbatory sex is a choice whose object includes a demeaning of the bodily person.

Of course, not every use of parts of one's body includes such denigration. To use parts of one's body, so long as one is treating them as parts of oneself, does not involve treating them as subpersonal objects. Also, in some types of dealing with other bodily persons, to abstract from their personhood (as when one considers a person as 175 pounds for purposes of estimating the maximum weight allowed in an elevator car) is not wrong. But masturbatory sex (whether solitary or mutual) necessarily involves more than just abstracting from the personhood of the body being used. It involves treating a bodily person as if he or she were not a person, for here the sexuality of the person, which includes both the body and personal expression, is used as a mere extrinsic means. This point requires explanation.

As Roger Scruton has shown, sexual desire of itself aims not just toward bodily contact and not just toward orgasm. Rather, in the sexual inclination, one naturally desires that the other person sexually desire oneself. Sexual desire aims at the other's body, but one's sexual desire tends toward the other's body precisely as animated by his or her own desire and, more than that, toward the other's personal, that is, freely chosen, involvement with one. That is, sexual desire, in persons, tends toward focusing on the other *person* as sexually embodied, and so one can say that it naturally *aims toward* a union that is both bodily and personal.[26] The desire tends not just toward particular sensations, but toward a recognition and affirmation (if not real, at least fantasized) included in (but not restricted to) reciprocal sexual desire from another. This is why it makes a significant difference to people (or, most people) who they have sex with, and why most people desire to have sex only with people they, at least, like and who like them (or at least with whom they can pretend to have this reciprocal personal regard). This is in marked contrast with how we feel, for example, about our barber, or a physical therapist – we are not uncomfortable (or at least not very uncomfortable) if we have just been introduced to these people who will touch our bodies. In other words, unlike most other bodily acts, sexual desire of itself strongly tends toward the expression of

[26] "In true sexual desire, the aim is 'union with the other', where 'the other' denotes a particular person, with a particular perspective upon my actions. The reciprocity which is involved in this aim is achieved in the state of mutual arousal, and the interpersonal character of arousal determines the nature of 'union' that is sought" (Roger Scruton, *Sexual Desire: A Moral Philosophy of the Erotic* (New York: Free Press, 1986), 89).

the person, of his or her personal involvement, or caring for, the one with whom one has sex.

This personal expressiveness of human sexuality, however, can be blocked or negated. This is illustrated most clearly in the phenomenon of the *obscene*. The obscene is the sexual viewed from a point of view outside a first-person perspective, that is, viewed as separate from the expressiveness of the personal involvement and attachment that sexual acts of persons tend toward. Thus, Roger Scruton points out that the copulation of human beings in public strikes most people as obscene. This is because such acts done in public are viewed from a point of view outside the first-person perspective of those engaged in it and thus as detached from any personal involvement.[27] Similarly, in the use of pornography, one deliberately obtains sexual pleasure from viewing a picture of a woman (to consider the most frequent type), and takes sexual pleasure in viewing, and perhaps fantasizing acts of the most profound intimacy with, someone with whom one has no personal relationship at all. In viewing pornography, one has divorced, in one's regard or intention, the sexuality of the woman from the other aspects of her being as an integrated and whole person and used that sexuality for one's own purposes (even if the woman used has consented to this use). Since sexuality of itself tends toward an expression of one's personal intentions (and not just an expression of one's sexual desire), to divorce the bodily (or animal, including the other's sexual desire) from the personal is not just to abstract from the other's personhood; rather, it is to treat the other's body, or sexuality, as if his or her body were a *sub*personal object.

To use the body-as-sexual for purposes which do not respect the integration of the personal and the bodily, is similar in some ways to sophistry. Sophistry is reasoning or arguing – an activity that necessarily involves the basic good of truth – but with a disregard for truth. To subordinate one's reasoning or argument to ends other than truth, and without regard for truth, is to fail in one's respect for the basic good of truth. Analogously, in sexuality the basic good of the capacity of a person to express himself or herself sexually is always at stake. Thus, to use sexuality but to disregard that personal expression (which, ultimately, as we argue later, can only be realized rightly within marriage) is to act with a disregard for, and thus a disrespect of, that basic good. More than that, to use one's sexuality (one's own and/or another's) and subordinate it to mere pleasure (pleasure not attached to a basic good) is to act *against* that integration, and thus to

[27] Ibid., 138–139.

violate that basic good directly. Thus, masturbatory sex is analogous to (though not the same as) lying. It is not itself a lie, since deception need not occur – the parties involved may be fully aware that the sexual act is detached from personal communion. However, like lying, it involves a direct detachment or a negation of an integration that is in itself a basic human good. In lying, there is a disintegration of the outer self from the inner self. In masturbatory sex there is disintegration, a separation, of the body-as-sexual, or the animal sexuality, from the whole person.

One's personal involvement is not of itself expressed in one's weight (recall the example of adverting only to a person's weight before entering an elevator); by contrast, one's personal involvement *is* of itself expressed in sexual acts. So, one can consider someone's weight and simply abstract from his or her personhood; but in a sexual act, to ignore a body's personhood (whether another's or one's own) is to treat that bodily person as if he or she were not personal, that is, to treat him or her (in his or her bodiliness) as subpersonal. Thus, in such acts, there is an implicit dualism and a depersonalization.[28]

The self-integration negated concerns, specifically, the sexual aspect of the self, the aspect of the self by which one is capable of giving oneself to another in a marital union. To regard the sexual aspect of the self as a mere object for use means viewing the sexual act, whether in oneself or in another, as a mere tool to attain extrinsic ends. One cannot view one's own body, or that of one's partner, as a mere extrinsic tool, without at the same time being disposed to view other bodily persons as similarly split or disintegrated. Thus, the specific self-integration included in the *marital act* and *marriage* is implicitly denied or denigrated. In the masturbatory act, one implicitly views the body-as-sexual as a mere tool, and so one implicitly denies the possibility of marriage as a truly two-in-one-flesh unity, that is, as a basic good in which there is a true bodily union of the spouses integrated with their emotional and spiritual union.[29] Hence masturbatory sex violates the basic human good of marriage.

Andrew Koppelman has objected to this argument, claiming that to act simply for the sake of pleasure need not be morally wrong. And, as a

---

[28] Almost always such masturbatory use of another involves using his or her animality, not just his or her body, for the one using the other usually desires not just physical contact but that the other desire him. This reciprocity, however, is not sufficient to make the sexual act an involvement with the other *as a person*. To divorce the animal *sexual desire* (not merely the body), in one's intention, from the personal is to treat the living body as subpersonal.

[29] Cf. Finnis, "The Good of Marriage and the Morality of Sexual Relations," 97–134.

consequence (he argues) a couple (whether heterosexual or homosexual) who "pleasure each other" – that is, aim immediately simply at pleasure – are giving each other a genuine gift and are therefore (contrary to our argument) sharing a genuine common good.[30] Am I not simply pursuing pleasure (Koppelman asks) unconnected to any good, when I scratch an itch? But certainly there is nothing wrong with scratching an itch. Or, when I take a hot shower, am I not just pursuing pleasure? But hot showers do not seem morally wrong.

However, regarding the scratching of an itch: what is remarkably different between scratching an itch and sexual activity, of whatever sort, is the simplicity of the former and the complexity of the latter. An itch is a discomfort in some part of the body and presumably an indication of some real, though mild, bodily disorder. There is usually no reason whatsoever against scratching to remove that discomfort – it is a simple and direct action aimed at calming the nerve endings at some part of the body. There is no pursuit of pleasure apart from a real fulfillment (or as isolated from the larger good of which it should be a part), as there is in the case of masturbatory sex. The same is true of eating for the pleasure of it (the activity sought is a real act of eating, which is really fulfilling) or of enjoying a hot bath (the relaxation of one's muscles being a healthy function). It is not that in these cases pleasure is a side effect; pleasure *is* sought, but as part or as connected to a genuinely fulfilling condition (however minor it may be).

Koppelman has also objected that obtaining sexual pleasure is the provision of a bodily need and that providing a bodily need realizes a basic good.[31] Now, it is true that an animal, including a human animal, finds sexual genital stimulation and orgasm pleasurable and so acquiring it has the effect of relief. But that is not the whole story. The situation with sex is similar (in this respect) to hunger and eating. Hunger involves a tension, and eating – even if what is eaten is not genuinely good for one – relieves that tension. But, understood more clearly, hunger is a desire and orientation to eating *food* or *nutrition*. In other words, the object of the *need*, as opposed to the chance object of the blind urge, is eating food, that is, a genuinely fulfilling activity – and so even if a person took pleasure in eating Styrofoam or plastic, this would not show that eating these

---

[30] Andrew Koppelman, *The Gay Rights Question in Contemporary American Law* (Chicago: University of Chicago Press, 2002), 85.

[31] Ibid. Gareth Moore raises the same objection, also using the example of scratching an itch, in Gareth Moore, O. P., op. cit., 232.

substances answers to a genuine need. Such desires are really disorders in the basic orientation or natural desire for real food.

Similarly, people have sexual desires that are in some ways similar to the way they have hunger pangs (though the desire for sex is, of course, much more complicated than the desire for food). But the question is, toward what really fulfilling condition or activity are these desires really oriented? As the desire to eat plastic, for example, is really a disordered desire for real food, so the desire for sexual pleasure or experience isolated from bodily and personal communion – indeed, marital communion – is a disordered desire for what sex offers which is really fulfilling, the expression or embodiment of a real interpersonal union. The issue is not what will bring some (temporary) relief to the urge, but what really fulfilling condition or activity is this desire oriented to? Just as hunger is not oriented to pleasure but to a really fulfilling activity that is pleasurable, so sexual desire is not oriented just to stimulation and orgasm, or even a complex *experience*, but to a really fulfilling activity that is pleasurable. So, again, pleasure is not itself the fulfillment – at least not by itself – but pleasure is fulfilling only when it is part of a condition or activity that is of itself fulfilling. Pleasure by itself cannot be the genuine good instantiated in a sexual act, and it cannot be the common good uniting two (or more?) in a sexual act, since in order for pleasure to be a genuine good it must be an aspect of an activity or condition that is already intrinsically fulfilling.

Thus, it remains that sex done just for pleasure, or masturbatory sex – whether it be solitary or with two or more participants – detaches the pursuit of pleasure from concern for what is genuinely fulfilling, involves a depersonalization of one's own or another's sexuality, and so is objectively morally wrong. To be morally right a sexual act must involve more than a fair and nonviolent pursuit of pleasure.[32]

III. Sex, Love, and Affection

So far we have argued that engaging in sex merely for pleasure is wrong in that in one's intention the person as bodily (both oneself and the other)

---

[32] We think it is important to note the logical link between solitary masturbation and other nonmarital sexual acts. Many philosophers and theologians hold that solitary masturbation is not in itself morally wrong, but hold that prostitution and promiscuity are wrong. We, however, doubt the coherence of such a position. If doing something by oneself is morally acceptable, then, unless some incidental injustice is committed when it is done with another, it is hard to see why doing the same thing with someone else's assistance should be wrong.

is viewed as a subpersonal, extrinsic instrument. So, unless the sexual act embodies or actualizes a real union of persons, it will involve the instrumentalization of both the other person(s) and oneself. We now argue that only in marriage can sexual behavior constitute a real union of persons. There are four types of nonmarital sexual acts: masturbation (solitary or mutual), sodomy, fornication, and adultery. We do not formally discuss adultery here: if masturbation and fornication are wrong, then adultery, which involves additional moral defects, is certainly wrong. We considered the morality of masturbation in Section I. In this section we discuss sodomy and fornication.

A. *Sodomy*

By "sodomy" here is meant (1) anal or oral intercourse between persons of the same sex or (2) anal or oral intercourse between persons of opposite sexes (even if married), if it is intended to bring about complete sexual satisfaction apart from vaginal intercourse. If a couple use their sexual organs for the sake of experiencing pleasure or even for the sake of an experience of unity, but do not become biologically one, then their act does not actually effect unity. If Susan, for example, masturbates John to orgasm or applies oral stimulation to him to bring him to orgasm, no real unity has been effected. That is, although bodily parts are in juxtaposition and contact, the participants do not unite biologically; they do not become the subject of a single biological act and so do not literally become "one flesh."[33] They may be doing this in order simply to obtain or share pleasure. In that case the act is really an instance of mutual masturbation and is as self-alienating, or depersonalizing, as any other instance of masturbation. However, they might intend their act as in some way an expression of their love for each other. They might argue that this act is no different from the vaginal intercourse they performed two nights before, except that this one involves a merely technical or physical variation – a rearrangement of "plumbing."

---

[33] John Corvino at one point claims that in homosexual acts, there is a physical unity. "But sex is often much more than that [namely, self-gratification], for heterosexuals and homosexuals alike. The physical union of the partners manifests and contributes to a larger union" (John Corvino, "Homosexuality and the PIB Argument," *Ethics* 115 (2005), 501–534, at 512–513). But in sodomitical acts, the two (or more) do not actually become organically one. Their bodily parts do not become functionally or teleologically, that is, biologically, one. There is contact and closeness (as there also is in hugging) but the specifically sexual aspect of the acts performed on each other does not make them organically one.

However, in sodomitical acts, whether between persons of the same sex or opposite sexes, between unmarried or married persons, the participants do not unite biologically. Moreover, an experience of pleasure, just as such, is not shared. Although each person may experience pleasure, they experience pleasure each as an individual, not as a unit. For a truly common good, there must be more than experience; the experiences must be subordinated to a truly common act or condition that is genuinely fulfilling (and as such provides a more than merely instrumental reason for action). If, on the contrary, the activities are subordinated to the pleasurable experiences, if the physical stimulation administered to one another is merely a means to attain what are (and can only be) individual, private experiences, then a real unity is not achieved.

What feature (or features) must a sexual act have so that one is not merely using another's body (and one's own)? The answer is that it must be an act in which a real good is realized or participated. If this is so, then it is an act in which the two share and therefore become one in jointly performing this act. In that case, their pleasurable experiences will be aspects of a real good, rather than their acts being subordinated to the pleasurable experiences. In the case of chaste marital intercourse, spouses participate in the real good of marital bodily union. In marital intercourse the man and the woman become organically one in an act of copulation, and this physical union initiates or renews their total marital communion: that is, distinct from the pleasurable *experiences*, there is an identifiable, real act and basic good in which they share and experience, namely, the act of initiating or renewing their marital union in their becoming organically one.

Confusion may arise on this point. It might seem that we are begging the question. For we are saying, first, that there must be some real act, definable independently of its pleasure, in which the couple share – a common good – in order for their act to be unifying. And yet we then say that with married people, the act that they share is their becoming one, their becoming one organism. Aren't we saying that the common act that makes them one is their becoming one? And if their common act can be their becoming one, why can't homosexuals (or, for that matter, heterosexuals) do this in sodomitical acts?

The answer is that there are three types of unity referred to here: unity of persons, unity of action (which promotes or actualizes the first unity), and the organic unity of male and female in coitus. For any two (or more) people, it is true in general that actions which they perform make them one only if there is a real, common good of their actions (unity of action). The common good could be health (sharing a meal), aesthetic experience (going to a play or movie), play (bridge, checkers), and so on. In each case there is a unity of action, that is, an action, sharing in a real, common good, performed jointly. Moreover, this unity of action promotes or actualizes interpersonal unity, or unity of persons. In the case of the sexual act of a married couple, their act of physically or organically becoming one (organic unity) is the common good, the shared pursuit of which (unity of action) also brings about or enhances their interpersonal unity (unity of persons). But if the participants in a sexual act do not become physically or organically one, then, whatever goods they may have as ulterior ends, the immediate goal of their act can only be either mere pleasure or an illusory experience. There is in such an act no common good, the common pursuit of which makes them one. There is no real unity of action to effect or enhance their interpersonal unity. So in that case, although they may intend or wish otherwise, their act is in reality a using of their own and each other's bodies-as-sexual as a means of obtaining a pleasurable experience, which might include the illusory experience of a union that they are not by this action promoting or effecting in any way.

B. Fornication

There must, then, be an organic unity so that there is a common good in the sexual act. But, as we showed in Section I, this organic unity is an instance of a real human good only if it is an aspect of a real union of the persons. If they are united as one organism, but are not united in other aspects of their lives or selves, then they are treating their bodies as extrinsic instruments. But suppose a heterosexual couple has a friendship and is even planning marriage in the future. They have intercourse and intend their act not just as an experience of pleasure, but (perhaps confusedly) as an embodiment of their personal but not-yet-marital communion. In this case they really do become biologically one in the sexual act, and so, their act *seems* to be a sharing in a common good. They become biologically one, and they intend this union to be an actualization and experience of their less-than-marital personal communion. What about this type of act, which has traditionally been designated as "fornication"?

The problem with this act, however, is that if sexual intercourse does embody a personal communion, it does not embody just some personal communion or other, or some generic type of communion or friendship. If sexual intercourse does embody a personal communion, it embodies the type of personal communion that is fulfilled by the man and woman's sexual complementarity, that is, the type of personal communion in which sexual acts can, or would, produce their full effect. Put otherwise, reproductive-type acts are able to embody only a reproductive-type community. But if such a community does not exist (or does not yet exist) between the man and the woman, then there is no such community to embody.[34]

In other words, an interpersonal communion is actualized only by an act that is proper to it. The interrelationship of family members, for example, is actualized and experienced in the family meal. Friends actualize and experience their relationship in conversation, and in pursuits of other common goods. Sexual activity does not actualize an ordinary friendship. But reproductive-type acts, acts in which the husband and the wife become one flesh (one organism) and share their procreative potentiality, actualize and provide experience of this specific type of personal communion. Only if they *are* married, only if they (publicly) consent to marriage, does their becoming biologically one actualize (initiate or renew) marriage. So, only if they have a truly marital relationship can their sexual act embody their personal communion.

In sum, in chaste marital intercourse the couple act in a fully integrated way. Each bodily person relates to the other precisely as a bodily person, because they become one physically and personally. In nonmarital sexual acts, however, either the participants unite in a bodily way but not as actualizing a personal communion (heterosexual fornication) or do not really unite but use their bodies as extrinsic instruments for the sake of an illusory experience of bodily unity or for private gratifications (sodomy, masturbation).

IV. Objections

There are four important objections to our position, and it will clarify matters to consider them.

Objection 1
First, it has been objected that this argument would entail that the sexual acts of sterile married couples are also immoral, and everyone recognizes that is not the case. Paul Weithman has called this "the sterility objection"

---

[34] As Germain Grisez expresses it: "[T]he part of the good of marital communion which fornicators choose, bodily union, is not an intelligible good apart from the whole. Although bodily union provides an experience of intimacy, by itself it realizes only the natural capacity of a male individual and a female individual to mate. Sexual mating contributes to an intelligible good, which fulfills persons, only insofar as it is one element of the complete communion by which a man and a woman become, as it were, one person" (Grisez, , op. cit., 651).

(an objection he does not himself advance).[35] Stephen Macedo argues as follows:

> If there is no possibility of procreation, then sterile couples are, like homosexuals, incapable of sex acts "open to procreation." What is the point of sex in an infertile marriage? Not procreation; the partners (let us assume) know that they are infertile. If they have sex, it is for pleasure and to express their love, or friendship, or some other shared good. It will be for precisely the same reasons that committed, loving gay couples have sex. Why are these good reasons for sterile or elderly married couples but not for gay and lesbian couples?[36]

Macedo argues further that the only reason why homosexual couples cannot perform sexual acts suited to procreation is that they lack "the physical equipment (the 'biological complementarity') such that anyone could have children by doing what they do in bed."[37] In other words, sterile married couples merely lack some physical condition that would enable them to procreate. But exactly the same situation obtains in the case of homosexual couples. Clearly, the objection concludes, sexual acts between sterile married couples can be morally right; therefore, there is no reason why sexual acts between homosexual couples cannot be morally right.

However, there is a clear difference between what homosexual couples do and what infertile married couples do. No one could have children by performing sodomitical acts. Yet, this is not true of the *type of act* performed by sterile married couples when they engage in vaginal intercourse. People who are not temporarily or permanently infertile *could* procreate by performing *exactly* the act that the infertile married couple perform and by which they consummate or actualize their marital communion. The difference between sterile and fertile married couples is not a difference in *what they do*. Rather, it is a difference in a distinct condition that affects what may result from what they do. However, the difference between any heterosexual couple engaging in vaginal intercourse and a homosexual couple is much more than that. The lack of

---

[35] Paul Weithman, "Natural Law, Morality and Sexual Complementarity," in *Laws and Nature*, ed. Martha Nussbaum (New York: Oxford University Press, 1996).

[36] Stephen Macedo, "Homosexuality and the Conservative Mind," *Georgetown Law Journal* 84 (1995), 261–300, at 278. George and Bradley, in reply, observe that pleasure and expressions of feeling are *not*, in truth, the justifying point of sexual relations between spouses; the justifying point is, rather, the intrinsic good of marriage itself considered as a one-flesh communion of persons consummated and actualized by acts which, qua reproductive in type, unite the spouses biologically and interpersonally. See George and Bradley, "Marriage and the Liberal Imagination," loc. cit.

[37] Macedo, op. cit., 278–279.

complementarity in homosexual couples is a condition that renders it impossible for them to perform the kind of act that makes them organically one.

If a married couple becomes infertile, it is obvious that this does not change what they have been doing in bed: they still perform the same kind of act they have been doing perhaps for years. Similarly, a fertile married couple may have sexual intercourse several times during a week. If conception results, they may not know which act of sexual intercourse caused it. Still, all of their acts are *the kind of acts* that could result in procreation. Their sexual acts later in life, for example, after the female spouse has become infertile, are still the kind of acts that could result in procreation; the difference is not a difference in *what they do* – the kind of act – but in a condition extrinsic to what they do.

Thus, the infertile heterosexual couple performs the kind of act that, given other conditions, reproduces; a homosexual couple (or indeed a heterosexual couple engaging in sodomy) performs acts on each other (for, they do not engage in a unified act) which of themselves are not apt, in any conditions, to reproduce. This indisputable difference is indeed morally significant. The heterosexual couple who engage in a reproductive-type act truly become biologically one, one body. And if they have given marital consent, then this act initiates or renews their marital communion. Their intercourse will be an aspect of this multileveled union and so will embody or renew that union. By contrast, the homosexual couple lack not just a condition enabling their act to be reproductive, but, first, a prerequisite for the formation of the kind of personal union which is initiated or renewed by sexual acts and, second, the biological complementarity enabling them to become biologically one. Of course, men have friendships with other men and women have friendships with other women; but sexual acts performed on each other do not biologically unite them and so do not actualize or embody such friendships.

Reproduction, or procreation, is not an action directly under our control. Its conditions are nonbehavioral as well as behavioral. What spouses do is an act that in some instances may result in procreation. Moreover – and here reproduction is distinct from other acts – by performing that act the man and the woman become biologically one, two-in-one flesh. When that one-flesh unity is an aspect of a total marital communion, it is a rational and sufficient motive and justification for that act. But humans (and other mammals) become one flesh (biologically one) only if they perform the type of act that in some instances procreates or only if they perform a reproductive-type act.

Still, one might object to this, as Andrew Koppelman has, that the sexual acts of a sterile or elderly couple *cannot* be described as reproductive in kind, since *these* acts do not have the power to procreate. Koppelman objects that our definition of *marriage* (that is, the definition proposed by traditional morality) is not adequately warranted, that it is in fact arbitrary: "Finally, there is not adequate warrant for accepting the NNL [new natural lawyers'] definition of marriage."[38] But to support that claim he argues that our classification of marital *acts*, as essentially distinct from homosexual acts, is unwarranted and arbitrary:

What sense does it make to postulate one type of sexual activity as normative in this way [our definition of marital acts], so that heterosexual intercourse is held to be an act of a reproductive *kind* even if reproduction is not intended and is known to be impossible? Why is it not equally plausible to say that all acts of seminal ejaculation are reproductive in kind, or to say that no acts of seminal ejaculation are reproductive in kind, and that reproduction is only an accidental consequence that may ensue under certain conditions? There is nothing in nature that dictates that the lines have to be drawn in any of these ways.[39]

The class of sexual acts we have described as reproductive in type, or "as such suitable for procreation," (Koppelman later says) might be just "an ex post mental construct."[40] After quoting John Finnis, who said that a marital act, even of a sterile or elderly couple, is of reproductive type because it is "behavior which, as behavior, is suitable for generation,"[41] Koppelman replies that such an act cannot be suitable for generation if the organs are not suitable for generation or do not have the power to procreate. He then adds:

A sterile person's genitals are no more suitable for generation than an unloaded gun is suitable for shooting.... Dependencies of deception and fright aside, all objects that are not *loaded* guns are morally equivalent in this context.... But the only aspect of reproductiveness that is relevant to the natural lawyers' argument, namely the reproductive *power* of the organ, does not inhere in *this* organ.[42]

So, Koppelman's claim is that one should not hold that marriage as we have defined it is normative and that it is arbitrary for us to single out heterosexual vaginal intercourse, which includes that of sterile and elderly

[38] Koppelman, *The Gay Rights Question in Contemporary American Law*, 86.
[39] Ibid., 86–87.
[40] Ibid., 87.
[41] Finnis, "Law, Morality, and 'Sexual Orientation'," 29.
[42] Koppelman, op. cit., *The Gay Right Question in Contemporary American Law*, 88.

couples, as morally significantly different from other types of sexual activity, such as homosexual sex acts.

Koppelman's argument has two parts, one about marriage and the other about sexual acts. First, let us reply to the part about marriage. Contrary to Koppelman's claim, marriage is not simply a historical accident, which can now be modified as our culture – or a small fraction of our culture – might choose. As explained earlier, the complexity of marriage stems from the fact that one aspect of the total good of marriage – bearing and raising children – requires a stable and loving environment formed by the children's parents. In order to form a stable and loving environment, this union cannot be a mere contractual and instrumental agreement entered solely for the sake of children – this would depersonalize both the children and the parental union. Hence the parents – and any couple who might become parents – should form a stable union of love *for each other*, an interpersonal union that is in itself good but that would be naturally fulfilled by bearing and raising children. But since this type of interpersonal union of man and woman is in itself good even if this natural fulfillment is not reached, it follows that sterile couples must be included within the extension of this kind of community – otherwise, marriage will be reduced to a mere means in relation to an extrinsic end and would cease once that end was completed or if it was found to be impossible of realizing.

Moreover, man and woman are complementary physically, but also emotionally, psychologically, and spiritually. So the union of a man and a woman, a union of complements, and in such a way as to provide a suitable environment for whatever children might come to be – such a community is scarcely an arbitrarily drawn class. Rather, the basic welfare of children and the romantic inclinations toward fulfillment in love in men and women are the bases in the natures of man, woman, and children, for delineating those committed man–woman couples and families as belonging to one class.

The *normativity* of this class stems from its being a basic and irreducible good perfective of human persons. Marriage, so defined – that is, defined as it has been for centuries in our civilization – is a basic good and therefore is worthy of pursuit, promotion, protection, and respect.

The second part of Koppelman's argument centers on reproductive-type acts. Here he claims that the classification of all heterosexual vaginal sexual acts as reproductive in kind is arbitrary. In turn, in the course of defending this argument, he makes two claims: (a) that marital acts performed by sterile or elderly couples are *not* reproductive in kind, but also (b) if they *are* considered reproductive in kind, then *any* seminal ejaculation could be classified as reproductive in kind. Claim (a), the key assumption in Koppelman's argument, is the following:

No act which cannot succeed (in a suitable environment under certain circumstances) in producing X can be of the kind that is oriented toward X.

Or, put more specifically:

No act in which the agents (or parts of the agents) lack the full internal resources (in a suitable environment, under certain circumstances) to produce X, can be internally oriented toward X.

Because the sterile man does not have all of the internal resources to procreate (together with a woman), then, says Koppelman, his sexual acts cannot be oriented toward procreation. In fact, says Koppelman, his sexual organs in that case are not genuinely reproductive organs at all – they are reproductive, he says, only in some "taxonomic" sense,[43] which seems to mean they merely can be classified that way, but without any present basis for that classification.

But these claims cannot be true. A composite entity may have several constituents internally arranged so as to cooperate to produce X. But this composite may have, or have acquired, a defect that prevents it from producing X. For example, a hand is oriented toward grasping objects, and remains oriented toward that, even though a defect – a broken bone, for example – prevents it from actually doing so. So a reproductive organ remains a reproductive organ in fact and not just in name (merely "taxonomically"), even if some defect in the agent makes actual reproduction impossible.

A similar point applies to a reproductive-type *act*. In the generative act, the male and the female perform an act (intercourse) in which the semen is deposited in the vaginal tract of the female. This act, performed by the male and the female together, is the first part of the process of reproduction. In performing this first part of the reproductive process together, the male and the female act as a single unit, even if the second part of the process cannot, for any of a variety of causes, be completed.[44] Of course, if the process continues, they continue (biologically) to act as a unit (though at a distance, by means of their gametes). A condition, or even a defect, which prevents the second part of the process cannot

[43] Ibid.

[44] Also see Alexander Pruss, "Christian Sexual Ethics and Teleological Organicity," *The Thomist* 64 (2000), 71–100.

change the fact that the male and the female did become organically one by engaging in the first part of that process.

Moreover, just as marriage is more complex than most other communities, so genuine sexual intercourse is more complex than other acts. The orientation of the first part of the process (sexual intercourse) is not related to the rest of the process in the same way that a simple means is related to a single end. Rather, the orientation of the sexual acts toward procreation belongs to the set of sexual acts, not directly to each act. And the only behavior that the couple have direct control over is the sexual intercourse itself in such a way that the male semen is deposited in the female vaginal tract – this is the only act, the only behavior, that they directly perform which disposes them to procreation. So, in doing that the male and the female do become one as one agent, namely, as together performing all of that part of the reproductive process over which they have direct control. So, when Koppelman says that only acts that have the power to reproduce are genuinely reproductive in kind, he is mistaken. Many sexual acts are reproductive in kind which will not actually succeed in reproducing and are known to be impossible of succeeding. So these are acts in which the male and the female become a single unit.

This explains (in part) why heterosexual acts of sterile and elderly couples are reproductive in kind. But, inversely, how can we hold that homosexual acts are *not* reproductive in kind? That is, how can we answer claim (b), namely, Koppelman's claim that if sexual acts of heterosexual sterile or elderly couples are considered reproductive in kind, then it is equally plausible to say that *all* acts of seminal ejaculation are reproductive in kind? (In effect, Koppelman wants to say that heterosexual acts of sterile or elderly couples are not reproductive – but *if* they are, then so are homosexual acts.) Do not the agents in homosexual acts also exercise part of their reproductive capacities and organs?

The answer is that of course homosexual couples make use of their reproductive capacities and organs, but, unlike sterile or elderly heterosexual couples performing vaginal intercourse, they do not jointly perform an act that constitutes the first part of the reproductive process. Both sets of acts (the homosexual and the heterosexual) may be *abstractly* described simply as "seminal ejaculation," but the homosexual act is not the joint performance by a male and a female, as a single unit, of all of the behavior under their control, which, given other conditions (for example, sufficient sperm count, ovulation) can reproduce. That is, *what the homosexual act is*, as opposed to *an extrinsic condition* of that act, makes it impossible to reproduce, and, as a consequence, if performed by two or more people, is not an act in which they become biologically one. Neither solitary nocturnal emissions nor instances of solitary masturbation are reproductive-type acts either, and for the same reason homosexual acts are not reproductive in kind. There is a *behavioral* difference in the act rendering it incapable of reproduction.

Koppelman could object that the infertility of the heterosexual couple is not an extrinsic condition (as we claim) but should be considered as modifying what they do – and so they are, after all, in the same boat as homosexual acts (in effect, that being reproductive in kind is not morally significant). But there are two reasons why this is not true. First, as pointed out earlier, every aspect of the behavior the heterosexual couple (in a marital act) chooses to perform may be the same on two different occasions, and yet one act may result in procreation and the other not. This indicates that the difference – actual procreation versus not actual procreation – is a difference extrinsic to *what they do*. Of course, if they know that procreation is impossible, then they cannot intend or hope for procreation. This is all that Koppelman's analogy of the unloaded gun shows: just as one cannot intend to kill with a gun one knows is unloaded, so one cannot intend or hope to procreate by an act one knows cannot in these circumstances result in procreation. But our claim is not that in a marital act, one must intend to procreate, hope to procreate, or even think that procreation is in these circumstances possible. Our claim is that a marital act is an act in which the man and the woman, as complementary, become bodily and organically one, in that they jointly perform a single act, single in that it is an act that is biologically oriented to procreation, though some other condition in the agents may prevent the completion of that orientation in this act.

Second, the marital acts of a sterile or elderly married couple proclaim and bear witness to the intrinsic goodness of marriage, though marriage is the kind of community that is naturally fulfilled by the bearing and raising of children. The marital acts of infertile married couples, as renewing and fostering their conjugal love and marriage, do contribute to the good of marriage in the whole community. And these marital acts, though infertile in themselves, do indirectly contribute to the aspect of the good of marriage, which their own marriage does not realize, namely, the good of procreation or the bearing and raising of children.

Objection 2

A second objection to the main argument is to claim that nonmarital acts – in particular, homosexual sex acts – *do* sometimes realize a basic, common good, that they do, sometimes, somehow embody or express a personal communion. We will consider here two variations on this. The first is to say that such acts *symbolize*, or *gesture*, the personal union of the participants, perhaps as a special *gesture*, and that in this way such acts contribute to or strengthen the participants' personal union.[45] But if that is so, then why can't sexual acts between partners of the same sex symbolize or gesture love or affection? And why must a couple have a community suited for procreation (i.e., be married) in order to validly express their love sexually?

It is true that chaste sexual acts are signs or symbols of personal union. However, sexual acts are in their immediate reality much more than symbols or gestures. The question is whether the reality that is more than symbolic will involve depersonalization. When one waves at someone, smiles at someone, or shakes one's hand, the gesture is of itself rather trivial, but partly through convention and partly through natural association, it signifies a cordial act of will or emotion. The same is true of a hug or a nonpassionate kiss. But insofar as these acts are symbols, the thought is moved away from the sign to the will or emotion which it signifies.[46] However, in a sexual act, there is a desire directed toward the body and the desire of the other. The participants' attention is riveted on the action itself. And the desire and attention is not just toward the physical presence of the other (as in a hug). So the action is not primarily a sign or gesture for some other reality. Indeed, sexual acts *are* symbolically powerful precisely because of what sexual intercourse between a man and woman is in reality.

Moreover, a morally right sexual act does not make present in an indeterminate way just some union or other. Rather, becoming biologically one in a sexual act is the sort of act specifically apt to make present *marital* communion, that is, the sort of union oriented to, and fulfilled by, procreation: *that* is the kind of communion it can embody (and if it does not, then it and the persons involved are being *used* for extrinsic purposes). Sexual intercourse is a real, biological unity, and if it is loving and respectful sexual intercourse within marriage, it embodies or makes present marriage: not just a gesture, but a joint act in which the two biologically become co-subjects and thus become one. Thus, it is fundamentally

---

[45] Cf. Gareth Matthews, O. P., *The Body in Context: Sex and Catholicism* (London: SCM Press, 1992), especially 92–109.

[46] In hugging, there also seems to be an enjoyment of the simple presence or closeness of the one hugged.

a real act and a real unification, and *because of that* it is a gesture with profound significance or meaning.[47]

It is true that someone may have sex with another to signify something as an ulterior end. For example, an otherwise unwilling teen girl may consent to have sex with her boyfriend in order to show him how much she cares. Still, the immediate reality of the sexual act is not a mere sign or gesture. And so if there is not a real union of which the sexual act is a part – in other words if it is not a marital act – then the bodily presence of the other, and the personal presence of the other as a bodily person, is used for the sake of the experience of the sexual act, even if that experience has as an ulterior end some signification. In other words, if doing X in itself involves treating the body as an extrinsic instrument, it does not cease to do so if one does X for the sake of an ulterior end, in this case, signification.[48]

Another variation on this argument is to say that there is, in some way, a real bodily unity in sexual acts not suited to procreation, that is, in sodomitical acts. Thus, Michael Perry poses the following question:

> The nonprocreative sexual conduct of a man and a woman in a lifelong, monogamous relationship of faithful love can be morally licit if it "actualizes" and "allows them to experience" their friendship as a sexual-spiritual union of profound depth and richness. Why, then, can't the sexual conduct of a man and a man or of a woman and a woman also be morally licit – why cannot it also be worthy of those who would be truly, fully human – if it actualizes and allows *them* to experience *their* friendship as a lifelong, monogamous, faithful, loving sexual-spiritual union of profound depth and richness?[49]

The answer to this is that not just any act will allow a couple to experience their unity. What is it about a sexual act that enables it to embody a personal communion? The fact that it gives intense pleasure is certainly not what enables it to do so, nor that the sexual desire is reciprocal, for pleasure and desire are good to begin with only if their object or content is genuinely fulfilling.

---

[47] On Pope John Paul II's theology of the body, and that it does *not* regard the sexual act as a mere gesture, see: Lee, op. cit., 107–120.

[48] One might also claim that the common good involved in nonmarital sexual acts is sharing a gift, namely, the gift of pleasure. But we replied to this claim in section I. Pleasure is not by itself an intrinsic good, but is really good only as an aspect of a genuinely fulfilling activity. So pleasure by itself does not constitute a fitting gift. If engaging in pleasure apart from participation in a real good by myself is not fulfilling for me (as shown earlier), then giving this experience, or enabling someone else to have this experience, is not a true gift.

[49] Michael J. Perry, "The Morality of Homosexual Conduct: A Response to John Finnis," *Notre Dame Journal of Law, Ethics and Public Policy* 9 (1994), 56.

No act – sexual or otherwise – can be *just* an experience of and actualization of a friendship. Friendship is a unity constituted by common pursuit of genuine goods such as health, knowledge, and play.[50] Thus, friendship is actualized and experienced only in the common pursuit or realization of other genuine goods.[51] In truly marital acts, the genuine, common good is their bodily, organic unity, as a noninstrumental aspect and biological basis of the overall (multileveled) reality of their marriage. But no actual organic unity is present in sodomitical acts, and there is not any other human good immediately instantiated by the act. So, sodomitical acts do not (in any substantial and morally significant sense) unify the two (or more) persons who perform them on each other's bodies.[52]

Objection 3

A third objection to our overall argument is to admit that in sodomitical acts, the body is instrumentalized, but to deny that instrumentalizing the

---

[50] As an intrinsic good, to be sure, play provides a basic reason for action. However, the good of play should not be equated with doing whatever one pleases. That would collapse play as a *reason* into a nonrational motive. Play, precisely as a rational motive, gives one reason to pursue more or less complex, frequently rule-based, activities (such as chess or football). It does not provide a reason to do whatever one wants to precisely because one believes that pleasure is to be obtained.

[51] Nothing in our analysis implies that friendship is merely instrumental to other goods. On the contrary, friendship is intrinsically valuable. See John Finnis, *Natural Law and Natural Rights* (Oxford: Clarendon Press, 1980), 88.

[52] Gareth Moore claims that "There is an obvious sense in which sensations *can* be shared: two people can have them together. You and I can share a delicious meal. It may be that your taste sensations are yours and mine are mine, but I can share my experience with you by sharing my food with you; I can give you the taste of mushrooms by giving you my mushrooms" (Gareth Moore, op. cit., 238).

Moore is of course right that when two people have similar experiences, especially when they aid each other to have them, they share *something* in common, namely, pleasurable experience. But the question is, is there a genuine common good the shared pursuit and attainment of which makes them one? If, for example, A and B view pornography together, they are sharing something, but their friendship is not promoted by that because what they share is not a good, is not something perfective of them. If A and B get drunk together, once again, although they share something, they do not jointly cooperate in realizing any basic human good (they may do so incidentally, say, in their conversation, but their obtaining their "highs" together would not be a joint participation in a common good). By the same token, if A and B have sex together, that sex must realize a basic good in order for it to be a genuinely unifying act. What they experience together cannot just be their oneness or their "intimacy": there must first be some real good the sharing of which makes them one or genuinely intimate. Pleasure cannot serve that role, since it is a good only if it is part of a larger activity or condition that is already fulfilling.

body is of itself morally wrong. Michael Perry expresses the objection as follows:

> Why is conduct morally bad simply because it involves one in treating one's body "as an instrument to be used in the service of one's consciously experiencing self?" [quoting from John Finnis's article] Assume that from time to time I choose to eat a food that is utterly without nutritional value (and so does me no physical good) but that it is otherwise harmless and satisfies my appetite for a particular taste or sensation. Assume, too, that I do not thereby fail to eat, or make it more likely that someday I will fail to eat, the nutritional foods I need. Have I thereby done something that "dis-integrates me precisely as an acting person?"[53]

Stephen Macedo also considers analogies with eating and argues that the sort of pursuit of pleasure which clearly does no damage to persons' self-integration in regard to our eating and drinking must similarly be judged harmless when it comes to sexual acts:

> Or as Sabl suggested to me, suppose a person lost his capacity to digest but not the capacity to eat, so that nutrition had to be delivered intravenously. Would it then be immoral to eat for the sake of mere pleasure, or perhaps for the sake of pleasure as well as the camaraderie of dining companions?[54]

The appeal to an analogy with eating could be construed in two different ways. On the one hand, one could use the analogy to support a claim that instrumentalizing the body is not of itself wrong. In other words, one would say that eating just for pleasure *does* instrumentalize the body, but eating just for pleasure is clearly not wrong, and so instrumentalizing the body is not always wrong (this is Perry's argument). On the other hand, one could argue that, although instrumentalizing the body is wrong, eating just for pleasure is clearly not wrong, so one can perform an activity – including sex – just for pleasure, without instrumentalizing the body. We reply that "eating just for pleasure" is not necessarily wrong, but that is because it does not involve treating the body as an extrinsic instrument.

First of all, to regard one's sexuality as an extrinsic instrument is immoral, because it involves a contempt for one's body; it involves treating one's sexuality as if it were outside oneself, a subpersonal object. To treat one's sexuality as a mere object is a violation of the basic goods of self-integration and marriage (see Sections I–III). With respect to eating, "to eat simply for the sake of pleasure" is not the same in its moral significance as having sex simply for the sake of the pleasure when it does not embody a marital communion. Often, one might choose to eat simply because one

---

[53] Ibid.
[54] Macedo, op. cit., 282, n. 85.

is hungry, and one might then take no thought of any intrinsic good, such as health. Still, what one chooses is an intelligible activity that is, at least to some degree, really fulfilling. (Even if for some reason, one can't digest one's food, the eating exercises part of one's digestive capacity and one chooses a nourishing-type act, of which the pleasure is an aspect.) Similarly, such acts as twiddling one's thumbs, tapping one's foot, or chewing sugarless gum are rightly enjoyed simply as physical activities, exercises of one's physical capacities; but that, of course, is not the central reality in a sexual act, for in a sexual act, one is focused on another's or one's own sexual desire and pleasure. One chooses *the activity of eating*, and the pleasure is a felt aspect of that activity. Such a choice is not *necessarily* wrong, though it could be wrong for reasons other than its relation to pleasure. Also, it would not be wrong, as we already mentioned, for someone who for some reason could not obtain nourishment from his food at all, to eat for the sake of exercising that part of his digestive system which still functions, for the camaraderie fostered by that common activity, and for the pleasure in the activity. Of course, it is wrong to allow one's mere desire for the pleasure of eating to cause one to eat excessively or to eat in an unsocial way (without manners). To do so is to commit the immoral act of gluttony. However, the wrongness of gluttony does not seem to consist, primarily, at any rate, in self-alienation.

Masturbatory or sodomitical sex is quite different. Here the physical activities (stroking, rubbing) are chosen as merely extrinsic means toward an effect in consciousness, the only thing chosen for its own sake (though there may be ulterior ends). Although someone who cannot obtain nourishment from his food can still perform that behavior which is suited to nourish (of which one is aware, at some level), the analogous point is not true of masturbatory or sodomitical sex acts. Such acts are not suited to reproduction: they are not, in our parlance, "reproductive-type acts."

V. Nonmarital Sexual Acts, Multiple Partners, Incest, Bestiality...

Most people recognize that incest, bestiality, and pedophilia, as well as promiscuity and group sex, are morally wrong. Nevertheless, it is not clear how such activities could be immoral if the explanation of the meaning and nature of sexual acts proposed by those opposing our view were correct. We have shown that sexual acts, when morally right, are not just signs or gestures of affection, but are real biological unifications that embody marital communion. But if the sexual act *were* essentially just a sign or gesture of affection, then it is hard to see why it would *not* be an appropriate sign to express to one's child, by an adult to his or her friend of minor age, or even to one's pet. If sex is essentially only a sign or gesture of affection, then why would it be improper to use to express one's gratitude to one's parents or one's teachers? No one sees anything wrong with sharing beautiful music with such people, or sharing a meal with several people at one sitting. Some parents at times give their children massages, to relax them or to help them sleep if they are extremely tense. But what is it about sex that makes it improper in such circumstances?

There must be some feature, or features, of sex that distinguishes it from activities which *are* appropriately shared with children, one's parents, in groups, and so on. But what is that feature or features? Being an intense and pleasurable sign of affection, or even a mutual desire to be desired – the only traits distinctive of sex according to many who oppose our view – provides no reason to refrain from sexual acts in those contexts. Our view, on the contrary, provides an intelligible answer: sexual acts are such that *either* they embody a marital communion – a communion that is sexually embodied only in reproductive-type acts between a man and a woman, in a marital relationship – *or* they involve instrumentalizing one's sexuality (and perhaps that of others) for pleasure, or for one's illusory experience or fantasy of marital union, an illusion or fantasy that is especially inappropriate with children, one's parents, and so on.

Replying to this argument (as presented in our earlier article, "What Sex Can Be") John Corvino contends that it oversimplifies what nontraditionalists on sexual morality hold about the sexual acts. He writes, "First, Lee and George seem to be contrasting their view with a straw man. This is partly because the phrase 'intense and pleasurable sign of affection' oversimplifies the good(s) their opponents attribute to sex."[55] It is true that proponents of the morality of nonmarital sex wax eloquently about the goods supposedly achieved by nonmarital sex. It is also true that many people *hope to* achieve or enhance a real unity by nonmarital sex acts. Corvino claims that a nonmarital sexual act "can realize a shared experience of intimacy, one that is unachievable alone."[56] He says that a sexual act (whether marital or extramarital, heterosexual, or homosexual) "can be a powerful and unique way of building, celebrating, and replenishing love in a relationship."[57] And he quotes Michael Perry, who claims that "Interpersonal sexual conduct, whether heterosexual or homosexual, can be a way of affirming and serving both the sexual and emotional wellbeing

---

[55] Corvino, op. cit., 524 (by "PIB argument," Corvino means the "polygamy/incest/ bestiality argument."

[56] Ibid., 520.

[57] Ibid., 512.

of one's lover. . . . " [58] But these assertions only amount to claims that the sexual act enhances the personal relationship. The question is, *how* does it do so? As we said earlier, an interpersonal communion can be enhanced only *in* or *by* a common pursuit or enjoyment of a substantive good, an activity or condition that is already genuinely fulfilling. What substantive good is instantiated in extramarital sex, the common pursuit or enjoyment of which is personally unifying? If there is not a biological unity as part of the good of marriage, then one can only say that it is a sign or gesture of love (and if love, why not simply affection?), or a sharing of pleasure. But then the problem remains: if the sexual act is in its immediate reality only a sign or gesture of affection, or a sharing of pleasure, then why restrict it to mature people in a stable (or quasi-stable?) friendship, why not allow it as an appropriate sign, or as pleasure, to share with one's children, multiple partners, or pets? [59]

---

[58] From Michael Perry, op. cit., 51.

[59] Corvino misconstrues our argument (that is, the argument proposed by Grisez, Finnis, ourselves, and others). After claiming that interpersonal intimacy is sought and achieved even by partners who intend not to procreate, he says the following: "This last fact seems obvious. Yet the new natural lawyers insist that, whatever such partners' intentions may be, they act only for their own self-gratification, not for any interpersonal (that is, common) good.' . . . Similarly, Lee and George claim that in non-marital sex, 'the physical activities (stroking, rubbing) are chosen merely as extrinsic means of producing an effect (gratification) in consciousness, the only thing chosen for its own sake'" (Corvino, op. cit., 520–521, quoting our "What Sex Can Be," at 155). But in that quote, we were not speaking of *all* nonmarital sex, only of masturbatory sex, which we *defined* as sex done for the sole immediate purpose of pleasure. We went on to say that often nonmarital sex is done for the purpose of experiencing unity, but we argued (and still maintain) that such sex does not *achieve* that unity and so is pursuing an *illusory experience* (thus the title of our article indicated that sex could be either one-flesh union (that is, marital intercourse) or self-alienation (as in masturbation, solitary or group)), *or* illusion. Corvino, however, claims that we argued that people can only *seek* or *aim at* either marriage or mere self-gratification. Then, Corvino points out that in nonmarital sexual acts, people usually desire something more than just physical pleasure, otherwise it would be difficult to explain why they seek a sexual partner to begin with. He then concludes, "The reason seems obvious: they want intimacy with a particular individual rather than a purely subjective experience. To claim that all such people want is 'self-gratification' is implausible, and in any case, is not knowable a priori. (note omitted) Where is the evidence for this radical revision of common sense? (note omitted) Finnis's view, and a fortiori, his PIB argument, must be rejected" (Ibid., 522–523).

But this was not the claim made by Finnis or any other new natural lawyer. When nonmarital sexual conduct is sought, usually at least *some* degree of personal, or at least animal, recognition and attraction is sought from the other. Indeed, both Finnis and we have explicitly noted that often unmarried couples *intend* their sexual act to be a way of realizing or promoting their personal communion, but that it cannot actually do so. That this was Finnis's point in the article Corvino referred to is clear from the following passage in that same article: "Why cannot non-marital friendship be promoted and

Corvino's attempted explanation of the immorality of adult–child incest – rather than answering traditionalist worries, as he intends – actually illustrates further the profound difficulties in the liberal, or nontraditionalist, view of sex. Corvino discusses the practice of males in the Etoro tribe, who require adolescent males to perform fellatio on the adults of the tribe, ostensibly because they believe the ingestion of seminal fluid is necessary for maturation. Corvino says that the Etoro practice could be morally innocent, given that their intentions are structured by their mistaken biological beliefs. However, Corvino claims, given the significance that sex has in our culture, adult–child incest is morally wrong. His explanation is as follows:

Our society has certain attitudes toward both intergenerational and intrafamilial sex. Those attitudes partially result from the harms that such sex can cause, but they also partially (and indirectly) cause some of those harms. Because sex has a particular meaning in our culture, participants in incest here are subject to certain psychological and social difficulties that their analogues in Etoro society are not. That fact gives incest a moral significance here that it might well lack for the Etoro. Since the persons in question in this example are children, we should be especially careful about protecting them from these difficulties.[60]

But this explanation is manifestly weak. In the first place, if the "moral significance" of the sexual act that makes it inappropriate and harmful for adult–child incest is a result of society's attitudes, then a proponent of such relations could simply argue that those particular attitudes of society should change. Second, Corvino has failed to specify what in our society's attitudes has that effect. The problem is just pushed back to the level of societal attitudes. Other than our society's continuing disapproval of incest (which would not by itself be sufficient to condemn it)[61] and our

expressed by sexual acts? Why is *the attempt to express affection by orgasmic non-marital sex* [emphasis added] the pursuit of an illusion?" (Finnis, "Law, Morality, and 'Sexual Orientation'," 28) And in our article, "What Sex Can Be," after defining sodomitical acts, as we have done so earlier, we went on to say that the participants may be doing this simply for pleasure, and in that case it is masturbatory, but also, "they might intend their act as in some way an expression of their love for each other" (Lee and George, op. cit., 146). And we then argued that such an act does not achieve biological unity and therefore is the pursuit of an illusory experience. The problem with a nonmarital sexual act is that, either there is not a real unity achieved in the act (if it is sodomitical) or the real unity is not part of the larger marital unity (if it is simple fornication), and so in either case the act does not embody or actualize a basic good. Unity may be *sought* in a sexual act, but a nonmarital sexual act cannot be a way of *achieving* unity.

[60] Corvino, op. cit., 530.

[61] A proponent of such acts could simply reply that this is an inconsistency on the part of our society. If our society adopts the attitude that sexual acts are essentially only symbols

society's persisting belief that sex should, ideally, be between a husband and a wife, what societal attitude (or attitudes) could make adult–child incest necessarily inappropriate or harmful? Corvino has failed to show why adult–child incest should be morally excluded.

Similarly, in replying to Hadley Arkes's suggestion that permitting homosexual acts would logically open one to permitting adult–child incest, Stephen Macedo's argument about incest is question-begging: "Incest, of course, would lead to a horrible and revolting form of vulnerability for children."[62] But if sex is essentially what Macedo claims it to be – an intense sign of affection – it is hard to see why extending it to children would in any way exploit their vulnerability, or why it would be "horrible and revolting." Only if sex necessarily involves more than expressing an extrinsic sign of affection, only if there is some *reality* made present or simulated[63] – a reality that is unfitting with a child or with one's parent, or with strangers, or in groups – can there be anything truly unfitting about adult–child incest.[64]

---

or gestures of affection, or even of love, the proponent of adult–child incest may argue that consistency demands an eventual acceptance of such acts.

[62] Macedo, op. cit., 288.

[63] If the couple (or group) are not married, then there is not a basic good made present in the act. Every couple performing heterosexual vaginal intercourse (and who have not intentionally rendered their act nonprocreative) *do* become biologically one, but this biological unity instantiates a basic good only if they are sharing their lives in a procreative union, that is, in marriage.

[64] Laurence Thomas argues that the harm of child sexual abuse is based on the facts that sexual acts generally involve a "dual-level reciprocal choice-worthiness" (that is, each one desires that the other desire him or her and is affirmed by that awareness), but that a child is incapable of that sort of desire or appreciation (that is, appreciation of the dual-level desirability). See Laurence Thomas, "Sexual Desire, Moral Choice, and Human Ends," *Journal of Social Philosophy* 33 (2002), 178–192, at 183. The child, Thomas explains, is unable to have "a sense of the expressive power of sexual interaction" (ibid., 182–185). However, while this is certainly true of younger children, it is not necessarily true of children twelve years and older. Moreover, this argument fails to explain the origin of sexual conduct's powerful expressiveness to begin with. That A desires B and desires to be desired by B, and is pleased by B's similarly structured desire, still leaves unexplained the substantive content of the desires – a content that must include more than simply pleasurable strokes, orgasm, etc. – that bestows upon this multilayered desire such powerful expressiveness. Thomas says that *ideally* one's sex life should be "animated by the personal sentiments that enrich our lives" (184). But, again, this leaves unanswered the question of just how personal sentiments – presumably love and commitment – become concretized in (how they animate) sexual acts. Our answer is that the sexual act aims at a real, biological union – a biological union that would be fulfilled by procreation, and then together raising the fruit of this act, the child – and so because of that reality, it also has (or normally has) an intense significance or expressive power.

If marriage and sex are related, as we have argued, one can easily see that marriage is the type of relationship that is incompatible with its parties also being parent and child, even when children have become adults. Because the marital relationship is by its nature the kind of relationship that is naturally fulfilled by bearing and raising children, it follows that it should be a permanent, mutual and equal sharing of lives. This mutuality and equality is incompatible with a parent–child "marriage." Although child and parent are equal in dignity as persons, there is an important respect in which they are *not* equal, that is, in the precise relationship of parent and child. The child always owes a certain debt of piety to the parent; this debt partially structures the parent–child relationship and renders it permanently incompatible with marriage between them. Since sexual relations involve a tendency toward, or a simulation of, marriage (as we have shown), such relations are incompatible with, and damage, the parent–child relationship and involve a grave betrayal of the trust included as part of that relationship. But because sexual liberals have not specified an intelligible good that sex must be for and because they do not morally require that sex occur only in genuine marriage, they cannot appeal to such an argument to exclude the morality of incest.[65]

Likewise, Corvino's argument against polygamy (in an attempt to show that a nontraditionalist on sex can morally exclude it) is strikingly weak. Our concentration in this section is on sexual *acts*, but it is worth examining Corvino's argument concerning polygamy, a relationship. Corvino claims that arguments against polygamy must appeal, not to the nature of the sexual act or to marriage, but to the broad effects such a practice would have on society. And, because of that, "If there are good arguments against these practices, they are as available to nontraditionalists as traditionalists."[66] His discussion of this issue does not make it clear whether he thinks polygamy is necessarily wrong, or simply something to be allowed

---

[65] We may also briefly address the question of incest between siblings. This, too, we believe is excluded because of the nature of the marital good, this time the marital good as including family. The encouragement or acceptability of sexual relations (and so, of marriage) between close-in members of the family is generically hostile to the maintenance of the kind of friendship and interdependence appropriate between siblings, and between parent and child. This argument is not merely consequentialist. What excludes incest is not the particular outcomes. Rather, the structure of the good of marriage (which is determined by its orientation to procreation and to the kind of relationship that is intrinsically fulfilled by bearing and raising children together) provides the required content of the form of life to be projected, intended, chosen, and lived out as a permanent and exclusive commitment of spouses. Again, such considerations are not available to sexual liberals.

[66] Corvino, op. cit., 528.

only with caution.[67] Corvino is right to suggest that polygamy's principal bad effect on society is inequality within the marital (or quasi-marital) relationship; indeed, polygamy leads to a view of women as inherently inferior to men. But this inequality results only if neither polyandry nor multiple partners of the same sex are viewed in society as a live option, and that is so only if marriage is viewed (rightly) as essentially linked to procreation. In fact, the basic, sound arguments excluding polygamy are not consequentialist at all. Polyandry is excluded as violating the good of procreation, since it precludes knowing who the father is of a particular child (and thus diminishes the natural personal bond that arises from the biological bond). And polygyny is excluded for the following reason. Because marriage is oriented to procreation, it requires a permanent sharing of whole lives – the dedication of the mother and the father *to each other* models for the child the goodness and equal dignity of both sexes. But polygyny of itself implies a gross inequality in the relationship itself, and a denial (implicit in such an arrangement) of the equal dignity of women. Thus, arguments excluding polygamy depend on a correct conception of marriage – namely, as a community naturally oriented to (though not merely instrumental to) procreation.

Even Corvino's argument against bestiality illustrates the inability of the liberal view of sex to provide intelligible reasons to exclude such acts. Corvino writes:

The bestiality analogy is the most far-fetched of the three [that is, polygamy, incest, and bestiality]. To compare a homosexual encounter – even a so-called casual one – with bestiality is to ignore the distinctively human capacities that sexual relationships can (and usually do) engage. As such, the analogy embodies the sort of reductionist thinking about sex that traditionalists typically attribute to gay-rights advocates. For that reason, however, the analogy is the easiest to rebut. I have argued that, prima facie, homosexuality appears capable of realizing the same goods as nonprocreative heterosexual relationships. Bestiality is not

---

[67] Discussing Jonathan Rauch's consequentialist argument against polygamy, Corvino writes: "Rauch's real concern is consequentialist, not Kantian: legalizing polygamy will result primarily in polygyny (one husband, many wives), and polygyny causes social problems. Whether these causal connections will actually ensue is an empirical question requiring additional data. Those data must include the fact that historically, polyandry (one wife, many husbands) is vanishingly rare and that polygyny is highly correlated with sexism. And they must include the fact that most polygamous relationships historically have involved inequality, with one 'head' making unilateral decisions. But they must also include the fact that very few people in contemporary Western societies seem interested in polyamorous relationships (a relationship with one partner is challenging enough) and that egalitarian relationships, though rare, do occur" (Ibid.). This is hardly a firm, well-grounded rejection of "polyamory."

comparable on this score, since (virtually by definition) it does not provide the same opportunity for interpersonal communication, intimacy, and so on.[68]

But this argument is simply beside the point. Our argument is that bestiality is immoral because, obviously, there can be no personal communion between a person and a beast and so the sexual act cannot instantiate a basic good, and, therefore, involves a depersonalization of our sexuality. But if one does not hold that the sexual act should involve the instantiation of a first-level, basic good (in this case, biological union of spouses), the joint participation in which effects personal union, then the sexual act will be essentially a form of signification, gesture, or communication. If that is so, then why need it be inter*personal* signification, gesture, or communication? One might argue: it naturally expresses personal communion and so is inappropriate where there is none, thus morally excluding casual sex *and* bestiality. But we examined this position in Section III. The problem with this argument is that, unless an act signifies by means of first instantiating a reality, there can be no moral objection to modifying what the act or gesture might naturally signify. Moreover, once sexual acts are put into the category of mere signs or gestures, proponents of bestiality (and of casual sex) could deny that sexual acts naturally signify a deep personal communion, or a *personal* communion at all; they could argue that they signify *affection*, on some level or another. And on that basis an argument could be made to defend the morality of bestiality. It remains that to exclude morally such acts as multiple partners, incest, and bestiality, one must defend a moral link between sex and a substantive good (such as a biological union embodying marriage), the joint participation in which actualizes a real personal communion.

In sum, in choosing to engage in sexual activity, one adopts an attitude toward the relationship between the body and consciousness in both oneself and others with whom one has sex, and one relates to the basic good of personal communion. To engage in sex merely for pleasure uses a person's animal sexuality as a mere extrinsic tool for gratification, thus depersonalizing the body-as-sexual, treating it as a subpersonal object. Moreover, sexual acts aimed at expressing affection or love but outside marriage are choices of an illusory experience, since either the biological union that embodies the relevant personal communion is lacking or the relevant personal communion is lacking. Only if there is a common good realized in and by the sexual act – making the couple one in this cooperative

---

[68] Corvino, op. cit., 532.

participation in that common good – do the participants treat each other and themselves as unified bodily persons (and, thus, with respect) and embody a real, basic good. For only then is their pleasure and experience an aspect of participation in a real good, rather than individual, private gratifications making use of activities or pursuits of illusory experiences. In marriage, the couple become biologically one, and this bodily union is an aspect of their total marital communion, actualizing (initiating or renewing) their marriage. Only if the spouses truly unite biologically and only if this biological union is an aspect of a total personal communion, does their sexual act aim at a genuine, common good. And the sexual act can be an aspect of the total personal communion – that is, actualize or make present their personal communion – only if the personal communion is of the sort that is naturally prolonged and fulfilled in procreation and the sexual act is a reproductive-type act, making them truly biologically one. And so, only in marriage can sexual acts realize a common good rather than induce self-alienation or an illusory experience.

Index

Made in the USA
Coppell, TX
14 January 2022

71634471R00142